Who Benefits From *State and Local*

Economic Development Policies?

Timothy J. Bartik

1991

W. E. UPJOHN INSTITUTE for Employment Research
Kalamazoo, Michigan

Library of Congress Cataloging-in-Publication Data

Bartik, Timothy J.
    Who benefits from state and local economic development policies? /
Timothy J. Bartik.
        p.   cm.
    Includes bibliographical references and index.
    ISBN 0–88099–113–5 (alk. paper) — ISBN 0–88099–114–3
(pbk. : alk. paper)
    1. Economic development. 2. Economic policy.   I. Title.
HD75.B367 1991
338.9—dc20   91–27375
                                                                      CIP

THE INSTITUTE, a nonprofit research organization, was established on July 1, 1945.
It is an activity of the W. E. Upjohn Unemployment Trustee Corporation, which was
formed in 1932 to administer a fund set aside by the late Dr. W. E. Upjohn for the
purpose of carrying on "research into the causes and effects of unemployment and
measures for the alleviation of unemployment."

Cover design by J.R. Underhill
Index prepared by Shirley Kessel
Printed in the United States of America

ACKNOWLEDGMENTS

I benefitted greatly from the extensive reviews of earlier versions of this manuscript by Peter Eisinger, Michael Luger, Robert Schwab, George Erickcek, Susan Houseman, and Allan Hunt. Each of these reviewers spent a great deal of time with my draft manuscript, and I thank them for their efforts. I also received helpful comments on portions of this research project from Ann Bowman, Richard Burkhauser, Shelby Gerking, Malcolm Getz, Janice Madden, Clifford Russell, and Robert Spiegelman. Helpful comments on this research were also provided by seminar participants at the University of Illinois, Michigan State University, the University of Pennsylvania, Vanderbilt University, and the annual meetings of the Association for Public Policy Analysis and Management and the Regional Science Association.

The publications staff of the Upjohn Institute did an excellent job with this large and complex manuscript. I thank Judy Gentry for her editing, Natalie Lagoni for turning the manuscript into camera-ready copy, and Sue McMurray for her work in publicizing the book. Leslie Lance and Ellen Maloney helped produce the figures in the book. Finally, Claire Vogelsong provided her usual excellent secretarial assistance throughout the many drafts of this manuscript.

Research assistance for this book was provided by James Vester and Martha Buckner, and I thank them for their help.

The support of the Upjohn Institute was essential to the initiation and completion of this research project. I appreciate the initial grant I received from the Institute for this project, before I joined the Institute staff, and the continued support after I became a staff member. I particularly appreciate the patience of the Institute's Executive Director, Robert Spiegelman, as I undertook the lengthy process of expanding a more narrowly focused research project into a book.

I would also like to thank the various influential teachers and mentors I have had over the years: Patricia Reifsnyder, Thomas Pangle, Sar Levitan, Eugene Smolensky, George Tolley, and V. Kerry Smith. I owe a great deal to each of them.

Finally, I am grateful for the support of my family: Deb Wickman, Alex Bartik, and Jonathan Bartik.

THE AUTHOR

Dr. Bartik received his PhD in Economics from the University of Wisconsin—Madison in 1982. He was Assistant Professor of Economics at Vanderbilt University and joined the Upjohn Institute as a senior economist in 1989.

He conducts research on regional economic development, focusing on issues of national interest as well as those of special concern to Michigan. He is currently studying the effects of industrial and regional change on growth of the urban underclass. He has studied economic development in West Michigan metropolitan areas using an econometric model.

Dr. Bartik's recent publications include "The Effects of Property Taxes and Other Local Public Policies on the Intermetropolitan Pattern of Business Location," in *Industry Location and Public Policy,* and "Small Business Start-Ups in the United States: Estimates of the Effects of Characteristics of States" in *Southern Economic Journal.*

CONTENTS

LIST OF TABLES

LIST OF FIGURES

— 1 —
Boon or Boondoggle?
The Debate Over State and Local
Economic Development Policies

Over the past 20 years, governors and mayors have assumed responsibility for economic development. While many regions have experienced high unemployment and declining real wages, federal action to deal with these economic problems has been constrained by budget deficits and a conservative political philosophy, and state and local governments have had to act. Almost every state and metropolitan area has expanded the size and scope of economic development programs. More money is being spent on subsidies to new branch plants than ever before, and even conservative states have intervened in the private market by subsidizing business research and industrial modernization, and by providing capital and business training to small business and entrepreneurs.

To most politicians, economic development means more jobs. More jobs are expected to bring many benefits: lower unemployment, higher wages, greater property values, increased profits for local businesses, more tax revenues, and reelection for the politician who can take credit for these boons. Politicians usually emphasize most the benefit of providing jobs for the unemployed.

But critics argue persuasively that state and local economic development policies cannot achieve these benefits. According to the critics, economic development policies do not help the unemployed and the poor, but mostly benefit capitalists and the propertied. The indictment against state and local economic development policies has three parts. First, the policies are argued to have little effect on the growth of a small region such as a state or metropolitan area. Second, even if these policies could affect job growth, so many in-migrants would be attracted that the local unemployment rate would quickly return to its original level.

1

Third, even if local growth lowered unemployment in one area, from a national perspective these benefits would be offset by increased unemployment in other areas.

This book presents evidence to counter these criticisms of state and local economic development policies. It argues that economic development policies can significantly affect the growth of a state or metropolitan area, that increases in the growth of a local economy can benefit its unemployed, and that state and local economic development policies can benefit the overall national economy.

While the argument relies, in part, on my interpretation of previous research, I also present new empirical research on how metropolitan growth affects the unemployed, workers, and property owners. That research shows that faster growth of a metropolitan area has significant long-run effects on its unemployment rate. Furthermore, faster growth leads to significant occupational upgrading to better jobs, particularly for minority and less-educated persons. Growth of a metropolitan area also increases its property values. But overall, the benefits of faster growth are probably distributed in a progressive manner, that is, the real incomes of low-income persons increase by a greater percentage than those of upper-income persons.

This is not to imply that cutting business taxes to spur economic development is always the right policy. Public services to business also affect the economic growth of a local area. Depending on the circumstances, the labor market benefits of local economic growth may be outweighed by the costs of environmental damage due to growth and the costs of government resources devoted to economic development programs.

Focus on Local Economies

To avoid confusion at the outset, my arguments for the potential benefits of state and local economic development programs are meant to be applied to programs that seek to affect growth for an entire small economic region, such as a state or a metropolitan area.[1] Programs aimed at individual towns or suburbs within a metropolitan area raise different issues. Metropolitan areas, or states, can legitimately be thought of as economic regions, because they have quasi-independent labor and housing markets. The trend in local economic development policy is towards metropolitan cooperation. In addition, states are increasingly prominent in organizing and financing economic development policy at all levels of government. Thus, the book addresses the types of state and local economic development policy that dominate the scene today and are likely to be even more important in the future.

What is Economic Development Policy?

Another source of confusion could be what is meant by "economic development policy." Growth and structural change in the economy of a state or local area are arguably affected by every government action, from the quality of public schools to the regulation of optometrists. Economic development policies discussed here, however, are those that provide *direct* assistance to businesses. Direct economic development policies assist businesses with cash, such as tax subsidies, for example, or with services, such as training individuals in how to develop a business plan for a new enterprise. Policies such as those related to public schools that *indirectly* affect economic development have broader purposes and are best evaluated from a broader perspective. This book focuses on direct economic development policies because their claimed success in promoting economic growth is their main rationale. Furthermore, economic development policies that assist businesses directly are politically controversial. Liberals are concerned that these policies give too much profit to business, while conservatives are concerned that these policies give too much power to government.

Table 1.1 lists the main types of direct economic development policies being pursued by state and local governments. These policies can be grouped into two types. Traditional economic development policies seek to provide financial and other incentives for businesses to locate and expand in an area. Most incentives are provided through the area's tax system and are targeted at attracting new manufacturing branch plants.

Table 1.1
A Typology of State and Local Economic Development Policies
that Directly Aid Businesses

Traditional Economic Development Policies
(Primarily Targeted at Branch Plant Recruitment)

Marketing Area As Branch Plant Location
Industrial development advertising
Marketing trips to corporate headquarters
Provision of site information to prospects

Financial Incentives
Industrial revenue bonds
Property tax abatements
Other tax relief
Provision of land at below-market prices
Direct state loans

Nonfinancial Incentives to Branch Plants
Customized industrial training
Expedited provision of site-specific infrastructure
Help with regulatory problems

"New Wave" Economic Development Policies
(Primarily Targeted at Small or Existing Businesses)

Capital Market Programs
Predominantly government-financed loan or equity programs
Government support for predominantly privately financed loan or
  equity programs

Information/Education for Small Business
Small business ombudsman/information office
Community college classes in starting a business
Small business development centers
Entrepreneurial training programs
Small business incubators

Research and High Technology
Centers of excellence in business-related research at public universities
Research-oriented industrial parks
Applied research grants
Technology transfer programs/industrial extension services

Export Assistance
Information/training in how to export
Trade missions
Export financing

What I call "new wave" economic development policies are an eclectic group of policies that became popular in many states during the late 1970s and early 1980s. These policies encourage various forms of innovation, such as applied research, industrial modernization, entrepreneurship, and business expansion into export markets. They also have in common a willingness to involve government much more with business decisions. Rather than just providing cash, they would have government provide services to businesses to help them determine their best market or technology.

Several prominent books on state and local economic development policies describe the many new wave policies and debate whether the new wave approach or the traditional approach is better.[2] While that debate is important, my focus in this book is on whether the general approach of assisting business for economic development purposes is likely to cause changes in business behavior that benefit other groups in society, and if so, who those groups are. All of the direct economic development policies have in common an attempt to reduce some sort of business costs, broadly defined. This even is true for new wave policies. For example, export information programs reduce the cost to businesses of acquiring information on markets in other countries; entrepreneurial training programs reduce the costs to potential entrepreneurs of developing a business and financing plan; applied research grants reduce the costs to high technology companies of developing an innovative product. Furthermore, the issue of the overall desirability of business assistance for economic development logically needs to be resolved before the issue of which type of business assistance is most effective. If the entire philosophy behind direct economic development policies is flawed—if these policies can only benefit the assisted businesses, or can only benefit property owners—then the debate over different types of policies is pointless.

Jobs Versus Other Goals
of Economic Development Policies

The analysis of this study emphasizes one particular goal of direct economic development policies, the goal of more jobs for the state or local area. Some direct economic development policies have additional goals as well. For example, many of the new wave economic development policies also aim at encouraging innovation.

Job creation is the primary goal for all direct economic development policies, traditional or new wave, from the perspective of politicians and voters. Governor Mario Cuomo of New York expressed the opinion of many state and local political leaders and voters when he said that "while there are no panaceas, nothing comes closer than one simple word: jobs."[3] Advocates of new wave economic development policies may tout their innovation benefits, but the policies will face political death if they fail to increase job growth.[4]

Despite all the publicity given new wave economic development policies, the evidence suggests that more resources are devoted to traditional policies whose primary goal is more jobs for the state or local area. Data from the National Association of State Development Agencies indicate that expenditures by state development agencies totaled about $1.5 billion in 1990 (National Association of State Development Agencies, 1990). Much of this agency spending is devoted to traditional rather than new wave programs. A State of Minnesota survey suggests that state spending on high technology economic development totaled $550 million in 1988 (Minnesota Office of Science and Technology, 1988). Some of this spending appears to be for university basic research, and there is overlap between the NASDA and Minnesota figures. But even if there were no overlap, and all of this $2 billion was devoted to new wave programs, these expenditures are dwarfed by the various tax subsidies, or "tax expenditures," that state and local governments give to business for economic development purposes. For example, in the State of Michigan alone, over $150 million annually is foregone from property tax abatements granted to businesses.[5] For just one manufacturing branch plant (albeit a large one), the General Motors

Saturn plant, Tennessee state and local governments provided subsidies with a net present value of $144 million, mostly in the form of property tax abatements.[6] Furthermore, in addition to these tax expenditures that are clearly linked to specific economic development projects, many of the recent tax reforms in the states have reduced business tax rates and provided business tax credits and deductions, largely on the rationale that these changes would help the business climate and promote economic development.[7] The "tax expenditures" caused by these development-oriented tax reforms vastly exceed what states spend on venture capital, entrepreneurial training, or other new wave economic development policies.

Do State and Local
Economic Development Policies Affect Growth?

Financial subsidies . . . are rarely a significant concern in wise business-location decisions and usually amount to little more than a government giveaway and burden on taxpayers, including corporate taxpayers forced to subsidize their competitors. (Page 36 in *Leadership for Dynamic State Economics,* Committee for Economic Development, 1986)

The first issue in analyzing state and local economic development policies is whether these policies have any significant effect on the job growth of an area. If they fail to increase job growth in the areas that adopt them, they cannot help the unemployed.

Many policy researchers have denounced the traditional economic development policies of tax and financial subsidies as ineffective in promoting state or metropolitan area job growth. The usual theoretical argument for this position is that state and local taxes are too small a percentage of business costs to affect business growth decisions. The usual empirical argument for this position relies on both surveys of business firms and econometric studies of the determinants of state or metropolitan area job growth. Surveys of business firms often show a low ranking of state and local taxes as a location determinant. Furthermore, until recent years, the overwhelming majority of econometric studies could find no significant statistical relationship between state and local business growth and state and local business taxes.

The theoretical argument that state and local business taxes are too small to affect business location is unpersuasive. Many states and metropolitan areas will be close substitutes from a business perspective, offering similar access to markets and supplies. Even small production cost differentials could prove decisive for a particular business location decision.

The problem with surveys of location determinants is that the questions asked are difficult to interpret. These surveys ask the business to list the most important, or essential, or crucial determinants of its current location choice. What "important" means in this context is difficult to define. What we really want to know is whether a different location would have been chosen if state and local business taxes had been 5 percent higher, or 10 percent higher. Answering this question requires a quantitative weighing of this site's advantages versus alternative sites, and most businesses would be unable or unwilling to provide such precise answers to a survey.

Recent econometric evidence indicates that variations in state and local business taxes do have effects on state or metropolitan area growth that are likely to be considered significant by most policymakers. Difficult methodological problems plague the estimation of how taxes affect state and metropolitan area growth. No existing study escapes all these problems. But compared to earlier studies in this area, recent studies generally use better data and methodologies. Recent studies mostly agree that state and local business taxes affect the growth of an area, and even agree on the approximate magnitude of the effect.

Major public services that benefit business, such as improvement in public infrastructure, are also estimated to spur state or metropolitan area growth in many of the newer studies of business location. An economic development policy of business tax cuts may fail to increase jobs in a state or metropolitan area if it leads to a deterioration of public services to business. An economic development policy of tax increases may succeed in increasing jobs if it significantly improves public services to business. Policymakers must consider both tax and public service effects on business if they are to successfully increase their area's job growth.

New wave regional economic development policies go beyond providing financial subsidies or general public services to providing specific services to small business and entrepreneurs. Many policy researchers who denounce state and local tax breaks are much more hopeful about these types of policies. At present, there is no good evidence on whether new wave economic development policies are effective. If new wave services have a higher value to business than their cost, they could have a greater effect on the growth of a state or metropolitan area, per dollar of government effort, than the more traditional business tax breaks. The cost effectiveness of state and local economic development policies is crucial to whether the policies make sense for a particular state or locality.

Does Local Growth Help the Unemployed and Lower-Income Households?

When jobs develop in a fast growing area, workers from other areas are attracted to fill the developing vacancies, thus preserving the same unemployment rate as before the growth surge. (John Logan and Harvey Molotch, Professors of Sociology at State University of New York at Albany and University of California—Santa Barbara, respectively, p. 89 in *Urban Fortunes: The Political Economy of Place,* 1987)

. . . the fortunes of numerous poor and unskilled urban residents of cities are often largely unaffected by even healthy expansion within local economies. (Page 5 in *Urban America in the Eighties,* Report of the Panel on Policies and Prospects for Metropolitan and Nonmetropolitan America, President's Commission for a National Agenda for the Eighties, 1980)

The next issue is whether the ability of state and local economic development policy to affect local growth makes any difference. Suppose some policy does increase job growth for a local economic region, such as a metropolitan area. The increase in local labor demand would be expected to lead to some short-term reduction in local unemployment and upward pressure on real wages. But if labor mobility is rapid enough, the increase in local labor demand will be quickly matched by an increase in local labor supply. The unemployment rate will increase back to its original level, and the real wage will drop back to its original level.

Migration statistics indicate that the United States is a mobile enough society that labor market effects of faster local job growth could plausibly be very short-lived. For example, during a typical four-year period, over 13 percent of the population moves between metropolitan areas (Marston 1985). This mobility rate far exceeds the likely unemployment rate differentials across metropolitan areas. Only a small portion of this normal flow of migrants needs to respond to changes in relative job growth rates across metropolitan areas for the labor supply change to be well-matched to the labor demand change.

Even if local labor supply quickly responds to labor demand shifts, economic development policies would still provide the benefit of higher land values. Increased local demand and supply of labor would increase both business and residential demand for land. The price of existing houses and buildings would increase. Land would be bid away from other uses (e.g., agriculture or speculation) and devoted to new residential and commercial development to accommodate the new businesses and residents. Even with this increase in developed land supply, the price of existing land would remain at a permanently higher level, as existing land presumably has some locational advantages over the newly developed land. Unlike the case of labor, sufficient land cannot "migrate in" to a local area to force land prices back down to their original level.

The benefits of higher land values lack the political or ethical appeal of the benefits of lower unemployment. Land is disproportionately owned by upper-income groups, so land value benefits would be distributed "regressively": the percentage increase in real income would be greater for upper-income groups than for lower-income groups. If land value increases are the only benefits of state and local economic development policies, it is questionable whether anyone other than property owners should be required to pay for these policies. Furthermore, in this case economic development policies would be unable to help solve the social problems of unemployment and poverty among minorities and other disadvantaged groups.

My argument for long-run labor market effects of local job growth is that what happens to people in the short run affects their long-run prospects. Suppose that an increase in local job growth leads, in the short run, to some currently unemployed residents getting jobs that they otherwise would not have obtained. These currently unemployed residents have a short-run advantage over potential in-migrants because in-migration does take some time to respond to shifts in labor demand. Because these current residents obtain jobs in the short run, they acquire skills that increase their employability and real wages in the long run, even after migration has had a chance to fully respond to the increased labor demand.

This dependence of a long-run equilibrium—in this case, the long-run equilibrium unemployment rate of individuals—on past history has been labeled _hysteresis_. Hysteresis was originally used in physics to describe how the electromagnetic characteristics of certain metals are permanently affected by the temporary application of certain magnetic forces.[8] More recently, some economists have suggested that an economy's equilibrium unemployment rate may be permanently increased by a temporary recession, or lowered by a temporary boom. If this is true, then macroeconomic policies that affect the short-run performance of an economy may also affect its long-run performance. The issue of whether equilibrium unemployment exhibits hysteresis has implications much broader than simply who benefits from state and local economic development policies.

The new empirical results of this book support the hypothesis that labor markets are subject to hysteresis effects. The results are based on analysis of average unemployment rates, occupational wage rates, and housing and other prices for 25 metropolitan areas from 1972 to 1986, and on analysis of the labor market success of 44,000 adult males in 89 metropolitan areas from 1979 to 1986. The results, extensively presented in four chapters of the book, can be briefly summarized here. The data suggest that a once-and-for-all shock to a metropolitan area's employment—that is, a shock that temporarily affects the employment growth rate but permanently affects the employment level—lowers the area's unemployment rate and raises labor force participation rates for at least eight years after the shock. Holding occupation constant, real wages are unchanged. Individuals with given education and experience are more likely to be promoted to higher-paying occupations in metropolitan economies that experience higher growth, however, and this upgrading in occupational status persists well after the temporary shock to growth has subsided. The effects of local growth on real earnings are highest for blacks and for less-educated workers. Local growth also raises property values; overall, however, it appears that faster local growth is likely to have a progressive impact on the income distribution. The percentage increase in real income is greatest for low-income groups, even accounting for the regressive distribution of the benefits from increased property values.

Can State and Local Economic Development Policies Benefit the National Economy?

I firmly believe that state government must resist the temptation to intervene directly in economic decisions of the marketplace. It is certainly true that the combination of reduced federal support for state and local programs and the devastating impact of our recent recessions has put enormous pressure on state governments to "do something." The reality, however, is that state actions have not always increased the country's net investment. On a national scale, the impact of state economic development initiatives on U.S. economic activity is dominated by monetary, fiscal, and trade decisions at the federal level. States, therefore, are merely competing at the margins *with one another* for their share of new investment. Little or no net gain for the United States as a whole is attained from these programs. (Ralph E. Bailey, chairman and chief executive officer, Conoco, Inc., memorandum of dissent on pages 88-89 of *Leadership for Dynamic State Economies,* Committee for Economic Development, 1986)

The argument is often made, as Bailey does in the above quotation, that state and local economic development policies are, even at best, a zero-sum game from a national perspective. It is argued that even if economic development policies succeed in increasing growth in one area, this growth is merely transferred from some other area, and overall national growth is unaffected. The lower unemployment and higher wages in one area are offset by the higher unemployment and lower wages in other areas.

My argument against this "zero-sum" game position is twofold. First, even if it were true that state and local economic development policies just reshuffled jobs among geographic areas, such reshuffling may benefit the nation. Individuals vary in the dollar value they place on getting a job, which determines how high a wage they will require in order to accept a job. For example, individuals may place a higher value on obtaining a job—that is, are willing to accept a very low wage—if they have few other income sources. Individuals may place a lower value on obtaining a job if they feel they make good use of their time outside the wage labor market, such as taking care of children. In low-unemployment areas, most individuals who place a high value on getting a job will get one fairly quickly. In high-unemployment areas, many individuals who place a high value on getting a job will remain unemployed for a long time. As a result, the average unemployed individual in high-unemployment areas will "need" a job more—in the sense of placing a higher dollar value on getting one—than the average unemployed individual in low-unemployment areas. High-unemployment areas will benefit more from an additional job than low-unemployment areas, as the social benefits from hiring the average unemployed person are higher.

The vigor with which states and governments pursue economic development probably reflects these differences in the social benefits of reducing unemployment. Common sense suggests that high-unemployment states and localities will face greater political pressures to expand economic development policies. The scanty empirical evidence suggests that high-unemployment areas respond to these pressures by more aggressively pursuing economic development. The competitive game of state and local economic development probably helps redistribute jobs to the most needy areas.

Second, state and local competition for jobs may increase national growth. Higher subsidies in many local areas for expanded business output and employment may reduce the average national unemployment rate and increase output. In addition, the transfer of jobs from low-unemployment regions to high-unemployment regions may reduce inflationary pressures and allow national policymakers to achieve lower national unemployment and higher output without increasing inflation.

One potential negative effect of state and local competition for jobs is that the national distribution of income may become more regressive, that is, more income may go to the rich instead of the poor. Competition for jobs may lead to reduced taxes on business owners. Wealthy business owners may benefit. But policymakers should offset these benefits for the rich by making the federal tax system more progressive, rather than by attempting to eliminate competition for jobs.

Is the Glass Half-Full or Half-Empty?

The focus of this book is on how state and local economic development policies can potentially provide benefits. This focus is necessary because the prevailing intellectual assessment of these policies is too negative. It should not, however, be interpreted as a blanket endorsement of all state and local economic development policies.

Empirical evidence presented here suggests that the benefits and costs of state and local economic development policies will often be close. Net benefits of economic development policies are most likely to be positive in areas of high unemployment and for programs that have large effects on business location, expansion, and start-up decisions per dollar of government spending.

Organization of the Book

The remainder of the book presents these arguments in more detail. Chapter 2 reviews what previous research shows about how state and local public policies affect business growth.

Chapters 3 through 7 develop the broad theme of the book: how metropolitan growth affects different groups in the population. Chapter

3 presents the theory of likely distributional effects of local growth. Chapters 4, 5, and 6 present empirical estimates of the effects of metropolitan growth on unemployment rates and other measures of labor market activities, prices, and wages. Chapter 7 examines the overall effect of growth on real earnings, and uses these results to simulate the likely quantitative magnitude of the distributional and efficiency effects of local growth.

Chapter 8 considers whether state and local economic development efforts help the national economy. Chapter 9 concludes with a discussion of the broader implications of these results for macroeconomic policy, antipoverty policy, and the role of local areas in national policy.

NOTES

1. The theoretical analysis of the book may also apply to groupings of counties in nonmetropolitan areas that constitute true regional labor and housing markets. Virtually none of the empirical work of the book deals with these nonmetropolitan economic regions, however, so extrapolation of the findings to nonmetropolitan areas is more uncertain.

2. I refer here to such recent books as *Laboratories of Democracy*, by journalist David Osborne (1988), or *The Wealth of States*, by several policy analysts associated with the Council of State Planning and Policy Agencies (Vaughan, Pollard, and Dyer 1985). Both these books argue against traditional economic development policies and in favor of some new wave economic development policies. A more scholarly account of this debate is provided by political scientist Peter Eisinger, in his comprehensive book on state and local economic development, *The Rise of the Entrepreneurial State* (Eisinger 1988). Case studies of how this debate has been resolved so far in various states are provided in *The New Economic Role of American States,* edited by Scott Fosler of the Committee for Economic Development, a national business think tank (Fosler 1988).

3. Eisinger (1988), p. 10.

4. Vaughan, Pollard, and Dyer, in their book *The Wealth of States*, are certainly aware of the political importance of creating jobs. One of their arguments for a greater focus on new wave economic development policies is that such policies are more effective than traditional economic development policies in creating jobs in the long run: ". . . in the long run, employment opportunities and wealth will be greater under an entrepreneurial strategy than under any alternative approach to development" (Vaughan, Pollard, and Dyer 1985, p. 128). Osborne also makes similar arguments in his book: "Businesses that fail to innovate do not last long; regional economies in which innovation does not flourish quickly stagnate." (Osborne 1988, p. 252).

5. These Michigan figures come from a report by the Citizens Research Council of Michigan (1986). Michigan is the only state I know of that keeps track of the volume of property tax abatements throughout the state.

6. These Tennessee figures come from a paper by Bartik, Becker, Lake, and Bush (1987). The figures are based on the in lieu of tax agreement between Maury County and Saturn, and on information from the Tennessee Department of Economic and Community Development on state expenditures on roads and job training for the Saturn plant. Stating the subsidy in present value terms is an appropriate way of emphasizing the large size of traditional economic development

subsidies. The present value of some flow over time of subsidies tells us what one-time subsidy, given today, would have the same value as that flow of subsidies. If all new manufacturing investment received the same present value subsidy as Saturn, the resulting flow of subsidies would be equivalent to spending $3.4 billion annually on subsidies. Total manufacturing gross investment in 1985 was $81.8 billion; $144 million times 81.8/3.5 would yield a total present value of new subsidy commitments of $3.4 billion. I should note that the Saturn subsidy was not particularly large for an auto plant; for example, the Kentucky subsidy to its Toyota plant was apparently much greater (Milward and Newman 1989).

7. Hal Hovey, editor of *State Policy Reports*, has stated that "state tax systems are evolving in the direction of [development-oriented] tax policies," which would eventually imply "eliminating *all* state and local taxes paid in operations, such as manufacturing, that have choices of where they locate and expand." (Hovey 1986, pp. 94-95). According to Steve Gold, former Director of Fiscal Studies of the National Conference of State Legislatures, "Interstate tax competition not only remains, but may intensify." (Gold 1988, p. 27).

8. Cross and Allan (1988) discuss the history of the hysteresis concept.

— 2 —
Can State and Local Policies Affect Economic Development?

> Business incentive policies, including tax credits and writedowns, loans, guarantees, subsidies (and even conditioning plant closures and relocations with an "exit" notice) are assumed to influence the cost-sensitive locational behavior of firms if they are large enough. . . . [This] widespread belief in the potency of incentives . . . is unsubstantiated by empirical evidence. (P. 43 in *Urban America in the Eighties*, Report of the Panel on Policies and Prospects for Metropolitan and Nonmetropolitan America, President's Commission for a National Agenda for the Eighties, 1980)

Critics of state and local economic development policies claim that these policies have little effect on employment growth of a local economy such as a metropolitan area or state. This chapter disagrees with that claim, and argues that state and local policies can significantly affect local growth. It analyzes four types of evidence on whether the policies of a state or local area affect its growth:

- evaluations of specific state or local economic development programs;
- surveys of businesses about the influence of state and local policies on their investment decisions;
- case studies of how changes in state and local policies might influence the behavior of an actual firm; and
- econometric studies of how state and local policies influence state and local growth, branch plant location decisions, and new firm start-up decisions.

17

Evaluations of Specific Programs

Relatively few studies have examined the effects of specific state or local economic development programs. Table 2.1 describes recent studies of specific programs. As shown in the table, there is evidence that enterprise zones, research parks, location incentives such as property tax abatements, and export promotion programs, make some difference to state or local economic growth. But not all studies find positive or statistically significant effects of these programs, and in one case, the study by James Papke of the Indiana enterprise zone program, the policy is associated with economic decline in the targeted regions.

These studies of specific economic development programs suffer from two major limitations. First, in some cases the programs are small compared to the areas whose growth they are supposed to affect (Luger 1987; McHone 1984; Coughlin and Cartwright 1987; O'hUallacháin and Satterthwaite 1990; Ambrosius 1989; and Feiock 1987).[1] For example, in Coughlin and Cartwright's study, state export promotion programs are minuscule compared to the size of any state's economy. Small programs could have effects that are large relative to program size. But relative to the size of the affected local economy, program effects are probably small enough to be overwhelmed by unobserved or random factors that alter the growth of that local area. Estimated program effects will either be statistically insignificant in this case, or will reflect the influence of unobserved local characteristics. Any statistically significant effects of the program are likely to be spurious.[2]

This mismatch of program size and local economy size is less important for studies of enterprise zones, a program designed to amass sufficient incentives to noticeably affect a small area.[3] But studies of enterprise zones and other relatively "large" economic development programs suffer from a second problem: it is difficult to determine what would have happened to the local area without the program. Enterprise zones are chosen in part because they are zones of low economic growth. Hence, their growth even after zone designation would be expected to be poor. Comparison of predesignation and postdesignation growth of the zone, as was done in the study by Jones and others (1985), may provide a better evaluation of program effects, but changes in zone growth could be due to more general economic forces, such as national booms or recessions, or changes in the overall national performance of specific industries. An even better approach is to compare changes in the growth of local areas targeted by an economic development program with changes in growth in control areas, as was done in the studies by Papke (1991), Luger and Goldstein (1990), Papke (1990), and Rubin and Wilder (1989). But choosing control areas—which ideally would be identical in all observed and unobserved characteristics to the targeted local areas—is difficult. Existing studies generally provide only brief discussions of how control areas were chosen, and only estimate effects using one set of control areas.

Three research strategies offer promise for better evaluations of the effects of specific economic development programs. First, for a program large enough to have a detectable effect on overall local growth, better methods for choosing control areas are needed.[4] For each targeted local area, researchers should select several alternative sets of control areas, based on different criteria for choosing characteristics on which to match controls to the targeted areas. The sensitivity of estimated program effects to the choice of different sets of control areas should be reported by researchers.[5]

For economic development programs that are too small to have an aggregate effect on the growth of a local economy, a promising research strategy for program evaluation is to collect micro-level data on businesses assisted under the economic development program, and on a control group of unassisted businesses.[6] The performance of the experimental group (the assisted businesses) and the control group would be compared on some measure of goals that is relevant to that particular program. For example, a technology transfer program might be evaluated based on the differences in productivity gains, technology adoption, or job gains, between the experimental and control groups of businesses.

Ideally, the experimental group of businesses and the control group of businesses would be randomly chosen. Random assignment ensures

Table 2.1
Studies of Specific Economic Development Policies

Author	Program Studied	Methodology	Findings
L. Papke (1991)	Indiana enterprise zone	Regression analysis of effects of EZ on inventories, machinery and equipment, and unemployment claims, using pre-and post-zone designation data on jurisdictions surrounding EZ, and control jurisdictions	Enterprise zones increase inventories and reduce unemployment claims, but also reduce machinery and equipment investment
Luger & Goldstein (1990)	Research parks	Comparison of changes in employment growth rates, before and after research park established in research park counties, to changes in growth rates in "control" counties; both comparisons of means and regression analysis	58% of parks "succeed" in that their counties have greater increase in growth than controls; older parks and parks with better university ties are more successful
O'hUallacháin & Satterthwaite (1990)	Enterprise zones, research partks industrial revenue bonds (IRBs)	Regression analysis of determinants of MSA growth by industry	Enterprise zones and research parks had positive effects in many industries, although seldom significant; IRBs did not have positive effect.
J. Papke (1990)	Indiana enterprise zone	Regression analysis examining pre- and post-zone designation level of capital in zones, compared to a control set of Indiana townships	Enterprise zones had significantly less capital (7%) after designation than before, compared to control townships.

Study	Policy	Method	Findings
Woodward (1990)	State offices in Japan and promotion efforts as recruitment tool for Japanese plants	Statistical analysis of whether state office or state industrial development index (Source: Luger (1987)) affects probability of Japanese plant choosing state	Presence of office in Japan was associated with close to double probability of plant choosing state; effect of industrial development index insignificant
Ambrosius (1989)	State revenue bond financing, public works, accelerated depreciation, various tax breaks, enterprise zones, job training	Regression analysis of whether level or trend in state manufacturing value-added per capita or state unemployment rate changed after adoption of particular incentive	Generally, insignificant effects, except tax break for land and capital improvements significantly associated with declining trend in unemployment rate
Coughlin, Terza & Arromdee (1989)	State expenditures to attract foreign direct investment	Regression-style analysis of whether state spending affected probability of being chosen for FDI	Large effect, usually significantly positive
Erickson & Friedman (1989)	Enterprise zones	Regression analysis of number of zone investments and jobs created as function of zone characteristics, zone incentives and MSA characteristics	Number of incentives often positively associated with better zone performance, although not significant in all specifications; number of zones in state often negatively associated with zone performance, although not always significant

Table 2.1 (continued)

Author	Program Studied	Methodology	Findings
Rubin & Wilder (1989)	Evansville, Indiana enterprise zone	Shift-share comparison of growth of enterprise zone industries with overall Evansville MSA	Enterprise zone gained significantly more jobs than MSA in warehousing, wholesale trade, retail trade, and services
Walker & Greenstreet (1989)	Wide variety of incentives, such as site-specific infrastructre, tax breaks, job training, etc.	Survey asking whether incentives were decisive in final location choice of firms looking for new site; logit analysis of which of two finalists chosen; regression analysis of in-situ expansion	Of plants offered incentives, 37% claimed were decisive; logit analysis showed significant effect of incentives on final site choice, holding other site characteristics constant; insignificant effect of incentives on in-situ expansion
U.S. General Accounting Office (1988)	Enterprise zone program in Maryland in first 4 years of operation	Time series analysis of breaks in trend of employment growth in EZ businesses that received EZ subsidies, and interviews with large employers responsible for breaks in aggregate trend	Although there were some increases in growth in zones, the large employers mainly responsible for those breaks in trend stated that factors other than EZ had influenced their decisions
Coughlin & Cartwright (1987)	State foreign export promotion programs	Regression analysis of dollars of state manufacturing exports as fundtion of state export promotion spending and other state characteristics	$1 of extra state promotion spending increases state exports by $432

Author (Year)	Policy	Method	Findings
Feiock (1987)	Counts of number of business incentive programs, special business services, promotional ads	Regression analysis of employment growth, new investment, and change in number of business establishments, for 92 cities	Generally positive effects of a city having larger number of economic development programs, particularly business services and ads
Luger (1987)	Financial/tax subsidies, recruitment efforts, R&D support capital provision, state-funded job training	Regression analysis of effects on state wage and unemployment levels and changes	State job training reduces wages and reduces unemployment; other estimates very imprecise
Jones, et al. (1985)	Enterprise zones	Comparison of zone employment growth before (1980-82) and after (1982-84) zone designation, using Dun and Bradstreet data	6 of 8 zones did better in after period
McHone (1984)	Special tax and financial incentives	Regression comparison of growth rates of counties in different states but same MSA	MSA counties in states with property tax abatements, accelerated depreciation, or state-run development bond programs tended to grow faster than rest of MSA

that any difference in performance of the two groups can only be due to the program. The random assignment approach is a feasible way to study entrepreneurial training programs that seek to develop business management skills; the use of the experimental method is well-established in the closely related area of job training, and the potential clients for entrepreneurial training are not likely to have the political clout to complain about being experimented upon. As of 1991, the States of Washington and Massachusetts were conducting experiment-based evaluations of entrepreneurial training programs for unemployment insurance (UI) recipients. Results from these experiments are expected in 1993.

Most economic development programs for existing businesses, however, would find it politically infeasible to randomly exclude some established business from the benefits of a government program.[7] This increases the difficulty of estimating program effects, but good estimates can still be obtained if the control group is carefully chosen to match the experimental group, and if the empirical research controls for other factors affecting business performance.[8] Finally, in some cases a valid control group is unobtainable. For example, grants to one firm for applied research may provide "spillover benefits"—such as encouraging other firms to adopt these technological innovations—for all firms in a specific industry in that geographic area. But some insights into program effects could still be obtained through case study interviews or surveys that asked businesses to identify program effects, in this case the spillover effects of government-sponsored research.

The key advantage of micro studies of economic development programs and specific firms is that these studies match the scale of the program and the measures of program effects. Small-scale programs— and programs in an ideal world should be experimented with on a small scale before full implementation—are more likely to have detectable effects upon specific firms than upon the overall economy of a state or metropolitan area.

A third strategy for evaluating the effects of specific economic development programs is to infer their effects from estimates of how more major cost factors affect state and local business growth. If state and local business growth is based on overall profitability offered by the area's economy, the percentage effects on business growth of a percentage change in some cost factor should be roughly proportional to that factor's share in total costs (see appendix 2.1). If one factor is 1 percent of business costs, and another factor is 20 percent of business costs, a percentage change in the second factor should have 20 times the effect on business growth of the same percentage change in the first factor.

The advantage of this research strategy is that it is easier to accurately detect the effects on business growth of major cost factors relevant to many firms in many local areas than of minor cost factors relevant to a few firms in a few areas. The disadvantage is that these inferences are only as valid as the theory underlying them, namely, that the dollar effect on profits determines business decisions. If business location and growth are strongly influenced by more subjective features of state and local economic development programs (for example, what these programs convey about the "business climate" of an area), then inferences about program effects on growth based on program effects on business costs will be imprecise.

The rest of this chapter focuses on whether significant state and local business cost factors—such as state and local business tax costs—can affect an area's business growth. Interpreted narrowly, much of the evidence considered only suggests whether overall business taxes, or public services, or other major policies, have effects on an area's business growth. But significant effects of state and local tax costs on area business growth can also be interpreted as implying that other policies affecting business costs can also significantly affect area growth. Even new wave policies—such as subsidies for business applied research, training for small business and entrepreneurs, and information on how to export—can be viewed as helping reduce business costs of acquiring information, as discussed in chapter 1. If tax costs and other business costs have minuscule effect on an area's business growth, then it is hard to see how new wave programs that reduce business costs could much affect area growth, unless these programs have very high ratios of business cost reduction per dollar of government spending, and are vastly expanded beyond their current small scale.[9]

Of course, ideally we would like to know more about the relative effectiveness of new wave economic development programs versus more traditional economic development programs of tax breaks and financial subsidies for business. We need to know whether new wave programs are more cost-effective than traditional economic development programs: per dollar of government expenditure or foregone tax revenue, which programs provide the largest real cost savings to business and greatest incentives for business growth?[10] With current data, we can only get good estimates of the effects of traditional economic development policies. Traditional policies receive most of the resources state and local governments currently devote to economic development, as noted in chapter 1, so estimates of the effects of these policies are of independent interest. Furthermore, as discussed above, whether traditional economic development policies have much effect may have general implications for whether any kind of state and local economic development policy has the potential of affecting an area's growth.

Survey Evidence on the Influence
of State and Local Policies

Surveys of firms are often used to determine how taxes and other major public policies affected a particular business location decision. The surveys differ greatly in design. Sometimes firms are asked to list "must" factors; other times, firms are asked to list "desirable" or "significant" factors. Some surveys ask about the decision to choose a particular metropolitan area or state; other surveys ask about the decision to choose a particular site within a metropolitan area or state.

The best recent studies suggest that taxes loom larger in location decisions as survey questions turn from "must" factors to "desirable" or "significant" factors, and as survey questions turn from the choice of a state location to the choice of a specific community within a metropolitan area. For example, Schmenner's (1982) survey of Fortune 500 companies found that only 1 percent listed taxes as a "must" factor in a firm selecting a particular broad region and state for a new branch plant, but 35 percent listed low taxes as "desirable if available and helped to tip scales in favor of this site." Premus's (1982) survey of high-tech companies found that 67 percent listed taxes as "significant" or "very significant" in influencing state growth decisions. Walker and Greenstreet's (1989) survey of new Appalachian manufacturing plants found that of plants offered tax and other financial incentives, 37 percent stated that these incentives were decisive in their final location decision. Finally, Rubin's (1991) survey of New Jersey firms receiving enterprise zone tax incentives found that 32 percent reported that these incentives were their primary or only reason to locate or expand their business in the zone.

In addition, some highly ranked factors in business location decisions are partly influenced by state and local public policy. For example, Schmenner (1982) found that the most frequently mentioned "must" for firms in choosing a particular region or state was a "favorable labor climate." "Labor climate" may be affected by state policy decisions on unemployment insurance, workers' compensation, minimum wages, and labor relations laws.

Although surveys provide useful information, their information on policy effects is too vague. Policymakers might want to know the growth effect of a 10 percent cut in taxes. Existing surveys cannot answer that question. Whether a firm lists low taxes as influencing a particular site choice does not help in answering the question. A particular firm may not see low taxes as influential, because all the site finalists had low taxes, but a 10 percent increase in taxes could still have altered the decision.

Another problem with surveys is that businessmen have political incentives to exaggerate the effects of taxes and other economic development incentives upon their location choices. A business executive who admits that the incentive received by his/her firm had no effect might cause political problems for the firm if specific survey responses became known. Furthermore, even if there is little risk of specific survey responses being released, executives responding to the survey might feel enough solidarity with business political interests to want the general findings of the study to indicate that tax and other incentives for business are needed.

The Case Study Approach

An alternative approach to examining how taxes and other major policies affect business location is case studies of actual firms. The purpose of such case studies would be to determine how much of a policy change would be needed for a firm to change its location decision. If the studied firm is "average," its responses give a rough idea of how policy changes affect overall business growth. Only one study (Bartik et al. 1987) has used the case study approach.

The study I did with my colleagues reconstructed the location decision of the General Motors Saturn plant. Using information on car demand by state and transport costs, we identified Terre Haute, Indiana as the site that would minimize the costs of transporting the Saturn car to market. We then examined more closely all sites in Indiana and nearby states that were near the intersection of two or more interstates. For each site, we looked at wage and tax costs. (The Saturn plant was to be unionized, but Saturn suppliers, many of whom were expected to locate near the plant, would pay regionally varying wages, and we calculated how these wage variations would affect the cost to Saturn of supplies.) Tax costs reflected all normal state and local taxes (before abatements), and were calculated by James Papke of Purdue using his "TAXSIM" model, which incorporates the known factor mix of a firm and detailed information on state tax laws. Summing these three costs (transportation, supplier wages, taxes) showed that the Nashville area was the lowest cost site for Saturn of the sites analyzed. Since the site actually chosen (Spring Hill, Tennessee) is 35 miles from Nashville, we have some confidence that the model captures the major quantitative factors considered by General Motors in siting the Saturn plant.[11]

Table 2.2 compares the estimated costs per car of the Nashville area to other possible sites for the Saturn plant. This table shows that politically plausible changes in state and local taxes could have altered the Saturn location decision. For example, if Lexington, Kentucky had lowered its taxes by 12 percent, its measured costs would have been lower than Nashville's. Tennessee offered Saturn subsidies, mostly in the form of property tax abatements, that reduced Saturn costs by $34/car from the

Table 2.2
Estimated Saturn Costs Per Car

Location	Average Cost of Transport to Market	Local Supplier Labor Cost	State and Local Taxes	Total Measured Costs
Nashville, TN	$426	$159	$118	$703
Lexington, KY	423	186	106	715
St. Louis, MO	419	172	134	725
Bloomington, IL	417	202	162	781
Kalamazoo, MI	430	244	116	790
Terre Haute, IN	413	209	168	790
Marysville, OH	427	219	169	815

costs listed in the table. It appears from table 2.2 that subsidies of this size could have determined which site was chosen for the Saturn plant.

Econometric Studies of State and Local Policies and Business Growth

The many econometric studies of business activity explain statistically how state and local business growth is affected by a variety of state and local characteristics. The "better" econometric studies appear to have reached some consensus about the effects of policies on a local economy. Judging some studies to be better than others implies criteria for a good local growth study. Hence, before summarizing the results from different studies, I will discuss some of the difficult methodological and data problems in estimating local growth models. I then summarize econometric studies on the effects on state and local business activity of taxes, public services, wages, unions, environmental regulations, and capital market imperfections—all potentially major location determinants that state and local governments can influence.[12]

Methodological and Data Issues in Business Location Modeling

The problems that must be dealt with by econometric models of the growth of a local economy include:

1. *Complexity of business location decision.* Most business location studies use aggregate data on state or local business activity levels or growth (e.g., aggregate employment). Modeling the determination of aggregate business activity is difficult. The aggregate level of business activity in an area is an amalgam of diverse decisions: new branch plant location decisions, small business start-up decisions, plant expansion or contraction decisions, and plant closing decisions. Because these decisions are so diverse, researchers examining aggregate state or local growth find it difficult to decide on the "specification" of estimating equations: what variables should help explain the aggregate level of business activity, how the effects of a change in a variable should

differ with the level of a variable,[13] and whether we might theoretically expect the estimated effects of different variables to be equal.

One solution to this problem is to pretend that decisions about aggregate state or local business activity are made by one decisionmaker seeking to maximize profits. This simplification helps in specifying an estimating equation. But the assumption of one decisionmaker might miss some crucial aspect of business location decisions.

Problems with modeling aggregate business location patterns increase the attractiveness of focusing on particular types of business location decisions, such as branch plant or small business starts. For a specific type of business location decision, the appropriate specification of an estimating equation may be more apparent to the intuition of the researcher.

2. *Durability of capital and agglomeration economies.* Because capital is durable, today's business activity will depend on yesterday's business activity. Furthermore, agglomeration economies—cost reductions due to having a greater concentration of a particular type of business activity in a local area—will also lead to some positive association of yesterday's business activity with today's business activity.[14]

Because of capital durability and agglomeration economies, equations explaining state and local business activity or growth should include some measures of lagged business activity. Including lagged business activity as a control variable helps avoid bias in estimating how state and local characteristics affect current business activity. But the importance of capital durability and agglomeration economies also implies that current economic characteristics will generally only explain a portion of a local area's current business activity. This makes it more difficult to precisely measure the effects of current economic characteristics on business activity.

3. *Problems in measuring many key location factors.* Many key economic characteristics of state and local areas are difficult to measure, or are inadequately measured for political reasons. These problems seem most acute for wages, public services, and taxes.

The ideal local wage measure holds labor quality constant. This requires preliminary estimation of how wages vary in different local economies, holding education, experience, and other labor quality measures constant. To avoid time-consuming preliminary estimations, most studies use rough measures of the cost of labor, such as the average manufacturing wage. The average manufacturing wage does not hold constant the quality of the local labor force, however.

An alternative to preliminary equations estimating the quality-adjusted price of labor is to include measures of labor quality in the equation explaining business activity or business growth. For example, the average educational level of the local area's population might be included as a rough measure of labor skill.

The effective quantity and quality of public services in a local area is also difficult to measure. Data are readily available on state and local public spending for different public services. But using current public spending data as a business location determinant has two deficiencies. First, many public services to business depend on public capital stocks, such as the amount of road, rail, and air transportation infrastructure, or the amount of water and sewer lines. Current public spending is only slightly correlated with the amount of these capital stocks. Unfortunately, data on state and local public capital stocks are difficult to obtain.[15]

Second, current spending does not control for the quality of public services. We want measures of public service output: the effectiveness of the state and local educational system, the impact of the local police force on crime, etc. Such output measures are difficult to find.

Finally, data on state and local business taxes are difficult to obtain. No federal statistical agency collects comparable data across states and local areas on business tax rates. Federal statistical agencies prefer avoiding controversies over which state and local areas have high business tax rates. Some research groups do publish data on business tax rates, but in many cases these are nominal tax rates and fail to control for differences across state and local areas in how the tax base is defined. Even when data are provided on effective business tax rates, these data are usually average effective business tax rates for business as a whole or for manufacturing in general. We know that effective business tax rates vary a great deal across different industries. Furthermore, the tax rates that would apply to one more dollar of investment by a new or existing firm—what economists would call "marginal" tax rates—may vary a great deal from average effective tax rates, as new investments are frequently granted property tax relief and state corporate income tax investment credits. Only one state (Michigan) systematically collects data on the magnitude of property tax abatements to businesses, and no state systematically collects data on the magnitude of other special tax incentives to new business investment. State and local policymakers may be concerned that publicizing the dollar amount of these tax breaks would lead to voter opposition.

Problems in measuring potential determinants of state and local business growth will tend to bias estimates of their effects towards zero. The more a variable we measure is meaningless "noise," the less it will appear to affect state and local growth.[16]

4. *Unobservable characteristics of regions, states, and local areas.* No matter how thorough the research, any empirical investigation will omit many potential location determinants. This omission causes "omitted variable bias": the estimated effects of variables included in the study will in part reflect the effects of these omitted variables.

For example, absent special controls, any variable that tends to be higher in the fast-growing South and West will appear to positively affect growth. Such variables as percentage of state land in national parks and average family consumption of iced tea will appear to be powerful growth determinants.

In a cross-section study, in which data on various local economies (e.g., states, metropolitan areas) are only available for one time period, the researcher can control for omitted effects of large regions (e.g., the Northeast, the South) by including dummy variables for these large regions in the estimating equation. Including regional dummies is equivalent to focusing on why business growth differs among the local economies within the larger regions; the regional dummies explain the differences in average growth rates among the larger regions.[17]

With panel data, cross-section data from more than one time period, the researcher can control for omitted characteristics of state and local areas. The researcher can include a dummy variable for each state or local area represented in the data. An equivalent procedure is to difference all variables from their means for that state or local area, or from last period's level for that state or local area.[18]

5. *Endogeneity of many crucial explanatory variables.* One problem of business location research is that many potentially important location determinants, such as wages, land prices, and taxes, may be endogenously determined by business growth. By this I mean that any omitted variable that changes business growth will thereby change these location determinants. This endogeneity problem is a more far-reaching criticism of state and local growth models than saying that *some* omitted variables may lead to biased estimates.

Higher state and local business growth from any source probably increases wages and land prices. If we do not hold constant the events that really caused the growth—and it is not possible to control for all variables that might affect local growth—then business growth, and local wages and prices, will have some tendency to be positively correlated. Unless statistical procedures are adopted to deal with the endogeneity problem, the estimated effects of wages and prices on growth will be less negative than the "true" effect of wages and prices, holding constant all other growth determinants.

For example, suppose that unbeknownst to the researcher, the growth of some local economy increases due to the location of a new defense base. The wages and land prices of the local area go up as a result of the faster local employment growth that results from the new base. But as the researcher tries to statistically explain why this area has grown faster than other areas, it will appear that higher wages and land prices have "caused" higher local growth.

Policy variables such as taxes may also be endogenous. This endogeneity is most likely when the researcher uses rough measures of business taxes such as total state and local taxes per dollar of personal income. An increase in business activity will increase the denominator of this expression, and decrease this measure of tax rates. In this case, higher local growth is causing state and local tax rates to be lower, but it may appear that lower tax rates are causing local growth to be higher. State and local growth models will tend to exaggerate the negative effects of taxes on growth.

This endogeneity problem may be less severe when more accurate measures of business taxes are used, but it can still lead to biases. Local economies that are particularly unattractive to business will tend to have lower tax bases per capita. Policymakers in this situation may attempt to maintain per capita service levels by increasing tax rates. In this case, lower state and local growth is causing state and local tax rates to be higher, but it may appear that higher tax rates are causing growth to be lower. Of course, policymakers in a slow growth area could also decide to lower business tax rates in an attempt to spark business growth. In this case, lower local growth is causing local tax rates to be lower, but it may appear that lower taxes are causing growth to be lower. In sum, the endogeneity of state and local taxes may cause growth models to either exaggerate or understate the negative effects of taxes on growth, depending on what one assumes about how growth usually affects tax rates.

The endogeneity of wages, land prices, taxes, and many other characteristics of local economies is difficult to deal with in business location studies. The needed statistical procedure is well known to econometricians. The researcher should find ''instrumental variables'' that are correlated with the endogenous explanatory variables but uncorrelated with unobserved factors affecting the dependent variable (e.g., business growth). The statistical estimation will then proceed by only examining shifts in the explanatory variables due to these ''instrumental variables.'' These shifts in explanatory variables are, by construction, uncorrelated with omitted variables. The practical problem is that convincing instruments are hard to find. A critic could usually suggest some reason why an instrument shifting local taxes, or local wages or land prices, would also be correlated with unobserved variables affecting local growth. It is difficult to disprove a criticism involving unobserved variables.

For example, one could argue that some political events, such as court orders to improve state prison conditions or equalize school spending across jurisdictions in the state, are ''exogenous'' determinants of state and local tax rates: these court orders could be argued to be not strongly correlated with business growth trends. The instrumental variable procedure is to examine tax effects on business growth by only considering tax changes caused by these court orders, ignoring evidence from all other tax changes. This procedure throws away a great deal of information. In addition, perhaps court orders are correlated with business growth trends. States whose economic prospects are worsening over time may be more prone to underfund their prisons and schools, leading to court intervention.

Taxes

[C]hanges in business taxes cannot be viewed as an effective means of influencing business locational decisions. . . . The reasons why changes in the state's business taxes are unlikely to be a successful policy can be summarized as follows. First, innumerable factors are important to a business in its decision about where to locate. . . . Second, taxes are one of the many costs of doing business and the magnitude of these other costs may easily swamp the amount of state taxes involved. . . . Third, state and local tax payments are deductible for purposes of the federal corporate income tax. . . . Fourth, differences in state and local taxes may reflect differences in the level and quality of state and local public goods and services, and these goods and services also affect business locational decisions. . . . Fifth, to the extent that tax rate differentials are capitalized, their impact will be reduced. . . . Sixth, most relocating companies plan to stay at their new site years longer than any group of elected officials is likely to be in office. Consequently, current tax levels, special concessions, or special features of the tax law may not be a reliable basis upon which to make a multi-million dollar investment. . . . Seventh, a state tax incentive that is granted by way of incorporating a similar federal provision may have no impact on a firm's decision making if the future of the federal provision itself is in jeopardy. . . . Eighth, . . . [i]f incentives are effective at all, a state will gain only a short-lived advantage over other states because the latter can be expected to adopt similar ones. . . . Ninth, some executives charged with the locational decision may be uninformed about the existence of tax incentives. . . . Finally, there are relatively few footloose firms that can be affected by tax incentives. (Richard Pomp, Professor of Law, University of Connecticut Law School, and former director, New York State Legislative Commission on the Modernization and Simplification of Tax Administration and Tax Law, in *Tax Notes*, November 1, 1985 issue)

The effect of taxes on state and local business growth is the most controversial issue in economic development policy. As pointed out in chapter 1, the resolution of this issue can affect the entire design of state and local tax systems.

The usual theoretical arguments against a large effect of state and local taxes on business growth are unpersuasive. The above quote from Richard Pomp summarizes the most common arguments. Some of these arguments only apply to special cases. The hypothesized ineffectiveness of tax incentives that are temporary or poorly publicized is irrelevant for well-designed state or local business tax policies.

Other arguments against significant effects of state and local business taxes rely on implicit assumptions about business behavior that need to be empirically tested. No doubt few firms are completely "footloose," that is lacking in any locational requirements. Also, many nontax characteristics of areas affect business costs, and taxes are only a small proportion of business costs. But this still leaves open the question of how responsive businesses are to variations in costs across areas.

There are strong theoretical arguments that many firms today may be quite sensitive to production cost differentials across different states or metropolitan areas, including the relatively small production cost differentials that can be brought about by state and local taxes. Over time, the costs of transporting finished products and supplies have declined relative to production costs, due to improved technology for transporting goods, and production innovations that reduce the weight of supplies needed to produce a given quantity of many products. For many firms, at least several metropolitan areas and states may provide similar access to markets and supplies. Even small differences in production costs among these several competing metropolitan areas or states may be enough to determine the firm's location decision.

The argument that public service cuts and tax responses from other states will offset any business tax cuts by one state also requires empirical investigation before being accepted. We can imagine circumstances in which these offsets will not occur at all: for example, a state business tax cut financed by cutting welfare payments, at a time when nearby states are facing budgetary problems. Thus, it is a policy-relevant issue what the effects of state business tax cuts are, holding business public services constant, and holding the tax policies of other states constant. We can then consider the effects of the tax cuts if accompanied by public service cuts or tax cuts by other states.

The "capitalization" argument is that cuts in state and local taxes will lead to offsetting increases in land prices. But even if land prices increase enough to keep profits constant, lower business taxes—which are mostly taxes on capital—and higher land prices will tend to attract land users who use a high ratio of capital to land ("capital-intensive" land users), and will give an incentive for any particular land user to substitute capital for land. The ratio of capital to land, and hence the total amount of capital, will increase in the jurisdiction. Because businesses are relatively capital-intensive land users, business capital per acre will increase even more.

Finally, because all costs are deductible from business revenue under the federal income tax, the deductibility of state and local business taxes does not reduce the effects of taxes versus other characteristics of state and local areas.

Thus the effect of state and local business taxes on economic growth can only be ascertained through empirical research. Table 2.3 summarizes the estimated effects of taxes on business location from a number of empirical studies. I attempted to summarize all empirical studies, published and unpublished, that have been done since Carlton's seminal research on business location decisions in 1979.[19] Appendix 2.2 provides a separate summary of each individual study.

Table 2.3 describes, for various categories of studies of taxes and business location, the percentage of studies that found at least one negative and statistically significant effect of state and local taxes on business locations. Table 2.3 also provides, for each category, the average long-run percentage effect on local business activity of a 1 percent across-the-board increase in all state and local taxes (the "elasticity" of business activity with respect to state and local taxes). Several possible measures of "average" elasticities are reported.

The most important conclusion from this table is that most recent business location studies have found some evidence of significant negative effects of state and local taxes on regional business growth. The findings of recent studies differ from those of studies in the 1950s, 1960s, and early and mid-1970s, which generally did not find statistically significant and negative effects of taxes on state and local growth.[20] Any individual study summarized in table 2.3 and appendix 2.2 can be criticized for some defect in methodology or data. But the consensus from so many studies limits the force of such criticism. If the consensus of significant negative tax effects is incorrect, the problem must lie in some systematic flaw that cuts across many studies.

Further support for significant tax effects on business location decisions is provided by the patterns revealed in table 2.3 in how estimated tax effects vary across different types of studies. Three important patterns can be noted in the table. First, tax effects on business location decisions are generally much larger for intrametropolitan business location decisions than for intermetropolitan or interstate business location decisions. We would expect this pattern because a potential business site is likely to have closer substitutes, offering very similar profits, within that same metropolitan area than in some other state or metropolitan area.[21]

Second, studies that control for fixed effects—unobserved state or local characteristics that affect growth—more consistently indicate tax effects on location and tend to indicate larger effects. The finding that tax effects persist even with controls for fixed effects suggests that these estimated tax effects are real. In addition, this pattern of results suggests that the lack of tax effects in some studies without fixed-effect controls may be due to omitted variable bias.

Third, controls for the levels of public services make a difference. Studies that include some measure of state and local public services are more likely to find tax effects on business location. We would expect the omission of public service measures to bias estimates of tax effects on business location towards zero. The pattern of results is consistent with the existence of this bias.[22]

In addition, some specific studies suggest patterns of tax effects that are consistent with our expectations based on simple economic principles. Table 2.4 shows three interesting patterns of results.

Table 2.3
Summary of Econometric Studies of Tax Effects on Business Location

	Percentage of Studies With At Least One Statistically Significant Negative Tax Effect (1)	Mean Elasticity of Business Activity With Respect to Taxes [Range] (2)	Trimmed Mean Elasticity (3)	Median Elasticity (4)
Inter-area studies	70% (57 studies)	-.25 (s.e. = .05) [-1.40 to .76] (48 studies)	-.22 [-.73 to .04] (38 studies)	-.15
Inter-area studies with controls for "fixed effects"	92% (12 studies)	-.44 (s.e. = .11) [-1.02 to 0] (11 studies)	-.43 [-.88 to -.07] (7 studies)	-.35
Inter-area studies with public service controls	80% (30 studies)	-.33 (s.e. = .09) [-1.40 to .76] (25 studies)	-.33 [-.77 to 0] (19 studies)	-.27
Intra-area studies	57% (14 studies)	-1.48 (s.e. = .54) [-4.43 to .62] (9 studies)	-1.36 [-2.70 to 0] (7 studies)	-1.59
Intra-area studies using specific community data	70% (10 studies)	-1.91 (s.e. = .60) [-4.43 to .62] (7 studies)	-1.91 [-2.70 to -.79] (5 studies)	-1.95

NOTES: See appendix 2.2 for details on the studies summarized in this table. Inter-area studies look at what affects differences across states or MSAs in business activity or business growth. Intra-area studies look at differences within MSAs in business growth. Studies are considered to control for fixed effects by including area dummy variables or first-differencing all variables. Studies are considered to control for public services if they include *any* measure of public service quality or quantity. Intra-area studies either examine relative business growth or activity among specific communities within the MSA, or examine relative overall city *vs.* overall suburban growth. Column (1) reports the percentage of studies in a particular category with any statistically significant negative tax variable; this does not indicate that *all* tax variables have significant negative effects. Significance is judged based on a one-tail, 5 percent test. Column (2) calculates the mean long-run elasticity of business activity—however defined—with respect to an across-the-board equal percentage increase in all taxes included in the study. This could only be calculated for a subset of all the studies in each category, and the number of such studies is indicated in parentheses. The estimated standard error of the mean is also reported; the probability is 95 percent that the true population mean is within two standard errors of the sample mean. In brackets, I show the range of estimated elasticities obtained in all the studies included in calculating the mean elasticity. The trimmed mean, column (3), calculates the mean elasticity for all studies except the 10 percent (to the nearest whole number) in each tail—that is, the 10 percent of studies with the highest elasticities, and the 10 percent with the lowest elasticities, are dropped before calculating mean elasticities. This procedure is intended to diminish the influence of outlier studies on the calculations. Column (4) calculates the median elasticity—that is, the elasticity for which half the studies fall below and half above. For categories in which there were an even number of studies, the median is halfway between the two middle studies.

Table 2.4

Selected Studies with Particularly Interesting Patterns of Tax Effects on Business Location

Study	Finding of Interest
Schmenner, Huber & Cook (1987)	New branch plants who say in a survey that they want low taxes are estimated to have significantly greater response to state and local taxes in making location decisions than other plants who do not state a desire for low taxes (−3.09 vs. −.50 elasticity).
Wasylenko & McGuire (1985)	Long-run elasticity with respect to taxes is −1.54 for manufacturing employment, −.85 for total employment.
Testa (1989)	Long-run elasticity with respect to taxes is −.93 for manufacturing employment, −.02 for nonmanufacturing.
Gyourko (1987)	Higher property taxes tend to increase labor intensity of an MSA's manufacturing base.
Newman (1983)	Negative effect of corporate tax on employment growth is greater for more capital-intensive industries.

First, Schmenner and his colleagues (1987) find that corporations that say taxes are important to their locational decisionmaking appear to behave consistently with that stated preference. In their study, "tax-sensitive" corporations are estimated to place a much greater weight on state and local taxes in deciding where to locate their new branch plants.

Second, both the Wasylenko-McGuire (1985) and Testa (1989) studies find that manufacturing location decisions appear to be more sensitive to taxes than nonmanufacturing location decisions. We would expect this pattern for two reasons: (1) manufacturers are more oriented to a national market, and hence local costs are a more important competitive consideration; and (2) manufacturing firms tend to be more capital-intensive, and most state and local business taxes are taxes on capital.

Third, both the Gyourko (1987) and Newman (1983) studies find that capital-intensive industries are more sensitive to business taxes on capital than other industries.[23] For example, Gyourko finds that metropolitan areas with higher relative property taxes tend to attract more labor-intensive industries.

The existence of these sensible patterns of results in tables 2.3 and 2.4 supports the conclusion that business taxes actually do affect location decisions. A critic of these findings must not only suggest some systematic flaw that is biasing the overall consensus of recent studies, but must also explain why this bias is varying the tax effects in reasonable patterns.

This recent research suggests a consensus on the likely magnitude of tax effects on business location decisions. The long-run elasticity of business activity with respect to state and local taxes appears to lie in the range of –0.1 to –0.6 for intermetropolitan or interstate business location decisions, and –1.0 to –3.0 for intrametropolitan business location decisions. That is, if a given small suburban jurisdiction within a metropolitan area raises its taxes by 10 percent, it can expect in the long-run a reduction in its business activity by from 10 to 30 percent. If an entire metropolitan area or state raises its taxes by 10 percent, the estimated long-run effect would be a reduction of business activity between 1 percent and 6 percent. These estimated tax effects assume public services are held constant as taxes change. Tax increases would have a less negative effect on an area's business activity—or even a positive effect—if public services were simultaneously changed in the same direction.

Most policymakers would interpret tax effects on state or local growth of this magnitude to be important. Political leaders are often eager to claim credit for attracting new industrial plants that add considerably less than 1 percent to the employment of a metropolitan area. A 10 percent tax reduction for a metropolitan area or state clearly will not produce an economic growth miracle. But if such a tax reduction actually would increase jobs in an area by between 1 percent and 6 percent, many political leaders might find this policy option attractive. Chapters 4 to 7 will estimate what economic benefits actually would occur due to this job growth, allowing a more objective perspective on whether the benefits are worth the costs to an area of lowering its business taxes.

The conclusion that state and local taxes affect business growth remains controversial among researchers, but the weight of academic opinion is shifting away from the old consensus that state and local taxes are irrelevant to business location. For example, Wasylenko's (1991) recent survey of the literature on interregional business location decisions states that "given [recent empirical evidence], it is increasingly difficult to argue that business climate, however broadly defined, does not influence interregional firm locations (pp. 27-8)." Another recent review of the empirical literature, by Blair and Premus (1987), states that "until recently, the conventional wisdom has been that taxes— and, by implication, other fiscal variables—do not deter industrial locations or economic growth. . . . However, most recent studies show tax-expenditure variables to be important" (p. 82).

Public Services

Why should public services matter to state and local business growth? A public service might be estimated to affect state and local business growth for at least four reasons: because the public service provides an unpriced input to production; because, although the public service to business is priced, the price is not known, and greater quantities of the public service are associated with lower prices for that service; because, although the public service is not directly used by business, greater quantities of the public service are associated with a lower price for some input that is used by business, and that lower price is not directly measured by the research; and because business growth causes production of the public service to change.

Examples of unpriced public service inputs include highways, police and fire services, and research and development (R&D) information obtained from higher education services. Such public services would increase productivity and reduce costs, thereby increasing business growth.

Examples of priced public service inputs include water and sewer services, energy utility services, and air transportation services. What really should affect business profitability and growth is the price of such services. However, such prices may be difficult to measure. It is difficult to control for implicit prices, such as the time cost in obtaining the services: the amount of time needed to wait for a utility hook-up, for example, or the average waiting time to get a flight to New York. Greater public spending on such services or greater capital stock associated with such services may, however, be correlated with lower prices. For example, the marginal cost of air travel, including waiting time, may drop as airports get larger and have more flights per day.

Public services such as education and welfare are not directly used by business.[24] They may affect business profitability, however, by affecting the real, skill-adjusted wage rate of labor. Education services may affect the skill-adjusted real wage in two ways. First, the additional supplies of skilled workers produced by educational institutions may cause the real wages of skilled workers to be lower. Second, better educational services may attract workers to a local economy and lower local real wages. Welfare may increase the skill-adjusted real wage for lower-skill workers by causing some to withdraw from the local labor market.

In theory, if skill-adjusted real wages could be perfectly measured, and businesses had perfect information on skill-adjusted real wages, education and welfare services would not be expected to directly affect an area's business growth, holding constant wages. But researchers lack perfect measures of skill-adjusted real wages. Furthermore, business information on real wages is also imperfect, and businesses may use educational and welfare services as an indicator of likely skill-adjusted real wages in a local area.

Finally, estimated effects of public services upon local growth may be biased if changes in local growth cause change in local public services. Growth clearly lowers welfare services, which will bias researchers towards finding that lower welfare services "cause" higher growth. For other public services, the situation is more complicated. If business growth produces fiscal benefits—that is, if business growth results in tax revenue in excess of the public expenditures required to service the businesses—then we would expect public spending on most services to increase. In this case, studies will be biased towards finding that higher levels of public services "cause" higher growth. But some measures of public services may lag behind growth trends. For example, it takes time to adjust the public capital stock. The state and local public capital stock per capita will be lower in areas that have recently been growing fast. In this case, studies will be biased towards finding that higher per capita public capital stock "causes" lower growth.

What do recent studies show about the effects of state and local public services on business growth? Table 2.5 and appendix 2.3 summarize the results from business location studies since 1979 that have included some measure of public services. Because the studies use such widely varying measures, I did not attempt to calculate comparable elasticities for the different studies. Instead, table 2.5 lists the percentage of studies that found some positive and significant coefficient on a public service variable, and some negative and significant coefficient on a welfare variable.

Table 2.5 provides some evidence that more public services are associated with faster state and local business growth, while welfare is associated with slower state and local business growth. Appendix 2.3 suggests that education and infrastructure variables have the most consistently positive relationship to local business activity and growth.

Table 2.5
Summary of Results from Various Studies
on Effects of Public Services on State and Local Business Growth

	Percentage of Studies With At Least One Positive and Statistically Significant Public Service Variable Coefficient	Percentage of Studies With At Least One Negative and Statistically Significant Welfare Variable Coefficient
All inter-area studies	60% (30 studies)	58% (12 studies)

NOTES: Results for individual studies and specific public service variables are summarized in appendix 2.3. This table, as well as appendix 2.3, focuses only on specifications for either total business activity, manufacturing activity, or closest dependent variable to those categories, and on model specification preferred by author of study. Study only needs one positive and significant public service variable coefficient to be counted as showing positive results. Of six studies with public service variables and controls for fixed effects, four show positive and significant coefficients. Two studies with controls for fixed effects and welfare variables both show negative and significant coefficients.

Studies use a wide variety of arbitrary definitions of public service quantities, so the exact magnitude of effects on state and local growth is difficult to calculate for most studies, and even more difficult to compare across studies. Most studies provide insufficient information to determine what would happen if taxes were raised to finance the expansion of particular public services. In three cases, however, some information on the relative strength of public service and tax effects on business location is available. Helms (1985) estimates that increasing state and local taxes, and using the revenue to finance anything except expanded welfare spending, will increase state personal income. Bartik (1989a) estimates that an across-the-board increase in state and local business taxes, used to finance increased fire protection and local school spending, will increase the rate of small business starts.[25] Munnell's (1990) estimates of the determinants of state growth in the 1980s, when combined with reasonable assumptions about interest rates and other economic variables, suggest that state and local tax increases to finance increased public capital will increase the growth rate of private employment. In her estimates of the determinants of state growth in the 1970s, public capital's effects are weaker; the net effect of tax-financed increases in public capital is positive in one specification, negative in another.[26] Based on these three studies, it is quite conceivable that state and local business tax increases, if used for particular public services, will encourage more business activity. Furthermore, Munnell's results suggest that public capital's role in state business growth is increasing over time.

As pointed out above, these results could be wholly spurious. All of these estimated public service effects on business growth could really be caused by business growth. But two studies (Munnell 1990 and Duffy-Deno and Eberts 1989) estimate that greater per capita public capital stock increases an area's growth. As argued above, estimates of the effects of per capita public capital stock on state and local growth should be biased towards zero. Hence, the findings of these two studies provide some reassurance that public services can actually increase state and local growth.

Wages

> . . . Inter-area wage differentials in the United States have had a significant effect on the location and relocation of firms. (John M. Levy, Associate Professor at Virginia Polytechnic Institute and State University and former Director of Economic Development for Westchester County, p. 35 in *Economic Development Programs for Cities, Counties, and Towns,* 1981)

Local wages are sometimes thought of as outside the power of state and local governments. But state and local governments can increase private sector labor costs by increasing state minimum wages, enacting labor relations laws that are more prounion than antiunion, increasing public sector wages, mandating particular fringe benefits in the private sector, increasing unemployment insurance or workers' compensation costs, or making welfare benefits more generous.[27] Hence, whether wages affect business location is relevant to the debate over whether state and local government policy can influence local economic growth. In addition, the effect of wages on state and local economic growth provides some evidence on the general effects of costs on growth.

Economic theory predicts that wages should have major effects on the growth of a local economy, as labor costs are a major share of business costs. Economic theory even leads to some predictions about the size of the business location effect of wages versus other cost factors. As discussed above, if business growth depends on the overall profitability and business costs of the area, then the effect on business location of a 1 percent change in the price of any cost factor should be roughly proportional to that cost factor's share in total business costs. The costs of locally supplied labor probably are about 14 times state and local business tax costs.[28] Thus, the elasticity of business activity with respect to wages (the percentage change in business activity for a 1 percent change in wages) should be roughly 14 times the elasticity of business activity with respect to state and local taxes. If the elasticity of business activity with respect to inter-area tax differentials is between −0.1 and −0.6, then the elasticity of business activity with respect to local wages should be between −1.4 and −8.4.[29]

Table 2.6 summarizes various studies that examine the effects of wages on business location. More details on particular studies are provided in appendix 2.4. Table 2.6 indicates that there is significant evidence that local wages influence business location. However, the magnitude of this wage effect is much less than one would expect based on the typical size of tax effects. The table suggests that long-run elasticities of business activity with respect to wages probably fall in the range from −.2 to −1.0; that is a 10 percent decrease in regional wages will increase local business activity by between 2 percent and 10 percent in the long run. Long-run wage elasticities may be a bit higher when business activity is measured by employment rather than by the quantity of local capital or output.[30] However, it is surprising that wage elasticities are around twice the magnitude of tax elasticities, rather than being 14 times greater, as we might predict.

Thus, if we believe the predictions of economic theory, empirical estimates of wage elasticities of business location are inconsistent with empirical estimates of tax elasticities. It would seem that either tax elasticities are biased upward in absolute magnitude—that is, away from zero—or wage elasticities are biased downward in absolute magnitude—that is, toward zero.[31]

It is more likely that wage elasticities are biased downward than tax elasticities are biased upward. Two arguments can be offered for this position. First, the measures of wages used in most studies of business location are subject to substantial error. Most studies just use average manufacturing wages, occasionally with controls for the average educational quality of the local labor force. Such measures of wages will be in error because they do not control for variations across states and metropolitan areas in industry mix, or in factors affecting labor quality, such as workers' experience. Measurement error in a variable such as wages will tend to bias estimates of its coefficient towards zero.

Business taxes, of course, are also measured with error. But measurement error for business taxes would cause a downward bias in measures of the absolute magnitude of tax elasticities, not an upward bias.

Second, wage elasticities may well be subject to substantial bias downward due to their endogenous determination by business growth.

Table 2.6
Summary of Results from Studies of Wage Effects on Business Location

	Percentage With At Least One Negative and Statistically Significant Wage Effect	Mean Long-Run Wage Elasticity	Trimmed Mean Elasticity	Median Elasticity
	(1)	(2)	(3)	(4)
All inter-area studies	62% (42 studies)	-.67 (s.e. = .24) [-4.39 to 1.66] (28 studies)	-.50 [-2.47 to .27] (22 studies)	-.36
Inter-area studies with fixed-effect controls	71% (7 studies)	-.64 (s.e. = .43) [-3.16 to -.27] (7 studies)	-.31 [-.58 to -.12] (5 studies)	-.27
Inter-area studies with employment dependent variable	60% (15 studies)	-.89 (s.e. = .35) [-3.16 to .18] (10 studies)	-.74 [-2.47 to -.05] (8 studies)	-.50

NOTES: This summary table is derived from appendix 2.4. In column (1), significance is judged based on a 5 percent, one-tail test. See table 2.4 for definition of trimmed mean and fixed-effect controls. In addition to mean elasticity across various studies, table 2.6 reports standard error of that mean and the range of estimated elasticities obtained in various studies.

Local wages increase when business activity increases. This induced positive correlation that occurs because business growth causes higher wages will tend to obscure the negative correlation we expect to observe due to higher wages causing lower business growth.

As noted above, estimates of tax elasticities may also be subject to an endogeneity bias. However, the bias of estimated tax elasticities due to endogeneity is of an uncertain sign. Furthermore, wages may be even more endogenous than tax rates. Political inertia is likely to be greater than any market rigidities that might constrain wage rate adjustments in response to business growth.

Despite these arguments, the relatively modest magnitude of wage elasticities casts some doubt on the magnitude of tax effects on state and local growth reported in table 2.3. Perhaps a 10 percent business tax reduction will not hike state and local growth by 2.5 percent, as predicted in table 2.3. If we believe the mean wage elasticity results reported in table 2.6 (wage elasticity $=-.67$), economic theory suggests that the tax elasticities of state and local growth will be about 1/14th as large as the wage elasticity, resulting in tax elasticities of only $-.05$ $(-.05 \approx -.67/14)$. A 10 percent business tax reduction would only increase an area's business activity by .5 percent, or one-half of 1 percent. Which tax elasticity figure is correct has major implications for how much it costs to create a given number of jobs using a business tax cut strategy.

A convincing reconciliation of our estimates of wage elasticities and tax elasticities of state and local growth can only be accomplished through better empirical research. As of yet, no study uses econometric techniques to convincingly adjust for the probable endogeneity of both tax and wage variables.

Unionization

We would expect increases in the unionization of a local area's economy to have some negative effect on business activity, because increased unionization would hike the local wage scale. However, in business location studies in which wages are included as a determinant of business activity, it is unclear whether unionization would be expected to have an independent negative effect on business activity. Several reasons why unionization might have an independent effect can be offered, and they have different implications for how unionization should be measured and how unionization effects should be interpreted.

First, independent unionization effects may simply reflect business fear of unionization's influence on nonwage elements of labor costs, such as fringe benefits or labor productivity. In this case, the unionization variable we would most like to measure would be the probability of a new or expanded establishment becoming unionized. This may only bear a loose resemblance to the average unionization percentage in the state. The percentage unionized in the state for that particular industry may be a better measure of the probability of a new firm becoming unionized in that industry. Smaller firms would be less affected by unionization in this case, as smaller firms are less likely to be unionized.

Second, unionization effects on state and local growth may really reflect the influence of the type of political and social climate associated with a high-unionization area. Some businesses may dislike the social climate that tends to accompany higher unionization. If state and local growth reflects these business preferences, then the average percentage unionized in the state may be as good a measure as any of this unionization influence.

Under the first interpretation of unionization effects, any estimated effect is one more cost of higher unionization. An opponent of unions would see this as another reason to limit their influence. A proponent of unions would see this business activity effect as one more reason for strong federal legislation promoting unionization, as state and local competition for new business will discourage state governments from any support for unions.

Under the second interpretation of unionization effects, unions are not really the issue. The real cause of lower business activity due to unionization is some element of the local social climate. Any policy response to this unionization effect must first discover what element of the social climate is actually discouraging business activity. Only then can a reasoned decision be made about possible policy changes.

What does the empirical evidence show about unionization effects? Table 2.7 shows recent business location studies that include some measure of unionization. Most studies show a negative unionization effect, although its magnitude varies widely. Some studies estimate huge negative unionization effects, while other studies estimate positive effects of unions on business activity.[32] As a result, the "average" effect of unionization on business activity is sensitive to exactly what subcategory of studies is considered, and exactly what procedure is used for calculating an "average" effect. Furthermore, the estimates of different studies vary so much that the mean long-run effect of unionization on state and local business activity, calculated over all studies, is always insignificantly different from zero, in a statistical sense: the true effect of unionization could be zero, and the mean results reported in table 2.7 could be due to chance. The mean effect of unionization is negative, but existing studies provide little basis for confidence that this finding will stand up as research progresses.[33]

The evidence is contradictory on whether unionization is acting as a proxy for social climate. Heywood and Deich (1987) found that industry-specific local unionization variables had much smaller effects on business growth than overall local unionization. This suggests a social climate interpretation. On the other hand, my research (Bartik 1989a) finds a greater effect of the average unionization of a state on branch plant location decisions than on small business start-up decisions. This finding suggests that the probability of being unionized may be influencing decisions about new business activity. A resolution of this debate awaits better measures of the marginal probability of different types of new business activity becoming unionized in a given state.

Environmental Regulations

Stricter state environmental regulations would generally be expected to discourage the location and growth of polluting firms. The belief that business location effects of environmental regulations would lead to excessively lax state environmental regulation has often been offered as a rationale for federal preemption of authority over environmental

Table 2.7
Summary of Studies of Effects of Unionization-Related Variables on State and Local Business Activity

	Percentage of Studies With At Least One Unionization Related Coefficient that is Statistically Significant and of Expected Sign	Mean Long-Run Effect of 1% Increase In Unionization Percentage on Business Activity	Trimmed Mean	Median
All inter-area studies	56% (27 studies)	-.86% (s.e. = .61) [-8.67 to 3.3] (19 studies)	-.52% [-3.28 to 1.32] (15 studies)	-.16%
Inter-area studies with controls for fixed effects	33% (6 studies)	-1.08% (s.e. = .99) [-5.46 to 1.32] (6 studies)	-.58% [-2.23 to .01] (4 studies)	-.05%
Inter-area studies that also include wage variables	60% (20 studies)	-.81% (s.e. = .80) [-8.67 to 3.3] (13 studies)	-.46% [-3.28 to 2.4] (11 studies)	-.16%

NOTES: More details on individual studies are in appendix 2.5. "1 percent increase in unionization" means increase as percentage of labor force; that is, an increase from 20 to 21 percent unionized is a 1 percent increase, not a 5 percent increase.

regulation, For example, the House Committee Report on the 1970 Clean Air Act states that:

> The promulgation of Federal emission standards for new sources . . . will preclude efforts on the part of States to compete with each other in trying to attract new plants and facilities without assuming adequate control of large scale emissions therefrom. (Page 3 in *Legislative History of the Clean Air Act.* U.S. Congress, Washington, DC, 1979)

Despite efforts toward a federally imposed uniformity in environmental regulations, state and local governments retain significant discretion over environmental regulation. States generally retain authority over enforcement and over the regulation of existing plants; new plants are generally only regulated by the federal government with respect to a few major pollutants. Hence, the issue of whether geographic variation in environmental regulation affects business location patterns remains current.

Only three studies have estimated the effects of state and local environmental regulation on business growth, one by McConnell and Schwab (1990), and two by Bartik (1988b, 1989a). On the whole, there is little evidence that environmental regulation has much effect on business location patterns. McConnell and Schwab find that state environmental regulation of the automobile industry has little effect on the choice of county for a branch plant unless the county is very far out of compliance with air quality regulations. My 1988(b) study of branch plant location decisions finds that the effects on state growth of a wide variety of variables measuring state environmental regulation are always statistically insignificant and usually can be shown to be substantively small; the exception is highly polluting industries, for which I cannot reject the possibility of a substantively large effect of environmental regulation, even though the estimated effect is statistically no different from zero. My 1989(a) study finds a negative and statistically significant effect of state environmental regulations on the state small business start-up rate. But the effect is small.[34]

The major limitation of all these studies is that environmental regulations are extremely hard to measure. Still, the weight of evidence shows that in our current regulatory structure, with federal constraints on the degree of geographic variation in environmental regulation, most business location decisions are little affected by environmental regulations.

Capital Market Imperfections

Only two studies have examined the effects of capital market imperfections on state and local business activity. My study of small business starts (1989a) found that states that relaxed their constraints on the opening of new branch banks between 1976 and 1982 had a greater increase in the small business start rate than states that did not relax regulations restricting branch banking. Bauer and Cromwell (1989) find that a variety of banking market structure variables affect the rate at which new establishments (both branch and independent) are formed in metropolitan areas. In particular, establishment formations are greater in metropolitan areas where banks are more profitable, where smaller banks are more prominent, and where more banks have recently entered the market.

Little can be concluded on the basis of two studies. Because many states have in recent years sought to intervene in capital markets to spur their economic development, more empirical studies of the effects of capital markets on business location patterns would seem to be warranted.

Conclusion

The most important conclusion from this chapter is that a wide variety of state and local policies can significantly affect the long-run level of business activity in a local economy. Business tax reductions may increase an area's business activity. But so may tax increases, if they are used to finance infrastructure and public services used by business.

We know much more about the effects on state and local growth of general state and local tax and public service policies than we do about the effects of specific economic development programs. No current research convincingly addresses the crucial question of whether new wave economic development programs, which offer specialized services to new and existing businesses, are more cost-effective in spurring state and local growth than traditional economic development policies of tax and financial incentives for business. Current research does suggest that state and local policies can change the local economic climate enough to make a difference to an area's growth. This suggests that new wave programs also have the potential of affecting area growth, but better empirical studies are needed to determine whether these new wave programs are succeeding in realizing that potential.

Given that state and local economic development policies can affect an area's growth, what then? The next chapters turn to analyzing what effects an increase in local growth will have on different groups participating in the local economy.

NOTES

1. The same point could also be argued for the state office in Japan variable in Woodward's study, even though his dependent variable is Japanese plants choosing the state rather than overall state economic growth. It is difficult to believe that state offices in Japan have enough of an effect to be detectable. Cause and effect may be reversed here; states that attract Japanese plants may open offices in Japan.

2. Other economists have also brought up this problem of the small size of many economic development programs, e.g., Netzer (1990); Hatry, Fall, Singer, and Liner (1990); and James (1991).

3. This may, in part, explain why enterprise zones have been evaluated much more than other specific economic development programs.

4. The ideal evaluation would randomly choose the targeted local areas from among candidate areas that satisfy whatever criteria policymakers wish to set for eligibility for the program. But it is probably not politically feasible to adopt this geographic experimentation approach on a large enough scale to yield meaningful results. At least 10 or 15 "treatment" areas and 20 or 30 "control" areas would probably be needed to have any chance of detecting statistically meaningful differences between the treatment and control regions. This scale of experimentation is not likely to be acceptable to the legislative representatives of the control areas.

5. An excellent recent review on the choice of control regions to analyze local economic change is provided by Isserman and Beaumont (1989).

An alternative to choosing different control regions is to keep the same control regions in the regression, but consider a variety of control variables that might affect both regional growth, and the selection of the region for inclusion in the economic development program. We should have more confidence in the results if they are not too sensitive to the choice of control variables. This strategy of considering different sets of control variables was essentially followed by Leslie Papke in her recent paper on the Indiana enterprise zone program (Papke 1991), and her results appear robust to different control variables.

This discussion of the choice of control areas is closely related to the discussion later in the text of how econometric models of state and local growth and business location may be biased due to the endogeneity of taxes and other policy variables. The distinction is that in the case of large-scale economic development programs targeted at particular small areas, the choice of the target area is clearly endogenous, while the endogeneity of state and local taxes and other policy variables is a more questionable hypothesis.

6. One study that moved in this direction was by Reynolds and Freeman (1987). This survey of Pennsylvania firms compared the size, growth, and export activity of firms that reported receiving assistance from the State of Pennsylvania with firms that did not report assistance. But, as the authors emphasize, this comparison by itself does not allow these state programs to be evaluated. As mentioned in the chapter text, at the very least we would want to add control variables for other factors affecting firm size, growth, or export performance. Reynolds and Freeman's survey did find that assisted firms were larger, had grown faster since start-up, and exported more, but this does not mean that the assistance caused these effects.

A recent Urban Institute manual by Hatry, Fall, Singer, and Liner (1990) on how to monitor economic development programs also suggests comparing the performance of assisted and unassisted firms. The authors point out that many states may be able to use their already existing "ES-202 data"—data from state unemployment insurance files—to make these comparisons of various firms.

Hatry and his co-authors also suggest extensive use of client surveys by economic development program managers. While client surveys are an invaluable tool for improving management and providing ongoing program evaluation, survey data are unlikely to convince skeptics that these programs work.

7. Perhaps random assignment of which businesses were most aggressively pursued as program clients would be politically feasible. For example, a sample of small and medium-sized manufacturing firms could be divided into a treatment group that would receive frequent requests to participate in a training program to increase exports, and a control group that would not be so aggressively targeted as clients of the program. The treatment group assignment variable could be used as an instrumental variable that would exogenously shift the probability of the business participating in the export promotion program.

8. In addition, if the variables determining the selection of program clients is well-understood, there are well-known econometric techniques that can be used to correct for "selection bias" and obtain consistent estimates of the effects of the program.

9. There must be some reasonable limit to the ratio of business cost reduction to dollar of government spending for new wave programs. If a program provided information that reduced business costs by $10 for every $1 spent on the program, one would expect private entrepreneurs to provide this service, given the huge potential profit margins. Of course, various "market failures" in information markets inhibit the development of such private services—for example, potential clients may distrust the sellers who claim to be able to provide valuable information. But are private markets so imperfect that profit margins of 90 percent are foregone?

10. Rasmussen, Bendick, and Ledebur have written several useful articles comparing the ratios of business cost reductions to government expenditures for a variety of traditional economic development incentives. See, for example, Rasmussen, Bendick, and Ledebur (1984). However, we have no equivalent information on the cost-effectiveness of new wave economic development programs.

11. One of the sites compared with Nashville was Kalamazoo, Michigan. Our model estimated that the Nashville site for Saturn would save General Motors at least $42 million per year over the Kalamazoo site. Our confidence in our crude model (only three cost factors considered) is increased by a *Nashville Banner* article that cited a "reliable source" as estimating that "General Motors saved more than $100 million annually by locating its Saturn plant in Tennessee instead of Michigan. . . . Taxes, wages, transportation costs, and workers' compensation premiums are all lower in Tennessee, accounting for much of the savings." (*Nashville Banner*, September 11, 1985).

12. The text does not explicitly discuss the empirical evidence on the influence of agglomeration economies—business cost savings that result from greater concentrations of particular industries, or business activity in general, in some local area—on subsequent business growth. Agglomeration economies may result in a type of multiplier effect of state and local economic development policies that may enhance their effectiveness. If an area succeeds, through tax reduction, service enhancements, or other policies, in increasing growth in some industry, agglomeration economies may attract additional growth in that industry.

13. That is, given that certain variables are in the estimating equation, what should the estimating equation's functional form be.

14. Agglomeration economy cost reductions are usually attributed to the development of specialized supplier markets for an industry, made possible by a greater concentration of the industry.

15. Some recent innovative studies have attempted to create such public infrastructure measures. Both Eberts (1991) and Munnell (1990) have used public investment data to estimate the magnitude of the public capital stocks in different metropolitan areas (Eberts) and states (Munnell).

16. Strictly speaking, this bias towards zero only holds if only one variable is mismeasured. The bias when a number of variables are mismeasured will depend in a complex way on the intercorrelations among the different variables. However, in practice one would expect any grossly mismeasured variable to have a coefficient estimate that is biased towards zero.

17. This restriction in the scope of the empirical examination throws away some of the information the data might contain on why state and local growth rates differ, but provides more assurance that the results are not simply due to omitted regional effects. With just one cross-section, omitted jurisdiction effects cannot be controlled for, as there is only one observation for each jurisdiction.

18. Some of these specification and functional form issues are discussed in more detail in an appendix available from the author.

19. I would certainly admit that I have probably inadvertently omitted some studies, particularly unpublished studies. But I have made no attempt to select studies whose findings match my own beliefs. Hence, the studies summarized can be considered at least a roughly random sample of recent studies on taxes and regional business growth.

20. John Due's (1961) study is the most commonly cited review of this early business location literature.

21. This negative tax effect appears to be greater for intrametropolitan studies that use data for specific individual communities rather than aggregating all suburban communities into one general suburban category. The two studies that aggregate all suburban communities into one suburb yield tax effects that are insignificant, and that are assumed to be zero in constructing the table. We would expect this pattern of results because aggregating all suburban communities ignores the possibility of a business locating in an individual suburban community with low taxes, even if average suburban taxes are high; hence, aggregating all suburban communities will tend to understate the effects on an individual community of raising its tax rates. In addition, while individual suburbs may be close substitutes for one another from a business perspective, city business sites may not be close substitutes for suburban sites.

22. A regression, using each inter-area study as an observation, of the estimated tax elasticity on a constant, and dummies for whether the study controls for fixed effects or public services, yields the following results:

Tax elasticity $= -.11 - .24*$Fixed dummy $- .16*$Pub dummy.
                    (.08) (.12)   (.10)

Standard errors are in parentheses below the estimated coefficients. This regression provides some evidence that the inclusion of both fixed-effect controls and public service controls matters to the magnitude of the tax coefficient estimated in a business location study.

23. In the case of the Newman study, the estimated difference across industries is not statistically significant.

24. Economists would generally refer to welfare as a transfer program rather than a public service. In this discussion, I simply use "public services" as a generic term for all publicly supported programs.

25. One might ask why fire protection spending and local school spending should be particularly beneficial to small business starts, compared to police spending or higher education spending, two of the other categories of public spending included in my 1989 paper. The effects of police spending may be biased by a positive correlation with crime, which will tend to discourage business growth. Furthermore, perhaps small businesses care more about the availability of moderately skilled workers than about the availability of college-educated workers. Finally, higher fire protection spending, in addition to reducing business insurance costs and fire damage costs, may reflect a general orientation towards the area's government focusing on providing good basic services to business and households, rather than on attempting to redistribute income.

26. Munnell's tax variable is state and local taxes as a percent of personal income, while her public capital variable is in dollars per capita. The present value per capita of changing taxes by 1 percent of personal income is $.01*Y/(r-g)$, where Y is per capita personal income, r is the real interest rate, and g is the annual rate of growth of real per capita personal income. This present value can finance an annual per capita payment stream of r times that present value. The annual cost per capita of K dollars per capita of public capital is $(r+d)K$, where d is the depreciation rate of public capital. Munnell's figures indicate that d is about .02. A reasonable figure for r is .03, while a conservative figure for average annual growth in real per capita personal income is 1.5 percent ($g=.015$). Under these assumptions, a change in state and local taxes of 1 percent of personal income can finance an increase in public capital per capita equal to $.01*Y*r*(1/(r-g))*(1/(r+d))=mY$, where m is .4 under these assumed values for r, d, and g. Using observed values for Y, and Munnell's parameters in her table 12, the estimated net effect of tax-financed increases in state and local public capital is strongly positive in Munnell's two sets of results for the 1980-88 time period, slightly positive for the 1970-80 time period, and negative for the 1970-88 time period. Different assumptions about r, g, or d would yield different results; the higher the value of m, the more public capital can be financed with a given tax increase. The minimum critical value of m to yield a net positive effect of tax-financed increases in public capital is .06 for the 1980-88 "changes" regression, .20 for the 1980-88 "levels" regression, .36 for the 1970-80 regression, and .63 for the 1970-88 regression. I thank Alicia Munnell and Leah Cook for providing me with additional background information on their parameter estimates and data, allowing me to make these calculations.

27. One additional state and local government policy that I omit is economic development policy towards what types of employers to attract to the area. There is certainly much anecdotal evidence that southern economic developers have sometimes attempted to avoid bringing in high-wage, unionized employers.

28. According to the July 1990 issue of *Survey of Current Business*, total U.S. employee compensation in 1989 was $3,079 billion. (Table 1.14, p. 45.) Total state and local receipts, excluding federal grants in aid, were $632 billion. According to a 1981 report by the Advisory Commission on Intergovernmental Relations (ACIR 1981), the business share of state and local taxes is around 33.9 percent. Applying this percentage to 1989 state and local receipts, total state and local business tax costs in 1989 would be estimated to be $214 billion. The ratio of employee compensation to state and local business tax costs is 14.4; the ratio of employee compensation to all state and local nongrant receipts is 4.9. Hence, if we believe that business taxes but not personal taxes affect business location, a 1 percent increase in labor costs would have around 14.4 times the

effect on regional growth of a 1 percent across-the-board increase in all state and local taxes. If all state and local personal taxes are shifted into higher business costs (which seems unlikely), a 1 percent increase in labor costs would have about 4.9 times the effect on regional growth of a 1 percent across-the-board increase in all state and local taxes. I regard the first calculation as somewhat more plausible, as I would expect only a small proportion of personal state and local taxes to be shifted to business.

The assumptions behind these calculations could be challenged. But I believe that any recalculation would still show that wage effects on an area's growth should vastly exceed tax effects on growth. 29. As mentioned in appendix 2.1, substitution effects may imply that elasticities of local employment with respect to various cost variables will not be exactly proportional to cost shares. But substitution effects should tend to increase the absolute magnitude of wage effects on local employment relative to the effects of capital taxes on local employment.

30. However, the wage elasticity is not significantly lower when employment is used as a dependent variable. A regression of each study's estimated wage elasticity on a dummy for the inclusion of fixed effects, and a dummy for an employment dependent variable, yields the following results:

Wage Elasticity = −.55 + .02 * (Fixed-Effect Control) − .34
                  (.34)   (.57)   (.51)
                  * Employment Dependent Variable
                  (standard errors in parentheses; 28 observations).

31. One could instead conclude that economic theory is wrong and business activity elasticities with respect to different variables have nothing to do with cost shares. But the general idea that relative effects on costs matter seems intuitively plausible, even if one does not accept many of the assumptions made by economists.

32. As can be seen in appendix 2.5, a very few studies, notably Bartik (1985), Woodward (1990), Newman (1983), and Helms (1985), account for the negative mean effects of unionization that are evident in table 2.7.

33. Regression analysis of the pattern of results does not help clarify matters. A regression of the unionization elasticity on dummies for fixed effect controls, wage controls, and on whether the study focuses on branch plants of large companies, yields the following results (standard errors in parentheses; number of observations is 19):

Union Elasticity = −.66 − .92*(Fixed) + .76*(Wage Control) − 1.61*Branch
                   (1.27)(1.56)   (1.56)   (1.80)

The pattern is sensible, but all coefficients are statistically insignificant.

34. A 1-standard deviation change in the environmental variable, the Conservation Foundation rating of the stringency of the state's environmental regulation, causes only a .01 standard deviation change in the small business start-up rate.

— 3 —
Theoretical Analysis of the Distributional Effects of Local Job Growth

Local policy will not determine the level of economic well-being. Because people and resources are mobile, all areas tend to share similar general levels of economic well-being. (Thomas Michael Power, Chairman, Department of Economics, University of Montana, page 43 in "Broader Vision, Narrower Focus in Local Economic Development," *Forum for Applied Research and Public Policy,* Fall 1989)

For those who count, the city is a growth machine, one that can increase aggregate rents and trap related wealth for those in the right position to benefit. (Pages 50-51 in *Urban Fortunes: The Political Economy of Place,* John Logan and Harvey Molotch, 1987)

In this chapter, I analyze the likely distributional effects of state and local economic development policies. The analysis is theoretical; subsequent chapters present empirical estimates of distributional effects.

The focus of the chapter is not on national income distribution but on local income distribution—on how the growth of a small economic region such as a metropolitan area affects the relative incomes and wealth of the different households and businesses within that local area. Chapter 8 considers how the competition of all states and local areas for jobs affects the national distribution of income.

In the short run, households are very immobile. As a result, the jobs attracted to a metropolitan area or other local economic area by economic development policy exceed the increase in labor supply due to in-migration in the short run. Labor markets become tighter: unemployment drops and wages increase.

63

In the long run, however, many households are mobile. As implied by Power in the above quotation, we would expect households to be attracted to a local area with tight labor markets, forcing unemployment up and wages down. In-migration would continue until unemployment and wages in the area were restored to their original level.

The long-run beneficiaries of growth would be expected to be landowners. State and local economic development policies attract businesses and households, increasing the overall demand for land. Since the supply of land does not increase due to in-migration, the price of land will go up. This leads to a natural suspicion, expressed by Logan and Molotch above, that political rhetoric about economic development masks its real purpose: using government to increase the wealth of a land-owning elite.

In this chapter, I counter this conventional view of the long-run effects of local growth with the argument that the short-run labor market experiences of individuals affect their long-run labor market success. Local economic growth helps individuals get better jobs today; because individuals get better jobs today, they can get better jobs tomorrow, next year, or indeed in the long run.

Immobility of Labor

The immobility of most households is widely accepted, but its full extent is not recognized. Some evidence for labor immobility is anecdotal. Journalists frequently describe families with poor economic prospects who refuse to leave such economically depressed regions of the United States as West Virginia and inner-city Detroit.

Survey evidence is also available on labor immobility. One of the best surveys on labor immobility is analyzed by Dunn (1979). The researchers surveyed 200 workers in a rural southern town who had recently been laid off due to the permanent closing of a textile mill. The workers were asked how much lower a wage they would accept in order to stay in their hometown; they were asked to assume that if they moved elsewhere they could obtain a job similar to their old job. The average worker said that he or she would accept 14 percent lower wages to remain in the hometown. Blacks, females, and older workers were the most reluctant to move. Follow-up interviews three years later found that workers who initially claimed a greater willingness to accept wage reductions were significantly more likely to actually stay in the town. Because the subsequent behavior of workers is consistent with their responses to the survey, it is reasonable to assume that the survey reflected the true feelings of the workers.

Econometric studies also indicate that households are extremely immobile. Venti and Wise (1984) and Bartik, Butler, and Liu (forthcoming) used information on household moving behavior from the Demand Experiment of the Experimental Housing Allowance Program to estimate how reluctant households are to move. The Demand Experiment, conducted by the federal government between 1973 and 1975 in Pittsburgh and Phoenix, examined how low-income renter households would change housing consumption in response to large, randomly assigned income and housing price subsidies.[1]

These two mobility studies with Demand Experiment data use different econometric techniques, but reach similar conclusions about household immobility. Venti and Wise observed housing choices of households that move, to infer the potential gains that "stayer" households are willing to forego. They estimate that the average stayer household is willing to forego gains from moving to a new house that are equivalent to 14 percent of household income.

The study I conducted with my colleagues estimated the increase in rent needed to increase the probability of moving of the median household to 50 percent. The required rent increase to reach the 50 percent probability was considered to be the household's "moving cost," where moving costs include financial costs and the psychological costs of leaving a familiar dwelling unit. We estimated that this moving cost averaged 10 percent of income in Pittsburgh and 17 percent in Phoenix. Higher moving costs were found for minority households, older households, and households with a longer tenure at their current dwelling.

Both studies focus on households' reluctance to move out of their current dwelling unit, regardless of whether the household stays in the same metropolitan area. The large moving costs found in these studies probably underestimate the resistance of the typical household to moving to a new metropolitan area.

Why households are so immobile is a difficult question. Moving costs of this magnitude are not likely to be due only to financial costs. Geographers, planners, and regional scientists talk about the importance to households of a "sense of place." Roger Bolton has recently written an intriguing essay analyzing a "sense of place" from the perspective of an economist (Bolton 1989a). He argues that a "sense of place" is a complex of familiar buildings, natural features, people, businesses, and social relationships that are valuable to residents because, among other things, they encourage trust in market and nonmarket relationships and save time in making decisions.[2]

A strong sense of place would make households uniquely attached to communities in which they had long resided. This attachment is a "psychological moving cost" which affects behavior as much as more tangible monetary costs of moving.

Short-Run Effects of Local Job Growth

The relative immobility of most households implies that local economic development policies will have short-run effects. Even with many immobile households, local job growth would lead to some in-migration of households and firms, and land values will go up. But this mobility is not extensive enough to eliminate all labor market benefits to households from the policy.

Table 3.1 summarizes the likely short-run effects of local development policies on different groups. The groups affected by the policy include households and firms that stay in the local area, landowners, local governments, out-migrants, and in-migrants.

The effects of direct development policies on households depend on whether they originally have a job, how wages are determined on their job, and whether they are renters or homeowners. Households with a job,

Table 3.1
Short-Run Distributional Effects of State and Local
Economic Development Policies

Group	Effect
Stayer Households	
Employed homeowners	Gain due to wage and property value increase
Employed renters in labor submarkets whose workers are relatively immobile	Gain because real wage increases
Employed renters in labor submarkets with inflexible wages	Lose because real wage drops
Unemployed who get jobs	Gain employment benefits
Unemployed homeowners who don't get jobs	Gain in property values, but lose due to increase in local prices
Unemployed renters who don't get jobs	Lose due to increase in local prices
Stayer Firms	
Subsidized firms	Gain due to subsidy
National market-oriented firms	Lose due to cost increase
Local market-oriented firms	Gain due to larger market
Landowners	Gain increased land values
Local Government	Gain if business in-migration predominates or excess capacity of public infrastructure; lose otherwise
Out-Migrants	Lose utility or profits before considering capital gains on land ownership
In-Migrants	Unaffected because other similar communities were already available

and whose wages are not determined by formal or informal contracts, probably benefit from a real wage increase. Real wages increase because labor demand probably increases faster than labor supply, given the greater short-run mobility of capital compared to labor. Households in this group who are homeowners also gain from the increase in their home values.

Households with a job, and whose wages are fixed by explicit or implicit contract, will suffer a real wage decrease as local prices increase. For members of this group who are homeowners, any adverse effect will be minimized because of the increase in their home's value.

Households who get a job because of the growth are probably net winners. Their benefit equals the wage on their newly acquired job minus the lowest wage at which they would have accepted a job.[3] Homeowners in this category also benefit from a capital gain on their home.

Unemployed or retired households who do not get a job are probably net losers. Their costs go up as local prices increase, and their incomes (Social Security, unemployment compensation, interest earnings) are not tied to the increases in local prices. This is probably true even for members of this group who are homeowners. Their capital gain on their home reflects an increase in the rent they are implicitly paying for that housing. As long as the household stays in its dwelling, the increase in implicit rents received just equals the increase in implicit rents paid. Only for households who want to move can the capital gain yield a tangible increase in wealth, and only then if the household is willing to move to a smaller dwelling.

Effects on local firms depend on whether they receive funds from these policies, and on whether they serve national or local markets. Firms that receive direct assistance from these policies can be presumed to, on net, gain because subsequent changes in prices and wages are probably of secondary magnitude.

Firms that do not receive direct assistance but that serve national markets probably, on net, lose. Their costs go up as local wages and prices increase. But because their prices are set in national markets, there is no compensating increase in revenues.

Firms that do not receive assistance but serve local markets probably gain, on net. While their costs go up, so do their revenues. The latter effect on profits will probably dominate, because a larger city will need greater supplies of local goods, and some increase in profitability will be required to elicit a greater supply.

Absentee landowners gain due to the increase in land values from the development.

Industries that serve local markets and are likely to benefit include development companies, banks, newspapers, retailers, and business service companies. Industries that serve national markets and are likely to lose include most of manufacturing. Within any given industry, small businesses, on average, are more likely to serve a local market than large businesses, so the small business share of employment in a given industry is likely to increase somewhat. In addition, small businesses may be able to more quickly respond to expanding market opportunities, which would also indicate greater benefits for small business. Finally, businesses with large land holdings, such as large developers, are likely to gain more than other businesses.

Local governments pay for the subsidy or service provided to businesses under the development policy. In addition, the policy has indirect fiscal effects: increased service demand and tax collections due to the increased numbers of households and businesses. Increasing numbers of households, particularly households with children, probably result in a net fiscal loss for local governments. Businesses with relatively low traffic demands, which would include most businesses except for retailers, probably pay more in taxes than they require in services. The net fiscal impacts of households without children, or commercial retailers, could be positive or negative. Whatever the mix of businesses or households attracted by the policy, the fiscal benefit is likely to be greater if the local public "infrastructure" (roads, schools, water and sewers, etc.) has substantial unused capacity. If there is little unused capacity and the local job growth will attract households with children, substantial fiscal benefits are unlikely.

Households moving away because of the policy presumably did so because the negative effects on their well-being outweighed any special attachment to the local area. Possible capital gains from selling their home may make such out-migrant households net winners, but this capital gain overstates the benefits.

Firms moving away presumably left because the changes in costs or character of the local market reduced their profits below an acceptable level, despite the "good will" they had acquired from their business experience. Capital gains on the sale of property may make business out-migrants into net winners from the policy, but the capital gain overstates the benefits.

In contrast to out-migrants, in-migrating firms and households will not be significantly affected by the direct development policy pursued by this community. From the perspective of outsiders, the community is just one of many that is attracting business and growing; it is impossible for changes in the rate of growth in this one community to have significant effects on the well-being of outsiders. If the community had grown more slowly, in-migrant firms and households could have moved to a similar rapidly growing community.

This asymmetry between in-migrants and out-migrants may seem surprising. The asymmetry occurs because the community is unique to out-migrants, but not to in-migrants. To out-migrants, the community is unique as their home community, and what happens to it can affect their well-being. To in-migrants, the community is just one of many similar communities.

This discussion does not imply that all job growth would be expected to have identical distributional effects. Low-skill workers are generally thought to be less geographically mobile than high-skill workers. Some types of economic development policies (such as branch plant recruitment and small business assistance) may particularly encourage businesses that use low-skill labor. If low-skill workers are less mobile, these types of policies will lead to relatively little in-migration and relatively large unemployment reductions. The employment benefits of this policy will be large, and the benefits to landowners and homeowners small. In contrast, consider policies that encourage high-technology businesses using high-skill labor. Such policies may lead to considerable in-migration, even in the short run. The benefits primarily go to landowners, rather than to workers or the unemployed.

Long-Run Effects of Growth

A more controversial issue is whether a once-and-for-all shock to an area's labor demand has long-run effects on local labor markets. By "long-run," I mean a period of 10 years or more. Many economists would argue that enough people move during 10 years that any increase in local labor demand will be offset.

The position that local labor demand shocks have no long-run effects has been most forcefully presented by Marston (1985) in an article analyzing differences in unemployment among U.S. metropolitan areas. Marston points out that "the movement toward equilibrium merely requires that a small part of the labor force be mobile. The fact that some workers are immobile may merely determine who will leave, but have little effect on unemployment differentials" (p. 66).

Marston argues that a labor demand shock to a metropolitan area will be completely offset over some time period if the normal migration flows between metropolitan areas over that time period greatly exceed the size of the demand shock. In that case, the shock can be offset by relatively small changes in normal migration patterns. Marston presents estimates indicating that normal migration flows between metropolitan areas are quite large. During a four-year period, 13.9 percent of the metropolitan population moves between areas; during an eight-year period, 25.9 percent of the metropolitan population moves between areas.[4] Economic development policies would be extraordinarily successful if they raised the employment of a metro area by even 1 percent during a year, compared to what employment would otherwise have been. Hence, over a four- or eight-year period, small increases in the normal volume of migration would completely offset a successful economic development policy. Also, even an extraordinarily large negative shock to an area's economy, such as several plant closings that reduced area employment by several percent, would be completely offset over a four- or eight-year period if a minority of the area's normal in-migrants chose other metropolitan areas. Marston concludes that "both the four-year and eight-year periods should be long enough that a shock at the beginning of the period could not cause a disequilibrium that would persist through the entire period" (p. 65).

Based on this reasoning, we might expect all of the benefits of state and local economic development policy to be reflected in higher land values after four years. Consider the likely long-run effects of an area's economic development policy on three different groups of area "stakeholders": households, firms, and landowners. Assume that all households and firms rent land from landowners; households and firms who own land can be viewed as renting it to themselves, and may benefit from local economic growth in their role as landowner as well as in their role as a household or firm. Assume also that the local area is in "equilibrium" before the economic development policy is implemented. Equilibrium means that the area, given its amenities, wages, prices, unemployment rate, and other characteristics, is able to attract a sufficient number of in-migrating households and firms, and new firms to at least keep population and employment stable, but does not attract so many as to cause explosive local growth. If an area could attract no new households or firms, it would quickly descend to ghost town status, since any area will lose some households and firms over time.

An economic development policy is implemented in the local area that provides direct assistance to business. Local job growth increases because the area is now more profitable to business. In-migration of households increases because the lower unemployment rate and higher real wages make the area more attractive to households. But as in-migration of households increases, unemployment rates go up and wage increases fall behind price increases, reducing the attractiveness of the area to households. Furthermore, as in-migration of firms and new firm births increase, local costs of land and labor go up, reducing the attractiveness of the area to business. A new equilibrium is reached when the local area's attractiveness to in-migrating households and firms is the same as it was before the policy was implemented—just attractive enough to prevent decline, but not attractive enough to cause explosive growth.

Landowners in the local area clearly gain from the growth of the area in the long run. But without further assumptions, it is difficult to determine the long-run effects of this economic development policy on the households and firms originally located in the area. A natural simplifying assumption is that households and firms originally located in the local area are similar enough, on average, to new and in-migrant households and firms that they are similarly affected by the growth policy. In that case, the development policy will not affect the original households and firms in the long run. Wages, prices, and unemployment rates adjust so that new and in-migrant households and firms find the attractiveness of the area unchanged in the long run; these same wage, price, and unemployment rate adjustments should leave the attractiveness of the area unchanged from the perspective of the original households and firms in the long run.

Of course, in the real world we would expect some differences between the original households and firms and new and in-migrant households and firms. But without some argument for systematic large differences, there is no basis for suggesting that the original households and firms systematically gain or lose from development policy in the long run. The only expected long-run beneficiaries are landowners.

In a simple version of this model, the development policy will have no effects on long-run unemployment, and will raise wages and prices (including land prices) by the same percentage in the long run. Assume that growth in and of itself—holding wages, prices, and unemployment rates constant—does not change the attractiveness of a local area. That is, firms and households are not greatly concerned over congestion, pollution, or other local characteristics that may change as an area grows. Then the simplest way to keep household well-being and firm profits unchanged is to keep the unemployment rate unchanged and increase wages and prices by the same percentage. The equal percentage increase in wages and prices must be just great enough to offset the initial spur to profits from the development policy.[5]

Long-Run Costs of Growth

One possible systematic difference between the original households and firms and those who move in is their attitude toward the characteristics that make a local area special. Households and firms originally choose a location because they find its amenities—any qualitative characteristics that affect household well-being or firm profits—particularly attractive. Over time, households and firms become accustomed to their home area. Households develop attachments to particular places and people. Firms develop linkages to customers and suppliers.

Growth changes many qualitative features of a local area. Congestion, crime, and air pollution may increase. Larger markets may attract more large-scale retailers and a greater number of specialized retailers and industrial suppliers.

Different households and firms will have different perceptions of the desirability of these changes. The in-migrants attracted will be those that find the changes most attractive or least unattractive. Wages, prices, and unemployment rate adjustments must only be sufficient to attract households and firms whose view of the qualitative changes caused by growth is relatively favorable.

But the original households and firms are likely to view these qualitative changes relatively unfavorably. They are accustomed to the local area as it originally was, and may even have chosen it for its particular qualitative features. As a result, the wage, price, and unemployment adjustments that are sufficient to attract new and in-migrant households and firms to the area are insufficient to compensate the original households and firms for the qualitative changes in the area.

For example, suppose that congestion increases as a city grows. The real wage must go up by some amount, or unemployment must go down, to enable the city to continue to attract in-migrant households. The in-migrants attracted will be those who best tolerate congestion, so the required upward adjustment in the real wage (or downward adjustment in unemployment) is modest. The original residents, on average, have a much greater preference for keeping their home city free of congestion. Some of them may have chosen to live in the city because it was not congested, while others may have become accustomed to lack of congestion. The real wage increase will not adequately compensate the original residents for the congestion increase.

If there were no costs of moving to a new city, the original residents' unhappiness with their changing city would be irrelevant because they could easily move to an uncongested city. But because of high mobility costs, the original residents will not move unless they perceive a sizable decline in their well-being at their original home city. Even if they move, their well-being is lower than if they had been able to stay in a home city that had not undergone change.[6]

A good example of losses due to growth is the effect on Spring Hill, Tennessee, a small rural community 30 miles south of Nashville, of the 1985 announcement that General Motors would locate its giant Saturn plant there. The announcement was welcomed by most Spring Hill residents, but some resented the threat posed by the plant to their way of life. For example, the *Wall Street Journal* reported an interview with one Spring Hill resident who said he "came here seven years ago because he wanted to live in 'a little one horse town.' Now, he says it's just a matter of time before he will have to move again. 'The people here have dollar signs in their eyes,' he complains" (*WSJ*, p. 1, 7/28/85, reported by Ed Bean and Damon Darlin).

Similar types of losses from growth can be experienced by businesses with strong ties to a community, either because the owner prefers living in the community, or because of built-up, firm-specific tangible and intangible capital (local reputation, unique plant and equipment that can not be sold, etc.). Some types of businesses may have production technologies especially suited to smaller communities. As growth occurs, these businesses are replaced by new businesses whose technologies are better suited to large communities. For example, small grocery stores may be replaced by large supermarkets. In a world of zero mobility costs, these businesses could just move on to similar small areas. But because of the particular ties of these businesses to their home community, a move could have large costs.

Spring Hill also provides an example of long-run costs of growth to resident businesses. A number of local farmers felt that the Saturn development threatened their way of life. One farmer complained that Saturn "will ruin farming in Spring Hill and have a negative effect on farming in all of Maury County." After the Saturn announcement, the town's farm implement dealership closed.[7]

Of course, if these original residents and businesses own land, their losses from the change in character of a community may be more than offset by the increase in the value of their land. But the increase in the value of land in a local area will overstate the benefits of an increase in local jobs, even in the long run.

The possible loss of the special characteristics of a unique place is an argument for economic development policies that only prevent decline of a local area, and against economic development policies that cause rapid growth. Preventing the loss of a sense of place is a possible benefit of only preventing the decline of an area. The loss of a sense of place is a possible cost of encouraging rapid job growth in an area. Although these benefits and costs may be important, measuring their dollar value or comparing them with other effects of state and local economic development policy is difficult. While this study does not attempt to estimate the value of a sense of place, this value should play some role in political decisions.

Hysteresis Effects of Local Job Growth

Faster job growth in a local area also causes systematic differences between the labor market experiences of persons who have lived in the area since before the job growth started and persons who move in afterwards. Due to faster growth, in the short run some persons in the area will obtain jobs who otherwise would be unemployed. In addition, some will move up to better jobs. The short-run experiences of these persons change their values, skills, self-confidence, and reputation. In economic jargon, these short-run experiences increase their human capital, as well as their human capital as perceived by employers. As a result, these persons are more likely to be employed in the long run, and more likely to be employed in a better job. Even though others will move in to this growing local area, many of the original residents will be better prepared to compete in the labor market. Even with new in-migrant workers available, employers will, in the long run, be willing to hire and keep the original residents in better jobs because of their improved human capital.

Long-run effects of one-time labor market shocks are referred to in economics as "hysteresis effects." Hysteresis is a term borrowed from physics and engineering. A system is said to exhibit hysteresis, or to be hysteretic, if its equilibrium is determined not only by current variables, but also by the history of the system. In other words, hysteresis signifies that history matters.

In physics and engineering, the hysteresis concept has been used to describe the behavior of magnetic fields in metals. Even upon removal of a magnetizing force, the electromagnetic properties of metals do not return to their original state.

In economics, the hysteresis concept has not been commonly used. Occasionally, economists have suggested that booms and recessions may have long-run effects on the equilibrium unemployment and wages of the nation. This theory has been most eloquently advanced by Phelps, in the following quotation from his 1972 book on *Inflation Policy and Unemployment Theory*:

> Of [the changes caused by a boom], job experience, with its op-
> portunities for learning by doing and on-the-job training, is possibly
> the most important. When people are engaged in sustained work
> of a kind with which they have not had any similar experience,
> they become different for it in a number of ways that are relevant
> for the equilibrium unemployment rate. Getting to work on time
> is just about the most important habit a worker can have in nearly
> every kind of job. . . . For many of the people who comprise the
> hard-core, most frequently unemployed group, getting to be
> "reliable" and learning to work with other people are necessary
> attributes for continuation in the job.
>
> For other people, the opportunity to acquire skills at more de-
> manding jobs in the skill hierarchy than they could ordinarily
> qualify for under normal always-equilibrium aggregate demand
> behavior may be the more important aspect. . . . The upgrading
> of many workers that results from a disequilibrating rise of ag-
> gregate demand may gradually lead to a true upgrading in the
> average quality of the labor force. (p. 79)

More recently, a few economists have suggested that hysteresis effects may explain why high unemployment was so persistent in the United States during the 1930s, and in many European countries in the 1980s. These unemployment rates vastly exceeded the prevailing national unemployment rates of previous decades. Furthermore, they showed little tendency to revert to their level of previous decades. This behavior of unemployment rates appears inconsistent with usual economic theories of the aggregate labor market, which assume that an economy experiencing a shock to labor demand will return to the previous equilibrium unemployment rate.[8]

Hysteresis theories of the labor market have not been subjected to many empirical tests. Observing one national economy over time does not provide sufficient information to tell whether changes in average unemployment rates are due to hysteresis effects or other factors. Equilibrium unemployment rates could change over time due to shifts in demographics, industrial structure, or technology.

Conclusion

This chapter has given theoretical reasons why local economic growth might affect more than land prices. The hysteresis argument for long-run labor market effects of local job growth goes as follows: households are immobile in the short run; as a result, local job growth has short-run effects on the labor market; these effects lead to long-run changes in households' human capital; these long-run changes affect unemployment and other labor market variables.

The next four chapters consider what the empirical evidence shows about the effects of local growth on local labor and housing markets, in both the short run and the long run.

NOTES

1. The random assignment of large income and housing price changes makes it much easier to uncover households' true mobility response to different opportunities. The random assignment implies that unobserved variables will not bias estimation of the effects of income and price changes. The large size of the changes means that observed responses would be expected to be large enough to allow for accurate estimation.

2. This sentence oversimplifies Bolton's essay, which discusses with some depth and subtlety what might be meant by a "sense of place," how it is created, and possible policy implications.

3. We should not assume that workers would be willing to work for nothing, and that the dollars gained by exchanging labor for wages measure the benefit from work over nonwork. Work has some cost to individuals over nonwork: less leisure, less time to deal with home and family responsibilities, less time to look for a better job.

4. Some readers of initial drafts of this book have wondered whether Marston's estimates of mobility rates across local labor markets are too high. I doubt whether any reasonable downward revision to Marston's estimates would appreciably affect the basic argument: gross migration flows are large enough that moderate changes in these flows could reasonably be expected to offset local labor demand shocks brought about by economic development policy.

The most recent published evidence from the Current Population Survey (Current Population Reports, Series P-20, No. 430, April 1989) indicate that MSA annual migration rates are quite high. Average annual MSA gross in-migration rates are around 6.56 percent, only slightly less than average annual county gross in-migration rates of 7.02 percent, and considerably greater than average annual state in-migration rates of 3.29 percent.

One cannot, of course, simply extrapolate annual migration rates to longer time intervals; among other factors, individuals who move once are most likely to move again. But migration rates do increase greatly as we extend the time interval considered. The most recent published information from the CPS on long-term migration, covering the period from 1980 to 1985 (Current Population Reports, Series P-20, No. 420, December 1987), shows average five-year county gross in-migration rates of 19.56 percent, and average five-year state gross in-migration rates of 10.48 percent. Average five-year MSA gross in-migration rates are not reported, but it would certainly be reasonable to assume that such rates would be 10 percent or greater.

One could question whether all migration in or out of MSAs really reflects movement across different local labor markets. Some of this migration may be to or from nearby counties or MSAs without the need for a job change. But mobility rates are surprisingly high, even if we restrict attention only to moves that almost surely are across different local labor markets. For example, the average five-year (1980-85) gross in-migration rate to states, from noncontiguous states or abroad, was 7.82 percent. Even this volume of gross migration—which almost surely understates gross migration rates across local labor markets—greatly exceeds the size of the employment increases that could plausibly be brought about over a five-year period by economic development policy. For example, based on chapter 2, a 50 percent cut in all state and local business taxes, holding public services to business constant, might in the long run hike local area business activity by around 12.5 percent. Helms' (1985) paper, discussed in appendix 2.2, suggests that business activity adjusts towards its long-run level by 8.96 percent per year. Hence, over a five-year period, a 50 percent business tax cut—which represents a huge policy change—might hike a local area's employment by 4.7 percent ($= [1-(.9104)^5]*12.5\%$), much less than normal gross migration flows in or out of the area over that time period.

5. This will hold true in the following simple model. Suppose that all households and firms are identical. In long-run equilibrium, utility (V) and profits (π) of a representative household and firm in the local area must equal the national equilibrium utility (V^*) and profits (π^*). Utility

in the local area can be assumed to depend upon local real wages (w), local unemployment (U), and local amenities that are relevant to households (S_w), while profits in the local area depend on local unemployment, local real wages, local land prices (r), and local amenities that are relevant to businesses (D). This gives rise to the following two conditions for a long-run regional equilibrium:

(1) $V(w, U; S_w) = V^*$ $\quad\quad$ $V_w > 0, V_U < 0, V_s > 0$

(2) $\pi(w, r, U; D) = \pi^*.$ $\quad\quad$ $\pi_w < 0, \pi_r < 0, \pi_U > 0, \pi_D > 0$

where subscripts indicate partial derivatives. These two equations have three endogenously determined unknowns: w, r, and U. To solve the system, we can suppose there is some type of normal relationship between the real wage rate and the unemployment rate. This relationship can be viewed as an ad hoc, intuitively plausible equation, or can be rationalized using efficiency wage theory (see appendix 4.1). The equation can be plausibly written as:

(3) $w = f(U),$ $\quad\quad$ $f_U < 0.$

Under these assumptions, suppose a demand shock to growth increases the profitability of the region. This would be a shock to D. The only way to still satisfy simultaneously equations (1), (2), and (3) is for w (real wages) and U (unemployment) to stay the same, and for r (regional prices such as land) to increase enough to offset the positive shock to profits from an increase in D. w and U cannot change because w and U would have to both change in the same direction to continue satisfying equation (1), while w and U would have to change in opposite directions to continue satisfying equation (3).

6. A hedonic imperfect mobility model showing that original residents often lose due to community changes is presented in Bartik (1986). This paper considers an intracity hedonic housing price model, but the same arguments could be made in an intercity hedonic real wage model.

7. These anecdotes about the effect of Saturn on Spring Hill area farming, including the quote from the local farmer, are taken from Garber and Fausey (1986), p. 22.

8. Human capital theory is only one of the theories offered by economists to explain labor market hysteresis. Other theories include business capital theory and insider-outsider theory. Appendix 3.1 discusses why these alternative theories do not explain hysteresis effects in *local* labor markets, but human capital theory does.

— 4 —

Effects of Local Job Growth on Unemployment, Labor Force Participation, and Weekly Hours

This is the first of four chapters reporting estimates of the effects of local growth on metropolitan areas. This chapter focuses on how local growth affects employment-related activities of individuals: whether they are unemployed, whether they choose to look for a job, and how many hours a week they typically work.

The initial focus on employment effects of growth—rather than effects on prices or wages—is because lowering unemployment is the key political rationale for state and local economic development policies. If unemployment is unaffected by state and local development efforts, politicians and voters are not likely to devote significant government resources to such programs.

Previous Research
on Local Growth and Unemployment

> Shocks that disturb the steady-state relationship among the unemployment rates of metropolitan areas tend to be eliminated by mobility within a year. (Stephen Marston, formerly Professor of Economics at Cornell University, p. 74 in "Two Views of the Geographic Distribution of Unemployment," *Quarterly Journal of Economics*, February 1985)

Previous research on local growth and unemployment is of three types. First, some research infers the unemployment effects of shocks to local growth by examining the correlation over time in metropolitan area unemployment rates. Second, some case studies of new branch plants seek to determine their effects on local unemployment. Third, a number of econometric studies estimate the effects of local growth by comparing different states or metropolitan areas.

The first research approach, examining correlations over time in metropolitan area unemployment rates, has been most prominently used by Stephen Marston (1985). The basic idea is that if a demand shock has persistent effects on a metropolitan area's unemployment, then the area's unemployment rate today should be positively correlated with next year's unemployment rate. The problem is that it is difficult to disentangle this hypothesized effect from other possible causes of positive correlation over time in local unemployment rates. For example, the equilibrium unemployment rate for a metropolitan area may differ from the national unemployment rate due to differences in the area's demographic makeup, industrial mix, or wage rates. Permanent differences in the unemployment rates of different metropolitan areas will also cause positive correlation over time in area unemployment rates.

Marston found an extremely low correlation over time in a metropolitan statistical area's (MSA's) unemployment rate, controlling for what he felt were permanent differences in metropolitan unemployment rates.[1] This finding was based on an examination of the unemployment rates of 30 MSAs for each year from 1974 to 1978.

The major weakness in Marston's research is his implicit assumption that over a four-year period there are no persistent effects of demand shocks. Differences across MSAs in average unemployment rates over the 1974-1978 period were assumed by Marston to be due to permanent "equilibrium" influences on unemployment, rather than demand shocks. But the discussion in chapter 3 revealed that unemployment effects of a one-year demand shock could persist for much more than four years. The one-year demand shock may have persistent effects because of its effects on human capital. Furthermore, the likely correlation over time of local demand shocks would further increase the persistence of demand influences on local unemployment rates.

Gramlich's (1987) research indicates that Marston's findings are sensitive to the assumption that demand shock effects persist less than four years. Gramlich estimates year-to-year correlations in metropolitan area unemployment rates over a 24-year time period. The implicit assumption behind Gramlich's approach is that over a 24-year time period, average metropolitan area unemployment rate differentials are not due to demand shocks. But demand shocks are allowed by Gramlich's approach to have effects that persist for 10 or 15 years. Gramlich finds year-to-year correlations in area unemployment that are over 20 times as great as the correlations found by Marston.[2]

A second approach to understanding how local growth affects unemployment is case studies of the unemployment effects of new branch plants. A book by Summers and his colleagues (1976) provides a comprehensive review and evaluation of case studies of the effects of new industrial plants in nonmetropolitan areas.

These case studies provide two types of evidence on the unemployment effects of new branch plants. First, many studies examine what percentage of the new plant's workforce were previously unemployed or out of the labor force. According to Summers and the others, case studies reach disparate findings: the percentage of previously "not employed" individuals (either unemployed or out of the labor force) hired by new branch plants varies from 2 percent to 43 percent in different studies. The average percentage of previously "not employed" workers hired by new branch plants is 15 percent.[3]

The problem with this evidence is that who is hired by the new branch plant may have little to do with its impact on local unemployment. For example, a new branch plant could hire only already-employed residents, but still affect unemployment because this hiring creates vacancies in other firms that are filled by the unemployed. Furthermore, the new branch plant may lead to increased employment in local consumer and intermediate goods industries. These "multiplier" effects may affect unemployment.

Some case studies also consider evidence on how new branch plants affected average unemployment in the local economic region around the plant. According to Summers and others' review, 11 of 16 case studies that examined average local unemployment rates found that unemployment dropped after the new branch plant began production.

But none of these studies appears to provide any standard to which to compare this drop in local unemployment. The drop in local unemployment should ideally be compared with some model estimating what would have happened to unemployment without the plant; failing that, the drop in local unemployment at least must be compared to national trends. Many of the studies reviewed were conducted in the early 1960s, when unemployment was dropping everywhere. Hence, a decline in unemployment in these local areas may be due to national trends, not the new plant's opening.

A third approach to researching how local growth affects unemployment relies on econometric analysis of growth and unemployment trends in different states and metropolitan areas. The basic idea is to examine whether faster growing states or metropolitan areas experience larger declines in unemployment and larger increases in labor force participation. Closely related research examines how local employment growth affects migration. This research is closely related because the jobs created by local employment growth can only be filled in three possible ways: an increase in the local labor force participation rate; a decrease in the local unemployment rate; an increase in net migration to the area. If few new local jobs are filled by net in-migration, then many of the new jobs must be filled by current residents who previously were unemployed or out of the labor force.

Table 4.1 summarizes the empirical results from previous econometric studies.[4] The studies suggest that many jobs from local growth go to in-migrants, but that local growth does affect the unemployment rate and labor force participation rate.[5] The studies disagree on what proportion of the jobs generated by local growth go to in-migrants, the resident unemployed, or new labor market participants.

There are several problems with previous econometric studies. First, these studies are unable to distinguish between the short-run and long-run effects of employment growth. They usually examine how the change in unemployment or labor force participation over some arbitrarily chosen time period is related to one growth variable, the employment growth over that time period. Any study's estimated effect of growth, derived from the coefficient on the sole growth variable, represents some combination, in unknown proportions, of short-run and long-run effects of employment growth.[6]

Second, previous studies generally fail to distinguish between the effects of different types of growth.[7] Successful state and local economic development policy increases labor demand in a local economic area. We would expect the following chain of causation: development policy increases the perceived profitability of a local area; local labor demand goes up; the increase in local labor demand reduces unemployment, increases labor force participation, and induces in-migration. The resulting correlation between local employment growth and unemployment would be expected to be negative. It is this negative effect of local employment growth on unemployment that we are trying to detect with our econometric estimation procedures.

Local growth can also be caused by a labor supply shock. Suppose an area for some reason becomes perceived as a more attractive place to live. The resulting in-migration increases unemployment and reduces wages. Either lower wages or greater availability of unemployed labor would encourage employment growth. The resulting correlation between changes in unemployment and employment growth would be expected to be positive. A simple statistical analysis might conclude that higher local employment growth was "causing" higher local unemployment rates.

In the real world, employment growth is caused by both labor demand shocks and labor supply shocks. Hence, the correlation between changes in unemployment and employment growth will reflect both influences. Estimation procedures that fail to distinguish between demand and supply shocks—such as those used by previous studies—will estimate an "effect" of employment growth on unemployment that is less negative than the true effects of employment growth caused by labor demand shocks.[8]

Third, previous econometric studies usually have not looked at how the effects of extra employment growth vary in slow-growth and fast-growth local areas. We might expect that a 1 percent differential in growth, in a metropolitan area already growing at 5 percent a year, would cause more migration response than a 1 percent growth differential

Table 4.1
Effects of Local Growth on Unemployment, Labor Force Participation, and Migration:
Estimates from Selected Studies

Study	Geographic Units Used in Growth Analysis	Growth Variable	Period Over Which Growth Calculated	Micro or Aggregate Data	Dependent Variable	Estimated % Effect of 1% Growth on Dependent Variable (Elasticity)
UNEMPLOYMENT STUDIES						
Holzer (1991)	MSAs, states	Sales	2 years 5 years	Aggregate	Unemployment rate	-.09 to -.24
Houseman & Abraham (1990)	States	Employment	1 year	Aggregate	Unemployment rate	-.10 to -.43
Moore & Laramore (1990)	Cities	Employment	10 years	Aggregate	Unemployment rate	0 to -.04
Summers (1986)	States	Employment	1 year to 15 years	Aggregate	Unemployment rate	-.2 for 1-year growth, closer to zero for 15-year growth
Fleisher & Rhodes (1976)	MSAs	Employment	2 years	Aggregate	Unemployment rate	-.07
LABOR FORCE PARTICIPATION STUDIES						
Holzer (1991)	States	Sales	5 years	Aggregate	Employment to population ratio	.26 to .37
Houseman & Abraham (1990)	States	Employment	1 year	Aggregate	LFP rate	-.01 to .60
Moore & Laramore (1990)	Cities	Employment	10 years	Aggregate	LFP rate	.03 to .08

Table 4.1 (continued)

Study	Geographic Units Used in Growth Analysis	Growth Variable	Period Over Which Growth Calculated	Micro or Aggregate Data	Dependent Variable	Estimated % Effect of 1% Growth on Dependent Variable (Elasticity)
Fleisher & Rhodes (1976)	MSAs	Employment	2 years	Aggregate	LFP rate	.01 for married women, −.04 for married men
MIGRATION STUDIES						
Houseman & Abraham (1990)	States	Employment	1 year	Aggregate	Population	.09 to .83
Treyz & Stevens (1985)	States	Employment	?	Aggregate	Population	.3
Greenwood & Hunt (1984)	BEA areas	Employment	1 year	Aggregate	Employed net migrants	.5 increase as proportion of employment increase
Bradbury, Downs & Small (1982)	MSAs	Employment	5 years	Aggregate	Population change	.5
Muth (1971)	Urbanized areas	Employment	10 years	Aggregate	Net migrants in labor force	.6 to .7 increase as proportion of employment increase

NOTES: Bradbury, Downs and Small results are from their tables 5.4 and 5.6. Fleisher and Rhodes results come from reduced form equations in their appendix. Sources of the other results above should be apparent from studies. Similar results to Greenwood and Hunt (1984) are reported in Greenwood, Hunt and McDowell (1986), and Greenwood and Hunt (1989). All unemployment and labor force participation "elasticities" show change in number of percentage rate points. For example, the Houseman and Abraham (1990) unemployment results in the table show that a 1 percent increase in jobs would reduce the unemployment rate by.10 percent up to .43 percent; for example, from 8 percent to 7.90 percent or 7.57 percent.

in an area currently declining at –2 percent a year. Hence, we would expect the unemployment and labor force participation effects of changes in growth to be greater in slow-growth areas than in fast-growth areas.

Fourth, most previous studies do not examine how the effects of local growth on unemployment vary across different types of individuals.[9] But how growth's effects vary with education, age, income, and race are important to voters and politicians.

Finally, some studies (Summers (1986); Treyz and Stevens (1985); Houseman and Abraham (1990)) use states as the unit of analysis. Yet metropolitan areas or other smaller areas are closer to our notion of a local labor market.

The new empirical work conducted for this book tries to overcome all these problems of previous studies.

New Estimates of the Effects of Local Job Growth

The new empirical work presented in this book uses both aggregate and micro data. Descriptive statistics on the data are given in appendix 4.3. The estimating equations are briefly described in table 4.2. A more detailed discussion of the econometric methodology is presented in appendix 4.2.

The model using aggregate data examines changes in the average local unemployment rate from one year to the next for 25 large metropolitan statistical areas, from 1972-73 to 1985-86.[10] The statistical relationship between these unemployment rate changes and the metropolitan area's employment growth is estimated. The estimation allows a time period effect for each yearly change in metropolitan area unemployment rates. Including time period effects means that the estimation is attempting to explain how variations in local job growth from the national average are related to variations in local unemployment changes from the national average.[11]

The model using micro data includes information from the Current Population Survey (CPS) on 44,015 adult males in 89 metropolitan areas.[12] The data come from the March CPS, which asks extensive

Table 4.2
Brief Outline of Data and Methodology Used
in Labor Market Activity Models

The aggregate model estimates equations of the following form:

$$(4.1) \ \Delta U_{mt} = B_0 + N_t + C(L)g_{mt} + V_{mt},$$

where ΔU_{mt} is the change in the unemployment rate from year t-1 to year t for MSA m, g_{mt} is the growth rate of nonagricultural employment from year t-1 to year t for MSA m, N_t is a dummy variable for the time period, B_0 is the constant term, and V_{mt} is the disturbance term. The "$C(L)$" term means that a series of lagged values in g_{mt} are also included in the estimation, with each lag allowed to have its own coefficient.

The micro model estimates equations of the following form:

$$(4.2) \ L_{imt} = B_0 + N_t + F_m + \mathbf{B}'\mathbf{X}_{imt} + C(L)E_{mt} + V_{imt},$$

where L_{imt} is either the labor force participation rate for individual i (defined as the number of weeks in the labor force during the previous year divided by 52), the employment rate (defined as the number of weeks employed divided by the number of weeks in the labor force), or the usual weekly hours the individual worked when working during the previous year. F_m is a dummy variable for the metropolitan area, $\mathbf{X}_{imt}$ is a vector of individual demographic characteristics, $\mathbf{B}$ is the estimated vector of coefficients on those characteristics, E_{mt} is the natural log of the level of nonagricultural employment in MSA m in year t, and $C(L)$ again indicates that the equation includes lagged values of E_{mt}. It can be shown that the micro "levels" equation can be derived from the aggregate "changes" equation. The inclusion of the MSA fixed effect implies that the model is examining how MSA job *growth* (not the MSA job *level*) affects labor market activities.

The estimation allows for up to eight lagged years in the employment terms. Reported results are based on the lag-length chosen based on the Akaike Information Criterion, a standard model selection criterion (Amemiya 1985).

The aggregate unemployment data are official estimates from the Current Population Survey. The micro data come from the March Current Population Survey. Nonagricultural employment data come from official "BLS 790" program estimates.

The years included are 1972 to 1986 for the aggregate model, 1979-1986 for the micro model. Twenty-five large MSAs are included in the aggregate model, 89 MSAs in the micro model.

More information on data and methodology are in appendices 4.2 and 4.3.

questions about the individual's labor market-related activities during the previous year. I pooled data from eight March CPS computer tapes, from March 1980 to March 1987. These tapes contain information on eight calendar years, from 1979 to 1986.

The micro data models examined the effects of a metropolitan area's job growth on several different types of labor market activities of the area's residents.[13] The labor market activities examined included: number of weeks the individual was in the labor force during the previous year divided by 52 (the labor force participation rate); the number of weeks the individual was employed divided by the number of weeks in the labor force (the employment rate, equal to one minus the unemployment rate); and, the usual weekly hours that the individual worked during the previous year when he was employed. These dependent variables were statistically related to the demographic characteristics of the individual and recent employment trends in the metropolitan area.

Both the micro data and aggregate data models allow for the effect of growth on labor market activities to vary freely over time for up to eight years after a growth shock. Statistical tests are used to determine how many years must pass after a one-time local job growth shock for the effect of that shock to stop changing, that is, to converge to some "equilibrium" long-run effect. These statistical tests always indicated that this stable long-run effect was reached in less than eight years.

Both micro and aggregate data models also attempted to distinguish between demand-induced local growth and local growth in general. One version of the models examined the effects on labor market activities of all types of growth. The models were then re-estimated to examine only the effects of growth caused by increases in the demand for the metropolitan area's export industries (that is, industries exporting outside the metropolitan area to the national market).

Figures 4.1 through 4.4 report the estimated effects on local labor markets of all types of local job growth, whether caused by demand shocks or supply shocks.[14] The figures show the estimated labor market effects if metropolitan area employment was permanently increased by

Figure 4.1

Estimated Cumulative Effects of a 1 Percent Shock to Local Employment on Average Local Unemployment Rate, Using Aggregate Data

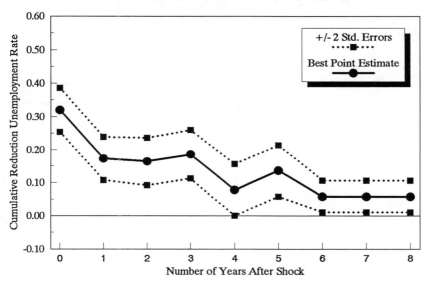

Estimates Underlying Figure

Cumulative Effect After:

Immediate effect = 0 years	1 year	2 years	3 years	4 years	5 years	Long-run effect = 6 years
.320	.173	.164	.186	.078	.136	.058
(.033)	(.033)	(.036)	(.037)	(.039)	(.039)	(.024)

NOTES: Standard errors of estimated cumulative effects are in parentheses. Bold line in figure shows best point estimate of cumulative effect of growth shock. Two dotted lines show two standard errors to either side of best point estimate; this interval has 95 percent probability of including true effect. Reported estimates are for specification that minimizes AIC. Long-run effect in 8-lag specification is .054 (.026).

As mentioned in notes to chapter 4, the cumulative effect after the number of lags included in the optimal AIC specification is an implied long-run effect. Minimizing the AIC after k lags implies no significant change thereafter. The figures here only carry this long-run effect out to eight years after the shock, as the empirical work never tested whether this long-run effect might decay after eight years. For comparison, the notes at the bottom of each table also report the estimated long-run effect in a specification with eight lagged employment variables. These long-run effects, as one would expect, are always quite similar to the optimal AIC long-run effects.

Figure 4.2
Estimated Cumulative Effects of a 1 Percent Shock
to Local Employment on Local Employment Rate,
Using Micro Data

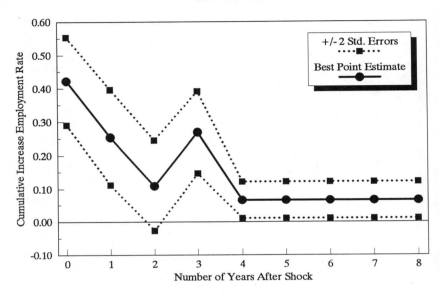

Estimates Underlying Figure

Cumulative Effect After:

Immediate effect = 0 years	1 year	2 years	3 years	Long-run effect = 4 years
.422	.254	.109	.269	.066
(.066)	(.071)	(.068)	(.061)	(.028)

NOTES: Standard errors of estimated cumulative effects are in parentheses. Bold line in figure shows best point estimate of cumulative effect of growth shock. Two dotted lines show two standard errors to either side of best point estimate; this interval has 95 percent probability of including true effect. Reported estimates are for specification that minimizes AIC. Long-run effect in 8-lag specification is .064 (.030).

Figure 4.3
Estimated Cumulative Effects of a 1 Percent Shock
to Local Employment on Labor Force Participation Rate

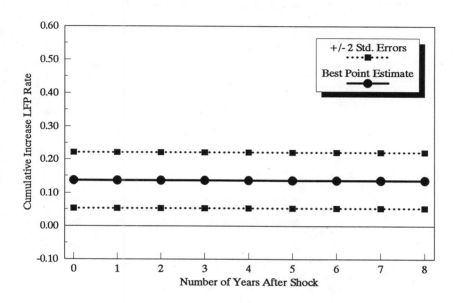

Estimates Underlying Figure

Cumulative Effect After:

	Long-run effect = 0 years
	.137
	(.042)

NOTES: Standard errors of estimated cumulative effects are in parenthese. Bold line in figure shows best point estimate of cumulative effect of growth shock. Two dotted lines show two standard errors to either side of best point estimate; this interval has 95 percent probability of including true effect. Reported estimates are for specification that minimizes AIC. Long-run effect in 8-lag specification is .148 (.053).

Figure 4.4
Estimated Cumulative Effects of a 1 Percent Shock
to Local Employment on Usual Weekly Hours Worked
When Employed, as a Percentage of Average Hours Worked

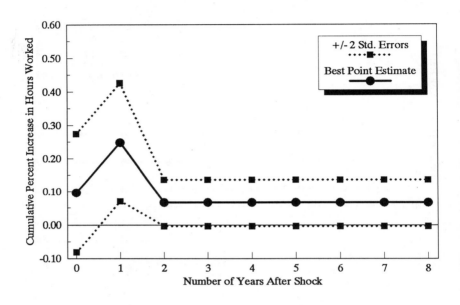

Estimates Underlying Figure

Cumulative Effect After:

Immediate effect = 0 years	1 year	Long-run effect = 2 years
.096	.248	.066
(.089)	(.089)	(.035)

NOTES: Standard errors of estimated cumulative effects are in parentheses. Bold line in figure shows best point estimate of cumulative effect of growth shock. Two dotted lines show two standard errors to either side of best point estimate; this interval has 95 percent probability of including true effect. Reported estimates are for specification that minimizes AIC. Long-run effect in 8-lag specification is .047 (.042).

1 percent above what it otherwise would be. The effects on metropolitan area unemployment rates, labor force participation, and employment rates are reported as the change in "rate points": that is, a change in unemployment of 45/100ths of 1 percent—from 8 percent to 7.55 percent, for example—is reported as .45 in the figure and table. The effects on weekly hours are reported as a percentage of the mean weekly hours worked by the sample.

The most important finding revealed by these figures is that local growth effects on unemployment and labor force participation are extremely persistent. A shock that permanently raises a metropolitan area's employment by 1 percent is estimated to reduce the area's long-run unemployment rate by 7/100ths of 1 percent (based on the micro data results) or 6/100ths of 1 percent (based on the aggregate data results). Long-run local labor force participation rates are estimated to increase by 14/100ths of 1 percent. While these growth effects may seem small, their persistence makes them important. The improvement in local unemployment and labor force participation due to the shock continues for many years. The long-run effects all seem very stable in the period from six to eight years after the shock. This stability suggests that the effects will not rapidly depreciate after eight years.

The estimated long-run effects can be restated to show who gets the new jobs from growth. Suppose some economic development policy creates 100 net new jobs for a metropolitan area. Based on these estimates, in the long run, 6 or 7 of the 100 jobs will go to local residents who otherwise would be unemployed, and 16 will go to local residents who otherwise would be out of the labor force.[15] The other 77 or 78 jobs go to in-migrants. These effects of new jobs on local residents are smaller than claimed by politicians. But the effects on residents' employment prospects are much larger than would be expected by many economists. Whether these effects are large compared to other alternative policies for improving individuals' employment prospects is discussed later in this chapter.

The time pattern of short-term versus long-term effects of growth shown in the figures and tables is about what one might expect. The short-run effects of growth on unemployment and usual weekly hours worked are greater than the long-run effects. Presumably, this difference reflects the greater migration response to growth as time goes by.

For labor force participation, the lack of any difference between short-run and long-run effects of growth is surprising. Perhaps labor force participation stays constant due to two offsetting effects. Lags in the labor force participation response to reduced local unemployment may increase the labor force participation effect over time. Some individuals take a while to decide to look for a job after the labor market has improved. Due to in-migration, however, the unemployment rate, after initially declining, begins to come back up again. This partial deterioration of the unemployment situation may discourage other individuals from looking for work.

Appendix 4.4 reports some additional empirical results on growth effects on labor market activity. In particular, the appendix shows that growth due to greater demand for a metropolitan area's exports has very similar effects to those of general area growth. There are two possible explanations for this result. First, metropolitan area growth differences may mostly be due to demand shocks, with supply-side factors playing a minor role. Second, even if supply-side factors play some role in explaining metropolitan area growth, labor supply shocks may be reflected in wages rather than unemployment rates or labor force participation rates. In that case, labor supply shocks will not induce any positive correlation between unemployment and local growth. This possible positive correlation was hypothesized above to bias estimates of the effects of local growth on unemployment.

The new results reported in this chapter are consistent with the hysteresis model of equilibrium unemployment discussed in chapter 3. In the short run, a shock increasing local growth allows some individuals to obtain jobs who otherwise would be unemployed or out of the labor force. This employment experience alters the "human capital" of these individuals: they obtain better job skills, or at least are perceived by employers as having better skills. As a result of improved human capital, they are more likely to be employed in the long run.

Effects of Growth Shocks
in Slow- and Fast-Growth Areas

> People are much more mobile in the face of job opportunities than in the face of job losses. If a factory in a small town closes and 100 jobs are lost, the number of residents who move out may be extremely small. The job loss will manifest itself through some increase in unemployment and some decrease in participation rates. . . . On the other hand, should a new factory open in a comparable small town, a very considerable number of people may come in to take the new jobs. The decrease in unemployment and increase in participation rates among the original population may thus be far smaller than a naive estimate would have indicated. (Page 4 in *Economic Development Programs for Cities, Counties, and Towns*, John M. Levy, 1981)

Many analysts believe that changes in growth will have much more effect on the employment climate in a slow-growing local area than in a fast-growing area. The hypothesis is that a declining area will have little in-migration, and that residents will remain attached to their homes, neighborhoods, or communities. Small negative or positive growth shocks will have little effect on out-migration, and in-migration will stay close to zero even if there are small positive growth shocks in the area. Hence, shocks to local employment can only affect unemployment rates and labor force participation.

In contrast, a fast-growing local area will have significant in-migration. Also, many of the residents will be relatively new and will not have developed strong attachments to the area. Negative or positive growth shocks may dramatically change the volume of in-migration, and many current residents will be willing to move out if the area becomes slightly less attractive. Shocks to local employment will be mostly absorbed by changes in net migration rates, with little change in unemployment or labor force participation.

The research conducted for this book investigates this hypothesis. The approach was to allow the effect of 1 percent extra employment growth to vary with the initial level of growth in the metropolitan area.[16]

Table 4.3 reports the results from this investigation. There is no strong evidence that local growth shocks have greater effects on the employment climate in slow-growing metropolitan areas. Unemployment and hours worked respond more in the short run to growth shocks in slow-growing metropolitan areas, but the labor force participation rate responds less in the short run. Combining the results for the unemployment and labor force participation rates, the overall probability of employment is affected about the same amount by growth shocks, regardless of the initial growth rate of the metropolitan area. The implication is that net migration responds similarly to growth shocks in slow-growing and fast-growing local areas.

Our intuition about the contribution of out-migration and in-migration to migration patterns in local areas with different growth rates appears to be incorrect. The empirical evidence from migration studies is that there is a great deal of out-migration and in-migration in all types of local areas. The relative volumes obviously vary between slow- and fast-growth areas, but gross flows in both directions are always surprisingly large. Hence, even slow-growth areas have many potential in-migrants who can respond to employment growth shocks. Thus, the net migration response to growth shocks could plausibly be quite similar, regardless of the initial growth rate of a local area.

Effects of Local Job Growth on Different Groups

Given the severity of the employment problems facing urban disadvantaged populations . . . it is at least arguable that many if not most of the jobs created by economic development programs will not materially ameliorate structural unemployment. (Franklin James, Professor of Public Policy, University of Colorado, and former Director of the Legislative and Urban Policy Staff, U.S. Department of Housing and Urban Development, during the Carter Administration, page 162 in "Urban Economic Development: A Zero-Sum Game?" in *Urban Economic Development*, Richard D. Bingham and John Blair, eds., 1984)

I now turn to the crucial issue of how local economic growth affects the employment prospects of different types of individuals. I focus on how effects vary with race, education, and age.

Theoretically predicting how demand shock effects vary across groups is difficult, as several influences work in different directions. Suppose we visualize the labor market as being imperfectly segmented by race, education, and age. Employers perceive these different types of labor as being imperfect substitutes.

Several factors in such a theoretical model will determine how the effects of growth shocks differ across groups. First, the relative geographical mobility of each group will matter. Other things equal, one would expect growth shocks to have larger effects on the employment prospects of less mobile groups. Older workers and less-educated workers are less mobile, so these groups should be more affected by growth, all else equal.[17]

Second, greater average growth may affect the relative demand for different types of labor. A 10 percent increase in local labor demand may not increase the demand for all types of labor by 10 percent. Franklin James, in the above quotation, is implicitly saying that labor demand expansion in metropolitan areas may not much increase the demand for less-educated workers. In addition, if blacks are concentrated in the inner cities while the bulk of employment demand increases occur in the suburbs, then metropolitan area job growth will tend to help whites more than blacks.

Third, groups may differ in their behavioral responses to changes in their employment prospects, above and beyond differences in mobility behavior. For example, older workers may find it more socially acceptable than younger workers to drop out of the labor force in response to poor economic prospects.

Considering all these influences, one could theoretically justify any observed pattern in how the effects of local growth vary with age, education, and race. Hence, how the effects vary across groups can only be determined by empirical research, to which I now turn.

Table 4.4 presents estimates of how the long-run effects of demand shocks on labor market activity vary with education, age, and race. The

Table 4.3
Nonlinearities in the Effects of Employment Shocks

	0 years	1 year	2 years	3 years	4 years
Labor Force Participation					
At mean growth rate	.224%	−.001%	.173%		
One standard deviation less than mean	.249%	−.228%	.173%		
Absolute *t*-statistic on difference	.27	2.63	---		
Employment Rate, Micro Data					
At mean growth rate	.395%	.228%	.102%	.249%	.044%
One deviation less than mean	.475%	.368%	.095%	.291%	.044%
Absolute *t*-statistic on difference	1.42	2.72	.15	.75	---
Unemployment Rate Reductions, Aggregate Data					
At mean growth rate	.30%	.16%	.15%	.14%	.06%
One deviation less than mean	.38%	.21%	.17%	.19%	.09%
Absolute *t*-statistic on difference	3.92	1.67	.51	1.26	.56

Weekly Hours

At mean growth rate	.070 hr.	.036 hr.
One deviation less than mean	.091 hr.	.036 hr.
Absolute *t*-statistic on difference	.71	---

NOTES: This table reports specifications that add terms in employment growth squared. The AIC prefers squared specification for all variables except weekly hours. The lag-length specification reported in the table is the one preferred by the AIC. The mean growth rate and its standard deviation vary with the sample and year; 2 percent growth is close to the typical mean, and 3 percent is close to the typical standard deviation. Table thus reports derivative of dependent variable with respect to growth at 2 percent growth and −1 percent growth. Reported *t*-statistic is *t*-statistic for appropriate growth squared term. Micro specification implicitly constrains long-run effect of growth shocks to always be the same regardless of initial level of growth.

Table 4.4
Differences Across Households in the Long-Run Effects
of Employment Shocks on Labor Market Activity

	Effect of 1% Employment Shock for Mean Household	Impact on Effect of Standardized Change in:		
		Education	Age	Black
Labor force participation	.164% (.050)	.006% (.002)	.013% (.002)	−.007% (.007)
Employment rate	.060% (.028)	−.004% (.001)	−.001% (.001)	−.012% (.004)
Weekly hours	.089% (.033)	−.002% (.002)	.003% (.002)	−.004% (.007)

NOTES: The table reports the effects of household characteristics on the long-run effect of growth for the lag-length chosen as "optimal" by the AIC for the interaction specification. This lag-length is four years for the employment rate, five years for labor force participation, and zero years for weekly hours. Household characteristic effects are reported for a one-unit change in race (from 0=white to 1=black), and for one standard deviation change in education (3.0 years) and experience (11.8 years). The impacts are calculated directly from the coefficients on the interaction terms in the regression (after multiplication by the "standardized change"). The labor force participation and employment rate results report effect in "rate units"; that is, for mean household, a 1 percent shock increases the labor force participation rate by .164 percentage points (from 88 percent to 88.164 percent, for example). The effect as a percent of the mean labor force participation rate would be higher. The weekly hour results are expressed as a percent of average weekly hours for that type of household. The standard errors are in parentheses. The AIC clearly prefers interaction specification for the labor force participation rate and the employment rate, but prefers the no interaction specification for hours.

table reports the mean long-run effect across all individuals for a specification that allows the effect to vary across groups. As one would expect, these mean long-run effects are similar, but not identical, to the long-run effects in the previously estimated specifications that do not allow effects to vary across groups.[18]

The most important lesson from table 4.4 is that growth shock effects are fairly similar across different groups. Most of the group differentials seem relatively small compared to the mean long-run effect for the sample. Thus, in this particular case it does seem that a "rising tide lifts all boats." The fears of some economists that metropolitan economic growth will fail to help less-educated workers and blacks are not supported by these estimates.

The largest differences across groups occur for older workers and blacks.[19] Labor force participation rates for older workers are significantly more sensitive to metropolitan area job growth. This may reflect the greater problems of older workers in gaining reemployment after a layoff, or it may reflect the greater social acceptance of an older worker's decision to drop out of the labor force.

Black unemployment rates are less sensitive to metropolitan job growth than white unemployment rates, but blacks are still affected. A 1 percent growth shock increases the black labor force participation rate by about 16/100ths of 1 percent, and reduces the black unemployment rate by about 5/100ths of 1 percent.[20]

Job Growth Versus Other Policies

. . . [P]romising strategies exist for addressing urban unemployment and poverty without recourse to economic development efforts. For instance, as has been suggested, the federal government might choose to help workers move from distressed communities with weak economies to other places where jobs are plentiful, a so-called "people to jobs" strategy. . . . A policy could include benefits like job training and wage subsidy vouchers for the disadvantaged.

[A]dvocates and administrators of economic development programs have largely failed to make a convincing case that economic
development programs are an effective or necessary element of
an urban policy. In particular, next to no evidence is available to
compare the impacts on urban poverty or unemployment of
economic development investments [with mobility programs or programs fostering the productivity of individuals seeking work].
(Franklin James, p. 179 in "Federal Economic Development Programs and National Urban Policy," in *Economic Development
Quarterly*, May 1988)

One practical question is whether encouraging state and local economic
development is the most cost-effective policy for reducing unemployment. The micro data model used in this book estimates the effects of
education as well as local growth on unemployment and labor force
participation, which allows some comparison of these two types of
policies. Examining the effectiveness of mobility subsidies would require a different kind of study.

Table 4.5 compares long-run growth and education effects on labor
force participation and unemployment. The table includes comparisons
of the effects of growth and education for different groups in the
population.

Table 4.5 seems to imply that the improvement of employment prospects is better achieved by increasing everyone's educational level than
by increasing local job growth. This conclusion overlooks two crucial
points: it is harder to change overall educational levels than overall local
job growth; local growth and education have differential effects on different generations.

On the first point, the table compares increasing educational achieve-
ment by one year with increasing local job growth by 1 percent. It is
probably harder to raise average local educational levels by one year
than to increase local employment by 1 percent.

One way of determining the relative ease of policy-induced changes
in local education and employment growth is to consider the maximum
feasible effect of state and local policy. For example, even if state and
local governments somehow got every current student in a metropolitan

Table 4.5
Comparison of Long-Run Growth and Education Effects
on Labor Force Participation and Employment Rates

	Labor Force Participation Rate	Employment Rate
Mean value of rates	87.5	94.6
Long-run effect of 1 percent growth	.137 (.042)	.066 (.028)
Effect of 1 year of education, white with mean education and age	.391 (.063)	.857 (.032)
Change in effect of education, for standardized change in:		
Education	−.358 (.074)	-.160 (.043)
Age	−.766 (.070)	−.277 (.040)
Black	.486 (.255)	.699 (.152)

NOTES: Standard errors are in parentheses. Results come from specifications with uniform effect of growth. Mean education is 13.0 years; mean age is 22.3 years of experience (implied age is 22.3 + 13.0 + 6 = 41.3). Standardized change is 3 years for education and 11.8 years for age (= 1 standard deviation) and a change from Black = 0 to Black = 1. Standardized changes are meant to be added to mean white effect to get implied effect. That is, someone with 16 years of education will find that the marginal effect on the employment rate per year of education is .857 + (−.160) = .697.

area to complete high school and college, it would take about 40 years (one generation) for average education to increase from current levels around 12 years to their final equilibrium level of 16 years, a rate of increase of 1 year per decade. A policy effect of this magnitude seems implausible. But perhaps better high schools, an increase in the school-leaving age, and more college financial aid could increase average educational levels at about half this rate, or about a one-half year increase in average educational levels per decade.

Consider for comparison the potential policy effects on local employment. State and local economic development policy, whether traditional or new wave, might have effects equivalent to removing half of all state and local business taxes, without reducing public services to businesses. Such a policy seems as feasible as increasing average educational levels by one-half year per decade through state and local policy. According to the empirical estimates of chapter 2, a 50 percent reduction in state and local business taxes (holding public services constant) would increase local employment by at least 10 percent in the long run. If half this long-run effect is achieved within a decade, the policy would increase local employment by 5 percent. Thus, from this thought experiment, a one-half year increase in average local educational levels is about as hard to achieve through policy as a 5 percent increase in local employment.

These lines of reasoning suggest that, to make the two alternative policies in table 4.5 comparable in difficulty, either the growth effects should be multiplied by 10, or the education effects should be divided by 10. Either adjustment would suggest that local job growth and education have effects on employment prospects that are of similar magnitude.

Turning to the second point, the education strategy and the job-growth strategy have different effects on the generations. An education and training strategy inevitably will find it easier to aid younger individuals. In contrast, increasing local job growth improves the employment prospects of all age groups. From the viewpoint of older residents, the job-growth strategy has a larger payoff than the education strategy. Thus, educational policy and state and local economic development policy should properly be seen as complements rather than as mutually exclusive alternatives.

This same point probably holds in comparing state and local economic development and labor mobility policies as strategies for reducing unemployment. The promotion of labor mobility is most likely to be successful with younger workers. Again, state and local economic development policies can potentially play a unique role in helping older workers, who generally will not want to move or be retrained.

Some Speculative Extensions to the Research Findings

The empirical analysis of this chapter only examines the effects of aggregate metropolitan employment growth on individuals' unemployment, labor force participation, and work hours. This should not be interpreted as implying that only total metropolitan employment growth matters. If increases in total labor demand have long-run effects on individuals' ability to get a job, as the evidence in this chapter suggests, then it seems reasonable to assume that the composition of labor demand—its distribution across industries, occupations, or neighborhoods within the metropolitan area—would also have some long-run effects on individuals' employment success.

For example, it would be reasonable to assume that individuals with low levels of education would be most helped by metropolitan employment growth that shifted the composition of employment towards industries with relatively modest skill requirements. Residents of inner-city ghettos would be most helped by metropolitan employment growth that was concentrated in the city rather than the suburbs.

These assumptions must remain speculative. This book does not directly examine the hypotheses because of the lack of detailed data on employment growth by industry and neighborhood within metropolitan areas. Overcoming these data problems poses a difficult challenge for researchers.

Even in the absence of data on the industrial and neighborhood composition of MSA employment growth, estimates of the effects of aggregate MSA employment growth are still important to policy. Estimated effects tell us the effects of job growth with a "typical" industrial and geographic composition. In addition, the finding here that labor demand shocks have long-lasting effects seems likely to be generalizable to industry- or neighborhood-specific labor demand shocks.[21]

Conclusion

This chapter has found effects of metropolitan area job growth on labor force participation and unemployment rates that are extremely persistent. These results are consistent with hysteresis theories of unemployment, which hold that short-run reductions in unemployment may lead to some long-run reductions in the equilibrium unemployment rate. The estimated long-run effects of local job growth on employment prospects are comparable to those of alternative policies, and they loom large for older workers.

NOTES

1. Specifically, Marston found a year-to-year correlation in metropolitan unemployment rates of only .02.
2. Gramlich finds year-to-year correlations in area unemployment rates that average .468 for all metropolitan areas in his sample, compared to Marston's finding of a .02 correlation.
3. Fifteen percent is a weighted average of the studies reviewed by Summers et al., using the number of branch plant workers included in each study as weights.
4. This table excludes the recent study by Browne (1990) of labor force participation rates in U.S. regions. Her study includes both employment growth and the unemployment rate as explanatory variables. From the perspective of the present study, the unemployment rate is an endogenous variable.
5. One study that does seem inconsistent with other studies is the research by Fleisher and Rhodes (1976). This study finds that areas with higher local employment growth from 1968 to 1970 had lower labor force participation rates for males in 1970. But this study differs from all the other studies in focusing on the absolute level of the area's employment climate—in this case, the level of the labor force participation rate—rather than on changes in the area's employment climate for individuals. But the level of the labor force participation rate, or the level of the local unemployment rate, is affected by so many unobserved attributes of local areas that it is very risky to rely on estimates of how growth is correlated with the level of an area's economic climate. It is possible that some of the unobserved demographic and industrial characteristics of an area that affect the level of the area's labor force participation rate also affect local growth. The resulting correlations between local growth and the labor force participation rate level could be spurious rather than reflect causation. Examining *changes* in an area's labor force participation or unemployment eliminates the influence of unobserved area characteristics that have a fixed effect on these aspects of an area's economic climate for workers. Hence, estimated effects of local growth on changes in unemployment or labor force participation are more likely to reflect true patterns of causation.

6. This proposition can be demonstrated formally, although it seems fairly intuitive. Consider the type of aggregate estimating equation used in this book (see appendix 4.2):

(1) $Y_{mt} - Y_{mt-1} = B_0 + B_t + C(L)(E_{mt} - E_{mt-1}) + U_{mt}$,

where Y_{mt} is some measure of local economic conditions (the unemployment rate, etc.) in MSA m at time t, E_{mt} is the natural logarithm of MSA employment, B_t represents a time-period dummy, $C(L)$ indicates an unrestricted polynomial in the lag operator, and U_{mt} is the disturbance term. As discussed in appendix 4.2, the cumulative effect of a growth shock after s years is the sum of the "C" coefficients up to the sth lag. Once the effect has reached its long-run level, coefficients on additional lag terms should be zero.

Consider now a different specification of the relationship:

(2) $Y_{mt} - Y_{mt-1} = B_0 + C(E_{mt} - E_{m,t-r}) + U_{mt}$.

$E_{mt} - E_{m,t-r}$ is the percentage growth in employment since r years ago, where r is assumed to be long enough for long-run effects to be realized. $E_{mt} - E_{m,t-r}$ is the sum of the various $E_{mt} - E_{mt-1}$ and lagged $E_{mt} - E_{mt-1}$ variables included in equation (1). Based on Lichtenberg's (1990) theoretical analysis of the effects in a regression of substituting a sum of independent variables for these independent variables, the coefficient C will be an average of all the coefficients embodied in $C(L)$. (Lichtenberg shows this will hold if the summed independent variables have the same variance; this seems likely here for the annual employment growth terms.) Hence equation (2) will estimate the long-run effect divided by r.

But the type of equation actually estimated by most researchers is of the form:

(3) $Y_{mt} - Y_{m,t-r} = B_0 + C(E_{mt} - E_{m,t-r}) + U_{mt}$.

$Y_{mt} - Y_{m,t-r}$ can be written as the sum of annual changes in Y. Because the expectation of a sum conditional on some X variables is the sum of the expectation of each component conditional on those X variables, we know that regression (3), which estimates the conditional expectation of the sum, will yield an estimated C which is the sum of the coefficients that would result from r separate regressions of annual changes in Y on $E_{mt} - E_{m,t-r}$. Each of these separate regressions is of the following form:

(4) $Y_{ms} - Y_{ms-1} = B_0 + C_s(E_{mt} - E_{m,t-r})$,

where s ranges from $t-r+1$ to t. Each C_s in these r separate regressions also equals the average of the coefficients, D, from the following regression:

(5) $Y_{ms} - Y_{ms-1} = B_0 + D(L)(E_{mt} - E_{m,t-r})$.

But in this case, unlike equation (1), the sum of the D coefficients will not represent the long-run effect if s is some years earlier than t. If s is enough years earlier than t, many of the D coefficients will be on employment growth in years after s, and should have coefficients of zero. Furthermore, for many of the earlier years some lagged employment growth terms with significant coefficients will be omitted from the regression. If we let G_k equal the true cumulative effect of a growth shock after k years, the estimated C_s in equation (4) will equal $((G_{r-t+s})/r)$, assuming there is no omitted variable bias from the omitted lagged growth terms. Hence, the estimated C in equation (3) sums r different C_s coefficients, some of which are $(1/r)$ times the long-run effect, and some of which are $(1/r)$ times the short-run effect, or

(6) $C = \sum\limits_{s=t-r+1}^{t} C_s = \sum\limits_{s=t-r+1}^{t} (G_{r-t+s})/r = (1/r) \sum\limits_{s=t-r+1}^{t} G_{r-t+s}$.

Thus, under these assumptions, the estimated C, from a regression of a change in Y over r years on the employment change over r years, is the average over r years of the cumulative effect after each of the r years.

This discussion assumes that the omission of some lagged growth terms will not change the coefficient on the remaining growth terms. But the reverse is quite possible. The coefficients on a typical included growth term will increase by $D_0 A_{i0}$, where D_0 is the true effect of the omitted growth term on the change in Y, and A_{i0} is the coefficient from an imaginary auxiliary regression of the omitted growth term on the included growth terms. We would expect the sum over all of the A_{i0} to generally be less than one, as we would expect a 1 percent increase in observed growth to be associated with less than a 1 percent increase in growth for other years, due to regression to the mean. Hence, the estimated C_s in equation (4) should be somewhat greater than $(G_{r-t+s})/r$, where G_k is the cumulative effect after k years. However, the estimated C_s will not in general be as great as $1/r$ times the true long-run cumulative effect. As a result, the estimated C will still be a weighted average of short-run and long-run effects, with a somewhat greater weight on the long-run effects.

7. Two exceptions are the studies by Bradbury, Downs, and Small (1982), and Houseman and Abraham (1990), which use methods similar to my own to distinguish demand shock growth from growth in general.

8. Appendix 4.1 develops a simple theoretical model that shows different effects of demand and supply shocks on the labor market equilibrium.

9. Houseman and Abraham (1990) examine how the effects of growth vary between men and women. In the United States, the effect of growth on female labor force participation is somewhat higher, and on population somewhat lower, than is true for men. Effects on unemployment seem similar. Houseman and Abraham also look separately at effects on prime-age workers versus the general population. Migration effects seem somewhat greater for prime-age workers. I should note that Houseman and Abraham are examining effects of growth of employment for that particular type of worker (i.e., growth of employment of prime-age males in regressions examining unemployment, labor force participation, and population of that group) rather than effects of overall employment growth.

Moore and Laramore (1990) examine how the effects of growth vary across four groups: black men, black women, nonblack men, and nonblack women. Local employment growth affects the labor force participation of nonblack men by about half as much as the labor force participation of the other three groups. Effects of growth on unemployment are greater for black men and women than for nonblacks.

10. MSAs were the focus of all analysis in this book as the closest statistical equivalent of a theoretical local labor and housing market. Local growth effects obviously could be different for rural labor and housing markets, or for neighborhood submarkets within an MSA.

11. A standard result in econometrics is that a regression including dummy variables for group membership is equivalent to a regression with all variables differenced from group means. Hence, including time period dummies is equivalent to differencing all variables from the national average for that time period.

12. Restricting the micro data analysis to adult males is obviously a limitation of the empirical work. Ideally, one would also want to estimate effects on females, youths, and individuals over 65. The restriction to adult males was adopted to save time. With limited resources, I decided to investigate effects of growth on adult males in depth rather than examine all groups more cursorily. Examining only adult males does have the advantage that there is probably less need, given current social norms, to be concerned about how the labor market experiences of other members of the family affect adult males. For stay-at-home youth or married females, a negative growth shock that hurts adult males' economic outcomes could well lead to increased labor force participation and earnings. For adult males, changes in individual earnings and labor force participation are probably more unambiguously linked to overall family well-being, at least on average.

13. The micro data estimation procedure allows for a "fixed effect" on labor market activities for each MSA, reflecting possible unobserved attributes of the MSA that might affect employment-related activities of individuals. This fixed MSA effect implies that even though the estimation expresses the level of individuals' employment-related activities as a function of levels of MSA employment, the estimation is really attempting to explain how the variation in employment-related

activities from their MSA average is related to variation in MSA employment from its average. See appendix 4.2 for more discussion of the specification.

14. Note that all the estimates in the figures and in the appendix tables report the usual OLS standard errors. As noted in appendix 4.2, the group structure of the micro data potentially implies that the true standard errors may be somewhat higher. However, as shown in appendix 4.2, table 4A2.2, this bias is small. For the micro employment rate dependent variable, the true standard errors may be around 6.8 percent higher than those reported. If all standard errors in employment rate regressions were adjusted upwards by this amount, no changes in inferences would need to be made. For the labor force participation and weekly hours dependent variables, there does not appear, as shown in table 4A2.2, to be any significant group structure in the data.

15. The percentage change in MSA employment is approximately the sum of the percentage change in the employment to labor force ratio, plus the percentage change in the labor force to population ratio, plus the percentage change in population. At the mean labor force participation probability of .875, the OLS estimated change in the labor force participation rate of .137 is a percentage change of .157 percent; at the mean employment probability of .946, the OLS estimated change in the rate of .066 is a percentage change of .070 percent.

These calculations assume that estimated effects for the adult male population can be generalized to the overall population. In the case of unemployment, the effects on overall unemployment are quite similar to the effects on adult male unemployment. Research by Houseman and Abraham (1990) and Moore and Laramore (1990) suggests that female labor force participation is more sensitive to regional growth shocks than male labor force participation.

16. This was done by including squared terms in growth in the estimating equations.

17. Blacks are more mobile than whites on average, but their mobility options are restricted by housing market discrimination. Hence, it is unclear how the relative mobility of blacks and whites would alter the relative effects of labor demand shocks on the employment prospects of these two groups.

18. The differences across groups are reported by considering a "standardized" change in each individual characteristic: a one standard deviation change (based on the standard deviation in this sample of individuals) in education (3 years) and age (11.8 years), and a change from a white individual to a black individual. This procedure allows one to get some sense of how important these differences across groups are, in terms of how much the normal variations in the sample across groups affect the long-run impact of growth. The estimated effects of these changes in characteristics are to be interpreted as adding to or subtracting from the effect for the mean individual. Thus, the .006 coefficient for education in the labor force participation row means that individuals with three more years of education than the average would be expected to have their labor force participation increased by .170 rate points in response to a once-and-for-all 1 percent employment shock in their metropolitan area, .006 points higher than the mean effect of .164 rate points.

19. Statistically significant differentials also occur with the individual's education, as shown in the table. However, while these differentials with education are statistically significant, they are substantively minuscule by any standard.

20. These figures differ from just adding the black differential effect to the effect for the mean individual. The mean individual in this sample is about 90 percent white and 10 percent black. Hence, the text calculates the black mean effect by adding 90 percent of the black differential to the effect for the mean individual.

21. Moore and Laramore (1990) do look at effects of changes in local industry mix as well as at effects of changes in overall local employment. They are able to get data to do this because they focus only on census years, and use relatively aggregated industry categories. They find

the expected effects of changes in the share of manufacturing in the economy (i.e., reduced manufacturing share raises unemployment and lowers labor force participation). For labor force participation, overall employment growth is much more important than changes in industrial sector shares. For unemployment rates, changes in the manufacturing share are of greater importance than overall changes in local employment.

— 5 —
Effects of Local Job Growth
on Housing Prices
and Other Prices

Everybody is talkin' these days about Tammany men growin' rich on graft, but nobody thinks of drawin' the distinction between honest graft and dishonest graft.

There's an honest graft, and I'm an example of how it works. I might sum up the whole thing by sayin': "I seen my opportunities and I took 'em."

Just let me explain by examples. My party's in power in the city, and it's goin' to undertake a lot of public improvements. Well, I'm tipped off, say, that they're going to lay out a new park at a certain place.

I see my opportunity and I take it. I go to that place and I buy up all the land I can in the neighborhood. Then the board of this or that makes its plan public, and there is a rush to get my land, which nobody cared particular for before.

Ain't it perfectly honest to charge a good price and make a profit on my investment and foresight? Of course, it is. Well, that's honest graft. (George Washington Plunkitt, Tammany Hall ward boss speaking in 1905, as quoted in *Plunkitt of Tammany Hall*, William Riordan, 1963)

This chapter focuses on how the growth of a small local area, such as a metropolitan area, affects prices, particularly housing prices. The key issue is the benefit to property owners of state and local economic development policies. Are these policies a modern version of "honest graft," a way for persons of influence to use government to increase their property values?

113

How Local Growth Affects Prices

Chapter 3 included an overview of how local job growth affects prices. Employment growth in a local economic region was argued to lead to in-migration, which raises land values, in turn raising the costs and prices of goods that use land as an input.

But economic theory provides further insights into the determinants of the price effects of local growth. The effect of local job growth on land prices increases with a greater in-migration response to employment growth. In addition, the land price response will be greater if the supply of developed land in an area does not increase much due to a given increase in prices. Finally, the land price response will be greater if local population density does not increase much due to an increase in land prices. The land price effect on density depends on households' demand for land, and on whether zoning rules and historical development patterns in the area allow redevelopment at higher densities.[1]

The prices of other goods and services will be directly affected by increases in the price of land. In addition, mutual interactions between overall local prices, local wages, and the prices of other goods will greatly augment the direct land price effect. Because land prices increase, the overall level of local prices will increase. This will tend to increase local wages, increasing the costs and prices of locally produced goods. The increase in the costs and prices of these local goods will increase the costs and prices of other local goods that use these goods as intermediate inputs. All of these augmenting effects will further increase overall local prices, hence local wages, and hence the prices of specific goods. The final equilibrium effects on local prices will reflect all these interactions. The price effect of local growth on local goods and services will increase with a greater share of local inputs in production.

Review of Previous Empirical Research

Previous research on local growth and land or housing prices[2] is of two types: case studies of a specific growth shock, and studies using econometric methods.

Two recent case studies have examined specific growth shocks and local prices. Erickson and Syms (1986) studied a particular enterprise zone in England. They examined industrial rents inside and outside of this zone, both before and after zone designation, and concluded that zone industrial rents rose enough to capture 60 percent of the financial incentives offered to industrial firms locating there.

The second recent case study was Gardner and others' (1987) examination of the effects of Chrysler/Mitsubishi's decision to locate their Diamond Star joint venture automobile plant in Bloomington, Illinois. This location decision was announced in October 1985. The plant was to employ 2,900 workers and was expected to bring an additional 2,900 supplier industry and retail jobs into Bloomington. The 5,800 jobs due to the plant are about 14 percent of the Bloomington metropolitan area's pre-Diamond Star employment level of 42,000.

Gardner and her colleagues used a "hedonic" housing price model to examine trends in housing prices in Bloomington before and after the Diamond Star announcement. Hedonic housing price models control for housing quality in measuring housing price trends. The study also used a hedonic model to ascertain housing price trends in Champaign-Urbana, a nearby metropolitan area of similar size to Bloomington. Based on these models, the authors found that housing prices in Bloomington increased about 10 to 15 percent after the Diamond Star announcement. Housing prices in Bloomington increased about 5 to 10 percent more than housing prices in Champaign-Urbana over this time period.

The second type of empirical research on housing prices and local growth uses econometric methods to determine whether metropolitan areas that grow faster have higher rates of housing or land price inflation. Table 5.1 reviews these econometric studies. The studies have reached a general consensus that local growth positively affects land and housing prices, although the exact magnitude of the effects varies across the studies.[3]

These econometric studies suffer from two statistical problems. Similar problems were analyzed in the chapter 4 review of studies on local growth and unemployment, so the discussion here can be brief. First, the

Table 5.1
Econometric Studies of Growth Effects on Housing and Land Prices

Study	Geographic Units Used in Growth Analysis	Variable Used to Measure Growth	Aggregate or Micro Data	Dependent Variable	Estimated Percentage Effect of 1 Percent Growth on Dependent Variable (Elasticity)
Treyz, Rickman & Shao (1990)	States	Population	Agg.	Housing price; exact definition unclear	.4
Manning (1988)	MSAs	Population	Agg.	Site prices per square foot for FHA home	Statistically significant, elasticity unclear
Thibodeau (1988)	MSAs	No. of owner households, no. of renter households	Agg.	Real rental and owner prices from hedonic	−.35 to +.35, statistically significant
Pollakowski (1988)	MSAs	Employment, population	Agg.	Real owner housing prices from hedonic price functions	.8 for pop., 6 for employment
Case (1986)	MSAs	Employment	Agg.	Average selling price of existing single-family home	.8
Hamilton & Schwab (1985)	MSAs	Population	Agg.	Price of quality constant FHA home	.3 to .4
Roback (1982)	MSAs	Population	Agg.	Site prices per sq. ft. for FHA home	1.0
Witte (1975)	MSAs	Population	Agg.	Site prices per sq. ft. for FHA home	Statistically significant, elasticity unclear

NOTES: All studies either look at growth or implicitly examine growth by including MSA dummies. Witte (1975) and Manning (1988) studies report "beta coefficients" (= raw coefficient times standard deviation of independent variable divided by standard deviation of dependent variable) without reporting standard deviation units, so elasticities cannot be calculated. Plausible values of standard deviations suggest their elasticities would be of similar order of magnitude to other studies.

studies in table 5.1 are unable to distinguish between short-run and long-run effects of local growth. The studies only include one measure of growth. Typically, this growth variable is the percentage change in employment or population over some recent time period. The coefficient on this one growth variable reflects some unknown combination of short-run and long-run effects of growth.

Second, previous econometric studies fail to distinguish the price effects of local growth caused by shocks that increase firm profitability and labor and land demand from the price effects of local growth caused by labor or land supply shocks. State and local economic development policies attempt to increase perceived profitability of a local area, and thus promote greater demand for the area's labor and land. Increased labor and land demand will raise land prices, and possibly wages; other prices go up due to the increase in land and labor prices; wages may further increase in an attempt to catch up with increases in the cost-of-living, putting some additional upward pressure on local prices; the final equilibrium effect of demand-induced growth on local prices and wages will reflect the interaction among all the various prices in a local economy.

Either land or labor supply shocks result in a different relationship between local growth and property prices. Consider a shock that increases a local area's effective land supply, such as relaxation of zoning constraints on new development, or the building of new roads that increase the accessibility of some land. Such supply shocks reduce the local area's land and housing prices. Lower housing prices attract labor, reducing nominal wages from what they otherwise would have been. The lower wages and land prices may attract additional industry. The resulting correlation between housing prices and local growth will be negative, the reverse of the correlation that results from a demand shock.

Labor supply shocks also lead to a growth and housing price relationship that differs from the relationship caused by a demand shock. Suppose amenities in a local area improve, attracting in-migrant households. Population and labor supply increase, raising land prices but lowering wages. The price-boosting effects of higher land prices are moderated by the lower wages. Thus, labor supply-induced increases in local employment will have a smaller effect on housing prices than demand-induced employment growth, as the supply shock will reduce wages of construction workers.

This chapter augments the existing research literature in two ways. First, results are presented from an additional case study, the land price impacts of the General Motors Saturn plant in Tennessee.[4] Second, empirical results are presented for econometric research on growth and prices that avoids the statistical problems of previous studies.

Effects of GM's Announcement of the Saturn Plant on Land Prices

On July 30, 1985, General Motors announced its decision to locate the new Saturn manufacturing plant in Spring Hill, Tennessee, a small town in Maury County near Nashville. Before the announcement, fierce competition among states for the Saturn plant had occurred. This case study will try to determine what effects the Saturn plant announcement had on land prices in Middle Tennessee.

As originally announced, the Saturn plant promised a significant boost to employment demand in Maury County and the Nashville MSA. The plant itself was originally supposed to provide 6,000 jobs. (This was subsequently scaled back to 3,200 jobs, but the cutback occurred well after the initial announcement.) Saturn officials claimed the plant would also lead to 14,000-16,000 ''support'' jobs in Middle Tennessee, as GM's ''just-in-time'' system would encourage suppliers to locate nearby. Even ignoring support jobs, 6,000 jobs are a significant proportion of Maury County employment. In 1985, Maury County's total employment was only 22,000. Saturn's planned employment would add over 27 percent to Maury County employment. Even compared to the Nashville MSA's employment of 489,000, Saturn jobs would add 1.2 percent.[5]

The case study analyzed land sales before and after the July 30, 1985 announcement, ranging from January to November of 1985. Sales in the eight days before the announcement were excluded because of the possibility of news leaks. The study looked at all land sales in the county "map areas" adjacent to the Saturn plant site. The 77 observed land sales averaged a distance of 3.1 miles from the Saturn plant site. The farthest away was 7.8 miles, the closest only 100 feet away. Thirty-three of the observed sales took place before the Saturn plant announcement and 44 afterwards.

Of the 77 land sales, 30 had some structure already present. Land values per acre for these parcels were calculated by subtracting the January 1, 1985 assessed value of the structures, adjusted to market prices using the average market value/assessed value ratio in Maury County.

Table 5.2 presents calculations based on these data.[6] An analysis that assumes all land within 7.8 miles of the site increased by the same amount indicates that land values went up by $408 million due to the announcement. An analysis that allows land further from the plant to increase by less indicates that the announcement raised land values by $243 million.[7]

A $200-$400 million land value increase is 20-40 percent of total Maury County market property value of $1 billion. As mentioned above, the Saturn plant increased Maury County employment by about 27 percent. The implied elasticity of property values with respect to employment growth—the percentage change in property values for a 1 percent change in employment—is close to 1.0, roughly consistent with the previous research summarized in table 5.1.

New Econometric Research
on Local Growth and Housing Prices

This section presents new estimates of how local variations in economic growth are related to housing price inflation. The next section presents similar estimates for nonhousing prices. The underlying model used in both sections is presented in table 5.3.

Table 5.2
Estimated Effect of the Saturn Plant Announcement
on Land Values: Two Approaches

1. Comparison of means

   $1,908 per acre average before announcement
   $5,237 afterwards
   Total of 122,326 acres within 7.8 miles of plant
   Conclusion: Land values increased from $233 million to $641 million, an increase of $408 million.

2. Estimation of land price gradient

   ln (Land Price/Acre) = 7.264 + 1.053 * (Dummy variable for sale
                                  (4.01)   after announcement)

   $-.148 \times 10^{-4}$ * ([Distance to plant] * [Dummy for after announcement])
   (−1.31)

   + .101 * (Ratio of Sales Value/Measured Land Value)
   (1.72)

   (t-statistics in parentheses)

Conclusions:

   • Based on this equation, land within 7.8 miles of the plant increased in value by $163 million

   • Land within 13.5 miles (where density gradient implies zero effect) increased in value by $243 million

NOTES: Both the comparison of means and the estimated density gradient are based on 77 observed land sales near the Saturn plant in 1985, both before and after the announcement. The maximum distance from the plant of any land sale in the sample is 7.8 miles.

Table 5.3
Outline of Model Used to Estimate Effects
of Local Economic Growth on Prices

The model estimates equations of the following form:

$$\Delta P_{mt} = B_0 + N_t + C(L)g_{mt} + V_{mt}$$

where ΔP_{mt} is the change in some particular price index in MSA m from year t-1 to year t, N_t is a set of dummy variables for the time period, g_{mt} is the percentage growth in nonagricultural employment in MSA m from year t-1 to year t, and V_{mt} is the disturbance term. The $C(L)$ term indicates that a series of lagged values of g_{mt} are also included in the estimation, with each lag allowed to have its own coefficient.

The estimation allows for up to eight lags in employment growth. Reported results are based on the lag-length minimizing the Akaike Information Criterion (AIC), a standard model selection criterion. Minimization of the AIC ensures that the reported long-run growth effects do not change significantly after the chosen lag-length, up to eight lags.

All equations are initially estimated by ordinary least squares (OLS), which show the estimated average effects of all types of employment growth. These are the estimates reported in the chapter text and figures. Equations are then re-estimated to focus on the effects of employment growth due to demand shocks; these estimates are reported in the appendices. Demand shock estimates are obtained by using the "share effect" as an instrumental variable for "two-stage least squares" estimation. The share effect reflects predicted growth if all local industries had grown at the national growth rate for that industry, and thus reflects trends in national demand for the area's exports.

The local Consumer Price Index (CPI) data come from the official CPI. The aggregate employment data are official estimates from the Bureau of Labor Statistics' "790" program survey.

Years included in the estimation are generally 1972-73 through 1985-86. For some price indices, data are only available for a shorter length of time. The 25 MSAs for which local CPI data are consistently available are all included in the estimation.

This chapter's model of how local growth affects prices is similar to the chapter 4 model of how local growth affects the average unemployment rate. The change in a metropolitan area's price index from last year to this year is statistically related to current and lagged values of employment growth for the metropolitan area. The estimation procedure allows statistical tests to determine when the price effect of an increase in employment "stabilizes" at some long-run effect, rather than arbitrarily assuming the length of time needed to reach a new equilibrium.

The effects of demand-induced growth on prices are examined, as well as the effects of all types of growth on prices. As discussed above, we might expect local job growth due to demand shocks to have different effects on prices than local growth due to land or labor supply shocks.

The price data used come from the official Consumer Price Index (CPI). Four different measures of housing price inflation are used. The shelter price index, available throughout the 1972 to 1986 period of this study, is meant to reflect overall household spending on the physical aspects of housing. This index is calculated as a weighted average, using the consumer expenditure weights, of the price of rental housing and the price of owner-occupied housing.

The effects of growth on rental housing prices and owner-occupied housing prices are also separately examined in this study. The rental housing price index, available throughout the period of this study, is calculated by the Bureau of Labor Statistics by examining how rents change for specific rental housing units. Each rental housing unit in the sample is followed over time and excluded from the price index calculation if the unit is substantially rehabilitated. Hence, the CPI rental housing index probably does a good job of measuring the average price change in the city for rental housing, holding quality constant. Given the heterogeneity of housing, holding quality constant is crucial in measuring housing prices.[8]

Measuring quality-constant prices of owner-occupied homes is more difficult. Homes are sold infrequently, which reduces direct information on their price. Also, home purchase decisions represent investment as well as consumption; the true "price" of housing in the CPI is its cost as a consumption good, not its value as an investment.

The traditional CPI measure of owner-occupied housing prices had several problems. In particular, the traditional owner-occupied housing price index was unable to control well for quality. BLS data collectors examined the average price per square foot, within classes of houses with different combinations of age and size, of FHA-insured homes. FHA-insured homes are a small and unrepresentative portion of the housing market. Furthermore, controlling for age-size class fails to control for many aspects of housing quality, such as the house's neighborhood.[9]

In response to criticism of the homeownership component of the CPI, the Bureau of Labor Statistics began in 1983 to use a new measure of homeowner prices. This new measure calculates changes in owner-occupied housing prices by examining the change in the rental price of housing units similar to nearby owner-occupied housing units. The rationale for this procedure is that economic theory implies that the true annual cost of homeownership must be equal in equilibrium to the rent for obtaining a similar home. If rents were less than true homeownership costs for identical houses, then households would switch from owner status to renter status, forcing up rents and forcing down homeownership costs. A similar argument can be made for how the market would force down relative rents if rents were greater than true homeownership costs for identical homes. While this procedure better controls for housing quality than the old homeownership measure, the resulting price index never directly measures the price of a single owner-occupied home. The measured index depends greatly on theoretical arguments about what relationships among rental and owner-occupied housing prices must hold in equilibrium.

BLS assumptions about the relationships between rental and owner-occupied housing prices may be inaccurate in the case of housing price changes caused by growth. How much people are willing to pay to buy a house depends in part on prevailing rent levels; all else equal, a given percentage change in rent levels should be associated with the same percentage change in home purchase prices. But the willingness to pay to buy a home also depends on how much the prospective buyer expects homes to appreciate in the future. If an increase in local growth today leads people to expect faster home value appreciation in the future, this expectation will push up home values. Growth's effect on home sale prices will exceed its effect on rental prices.[10]

This study examines the effects of growth on both the old and new homeownership measure; for our purposes, it is unclear which measure suffers from fewer defects.

Figures 5.1 through 5.4 present empirical estimates of the effects of overall local growth—whether due to demand shocks or supply shocks—on the various measures of housing prices. Several points stand out in these figures. Most important, there is clear evidence that housing prices are significantly affected by local growth in the long run. A 1 percent once-and-for-all shock to employment raises housing prices in the long run between .25 and .45 of 1 percent. The estimated magnitude of this effect is roughly similar to the estimates of previous studies reported in table 5.1.

A second point is that figure 5.2 implies that rental housing prices, in response to a positive growth shock, tend to overshoot their long-run equilibrium in the short run. This result makes intuitive sense. The increase in rental housing demand caused by the growth shock hikes rental housing prices of the relatively fixed short-run housing supply; builders respond after some lag to these higher prices, which brings prices down somewhat. However, long-run prices are still higher, despite this supply response, because land and construction labor costs are permanently higher due to growth.

Third, there is some evidence that local growth has somewhat higher percentage effects on home values than on rental prices. The original BLS homeownership price index is increased more in the long run by growth than either the price index for rental housing or the new "rental equivalent" measure of homeowner prices that looks at the rent charged for "comparable" houses to owner-occupied homes.

In addition to examining effects of all types of local growth on housing prices, effects of growth clearly due to demand shocks were also examined. While this examination revealed some statistically significant differences in the pattern of effects, on the whole the conclusions are unchanged: a once-and-for-all shock to an area's employment permanently raises housing prices. Appendix 5.1 presents these demand shock results in more detail.

Figure 5.1
Estimates of the Cumulative Percentage Effects of a 1 Percent
Once-and-for-All Local Employment Shock
on the MSA Shelter Price Index

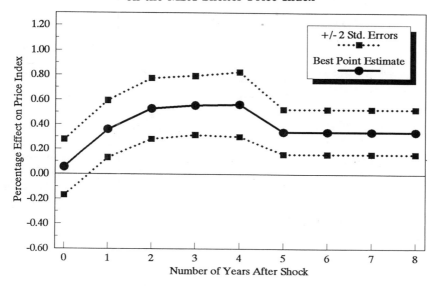

Empirical Estimates on Which Figure is Based

Cumulative Effect After:

Immediate effect = 0 years	1 year	2 years	3 years	4 years	Long-run effect = 5 years
.054	.361	.528	.554	.562	.340
(.112)	(.116)	(.123)	(.119)	(.131)	(.092)

NOTES: Bold line in figure shows best point estimate; dotted lines show point estimate ± two standard errors, approximately a 95 percent confidence interval for the effect. (That is, probability = .95 that true effect is in that range.) Standard errors are in parentheses. Estimates are for optimal AIC lag-length. Long-run effect in 8-lag specification is .312 (.097).

As mentioned in notes to chapter 4, the cumulative effect after the number of lags included in the optimal AIC specification is an implied "long-run" effect. Minimizing the AIC after k lags implies no significant change thereafter. The figures here only carry this long-run effect out to eight years after the shock, as the empirical work never tested whether this long-run effect might decay after eight years. For comparison, the notes at the bottom of each table also report the estimated long-run effect in a specification with eight lagged employment variables. These long-run effects, as one would expect, are always quite similar to the optimal AIC long-run effects.

Figure 5.2
Estimates of the Cumulative Percentage Effects of a 1 Percent
Once-and-for-All Local Employment Shock
on the MSA Rent of Dwelling Price Index

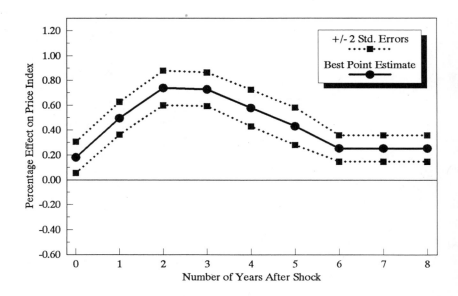

Empirical Estimates on Which Figure is Based

Cumulative Effect After:

Immediate effect = 0 years	1 year	2 years	3 years	4 years	5 years	Long-run effect = 6 years
.180	.494	.738	.727	.577	.430	.252
(.063)	(.066)	(.070)	(.068)	(.074)	(.075)	(.053)

NOTES: Bold line in figure shows best point estimate; dotted lines show point estimate ± two standard errors, approximately a 95 percent confidence interval for the effect. (That is, probability = .95 that true effect is in that range.) Standard errors are in parentheses. Estimates are for optimal AIC specification. Long-run effect in 8-lag specification is .238 (.055).

Figure 5.3
**Estimates of the Cumulative Percentage Effects of a 1 Percent
Once-and-for-All Local Employment Shock on the
MSA Homeownership Price Index (Original Version)**

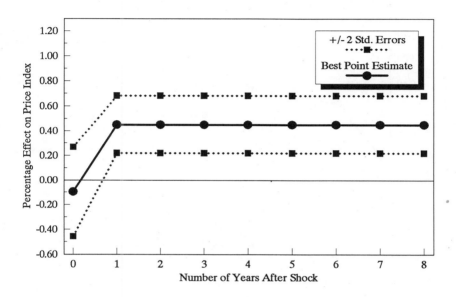

Empirical Estimates on Which Figure is Based

Cumulative Effect After:

	Immediate effect = 0 years	Long-run effect = 1 year
	−.095	.451
	(.181)	(.116)

NOTES: Bold line in figure shows best point estimate of effect. Two dotted lines show two standard errors to either side of best point estimate; the probability is .95 that true estimate is in this range. Standard errors are in parentheses in table. Estimates are based on optimal AIC specification. Long-run effect in 8-lag specification is .540 (.146).

Figure 5.4
Estimates of the Cumulative Percentage Effects of a 1 Percent
Once-and-for-All Local Employment Shock on the
MSA "Owners' Equivalent Rent" Price Index

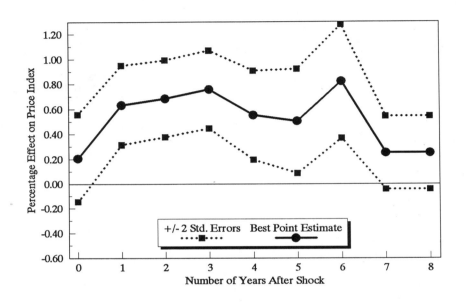

Empirical Estimates on Which Figure is Based

Cumulative Effect After:

Immediate effect = 0 years	1 year	2 years	3 years	4 years	5 years	6 years	Long-run effect = 7 years
.205	.632	.684	.757	.551	.503	.822	.250
(.176)	(.159)	(.154)	(.156)	(.178)	(.209)	(.227)	(.146)

NOTES: Best point estimates are shown by bold line in figure. Dotted lines show two standard errors to either side of best point estimate. Probability is .95 that true point estimate is in interval between two dotted lines. Standard errors are in parentheses in table. Estimates are based on optimal AIC specification. Long-run effect in 8-lag specification is .220 (.152).

Effects of Local Growth on Nonhousing Prices

Similar econometric techniques were used to estimate the effects of local growth on nonhousing prices. Growth effects were estimated for all the major categories of the Consumer Price Index. Table 5.4 summarizes the estimated average effects of growth—whether due to demand shocks or supply shocks—on each major category of consumer prices, and on overall consumer prices.[11]

The overall pattern of these estimated effects is as expected. Nonhousing prices are less affected by growth in the long run than housing prices. Some categories of prices, such as household fuel and furniture prices, are apparently largely driven by national markets rather than local growth. This makes sense because relatively little of the value of these products is produced in the MSA where they are consumed.

But the magnitude of some of the nonhousing price effects is surprising. Prior to seeing these results, I expected the effects of local growth on such categories as food and apparel prices to be extremely small. But the estimated long-run effect of growth on food and apparel prices is almost half as large as the effect of growth on housing prices.

A closer examination of the U.S. product distribution system makes these results more understandable. Depending on the data source one uses, from 35 to 50 percent of the value of sales in the food and apparel consumption categories appears to be absorbed by local distribution costs.[12] This local share is a bit more than one might anticipate. It is easy to make reasonably plausible assumptions about the share of local labor and real estate in these local distribution costs, along with assumptions about growth effects on overall prices (hence wages) and real estate prices, that will yield increases in costs in the food and apparel sectors close to the estimated effects on food and apparel prices.[13]

Effects of demand-induced growth on local prices in these consumption categories were also examined. The results are reported in appendix 5.1. None of the estimated effects of demand shocks substantially alters the conclusions from looking at the effects of overall growth.

Table 5.4
Estimated Percentage Effects of a 1 Percent Once-And-For-All Shock to Local Employment on Different Categories of Consumer Prices

	Percentage of Consumer Budget	Immediate Effect	Cumulative Effect After:					Long-Run Effect
			1 year	2 years	3 years	4 years	5 years	
Shelter	27.7	.054 (.112)	.361 (.116)	.528 (.123)	.554 (.119)	.562 (.131)	.340 (.092)	.340 (.092)
Food	17.8	.014 (.043)	-.001 (.043)	.147 (.032)				.147 (.032)
Transportation	17.2	.072 (.039)						.072 (.039)
Household fuel and utilities	7.9	.025 (.098)						.025 (.098)
Household furnishings and operations	7.2	.080 (.036)						.080 (.036)
Apparel	6.3	.136 (.046)						.136 (.046)
Medical care	5.7	-.092 (.056)	.006 (.057)	.003 (.060)	.139 (.044)			.139 (.044)
Entertainment	4.4	-.132 (.090)	.060 (.092)	.129 (.096)	-.119 (.098)	-.069 (.111)	.114 (.075)	.114 (.075)
All other goods and services	5.8	.031 (.053)	.044 (.054)	.137 (.041)				.137 (.041)
Overall Consumer Price Index	100.0	.022 (.041)	.118 (.042)	.200 (.031)				.200 (.031)

NOTES: Budget figures are from BLS Handbook of Methods, p. 187. Shelter index includes the residential rent (6.1 percent) and homeowners' equivalent rent (19.1 percent) indices examined in figures 5.2 and 5.4, as well as other housing costs. Estimated effects are for the lag-length for each category that minimized the AIC. This implies that the effect does not change significantly from that lag-length to the "long-run." As lag-lengths up to eight years were tested, this implies no significant change from that optimal lag-length up to eight years after the shock. Standard errors are in parentheses below estimated effects. Estimated effects are stated in percentage terms. For example, the .200 long-run effect for the overall CPI means that the CPI increases by 2/5the of 1 percent in response to a 1 percent shock to local employment.

Are Effects on Housing and Land Prices Large?

A key policy question about these estimates is whether local growth has effects on land and housing prices that are large from a practical perspective. The "statistical significance" of the effects does not necessarily imply that they would be considered important by individuals or governments. I will argue in this section that the effects of growth on property value are large from the perspective of property owners, but in the aggregate are smaller than the employment benefits of growth.

On the first point, effects of local growth on housing prices can substantially influence the rate of return to owning housing. Consider the effects of an extra one-half percent per year employment growth over a decade, or a total of 5 percent extra employment over the decade. Based on the results, this might raise housing prices by about 2 percent over the decade, or about .2 percent per year. Suppose housing normally earns about a 3 percent real return per year to its owner. This return is an explicit financial return to the owner of rental housing; it is an implicit consumption return to the homeowner, in that he/she could have earned that real return on other assets, but chose to buy a home instead.

Assume that 80 percent of the value of the housing is financed by a mortgage. Then this one-half percent extra growth per year will increase the annual return to equity investment in housing from 3 percent to 4 percent, a 33 percent increase over the normal rate of return. (The overall increase in the total housing price per year by .2 percent increases the value of the owner's equity by 1 percent, as the equity is only 20 percent of the total housing price.)

With respect to the second point, the increased implicit income in the MSA resulting from property value effects of growth is likely to be smaller than the increased income resulting from the greater labor force participation and reduced unemployment caused by growth. Based on the results in chapter 4, a 5 percent shock to employment will raise labor force participation by about .8 percent above its average value, and raise the employment rate (conditional on participation) by about .3 percent above its average value.[14] As a result, annual earnings will increase by 1.1 percent even if wage rates are unchanged.[15] Because earnings average about 70 percent of income, total income will increase by (.7)(1.1 percent), or around .8 percent.[16]

The 5 percent employment shock would cause a one-time increase of about 2 percent in property values. Total real estate value appears to be around 264 percent of income[17] in the typical MSA, so the one-time property value increase is about 5.3 percent (= 2.64 times 2 percent) of annual income. At a 3 percent real interest rate, this one-time increase is equivalent to a permanent increase of .2 percent in real income. This effect is only one-fourth of the income effect due to increased employment caused by growth.

Chapter 7 will return to this topic of comparisons of the various types of effects of employment shocks. The reader should note here, however, that the actual "benefits" to a local area may not correspond to these income effects. For example, in a local area with low unemployment, many of those who receive jobs may place a high value on their foregone leisure time, so their benefit is less than the effect on their incomes. Also, some property owners may live outside the local area. These average income effects, furthermore, conceal differences across individuals. Some individuals get jobs, and others do not. Property owners with developable land gain more from growth than others.

Conclusion

This chapter showed that shocks to local employment permanently increase housing prices. These housing price effects are large enough to significantly affect the return to owning property. Measured by their impact on real income, property value effects of growth are about one-fourth as large as employment effects of growth.

Somewhat surprisingly, growth also appears to have relatively large effects on local nonhousing prices, although the effects are less than for housing prices. Higher costs for distributing goods in the local area provide an explanation for these effects on nonhousing prices.

NOTES

1. An unpublished appendix available from the author shows that standard urban economics models imply that 10 percent more population increases land prices around 10 percent, but these models' assumptions may bias their conclusions. For example, the models assume all employment is in the central business district. In addition, the models assume that long-run development patterns are dictated by household demand rather than zoning or historical development patterns.

2. I have been unable to locate any previous studies that focus on how growth affects nonhousing prices, or overall prices.

3. The one exception is the study by Thibodeau (1988). His measure of growth, however, is quite different from the other studies. Rather than examining population or employment growth, Thibodeau examines the effects of the number of homeowner households on home prices, and the number of renter households on rental prices. But the number of households of a particular tenure type is a much more endogenous variable than total population or total employment. For a fixed population, the number of households will tend to decline as housing prices increase; for a fixed total number of households, the number of owner (renter) households will tend to decline as owner (renter) housing prices increase. Thibodeau tries to control for this endogeneity by including a control for the number of persons per household, but this attempt may not be totally successful.

4. Preliminary versions of some of these case study findings were presented in Bartik, Becker, Lake, and Bush (1987).

5. Maury County was not officially part of the Nashville MSA in 1985. However, the Spring Hill site is just south of Maury County's border with Williamson County, which is part of the Nashville MSA.

6. The last term in the land price estimating equation, Ratio of Sales Value to Measured Land Value, is included to correct for possible underassessment of the market value of structures. For parcels with structures, the dependent variable (land value per acre) is measured as $\ln((T-\hat{s})/L)$, where T is the sales price of the parcel, $\hat{s}$ is the market value of the structure based on assessment records, and L is the number of acres involved in the sale. Suppose that $\hat{s} = aS$, where S is the true market value of the structure, and $a < 1$ indicates underassessment. This results in the dependent variable being subject to measurement error. The equation we want to estimate is $\ln((T-S)/L) = Bx$. But we can only estimate $\ln((T-\hat{s})/L) = Bx + \ln((T-\hat{s})/L) - \ln((T-S)/L)$. A Taylor series expansion shows that $\ln((T-S)/L) = \ln((T-\hat{s})/L) + [1/((T-\hat{s})/L)](-1/L)(S-\hat{s})$. The last term in this expansion can be rewritten as:

$$[1/((T-\hat{s})/L)](-1/L)(S-\hat{s}) = (\hat{s}-S)/(T-\hat{s}) = [(a-1)/a][\hat{s}/(T-\hat{s})].$$

Adding and subtracting $(a-1)/a$ to this last term, we get $\ln((T-S)/L) - \ln((T-\hat{s})/L) = -(a-1)/a + [(a-1)/a][T/(T-\hat{s})]$. Hence, $\ln((T-\hat{s})/L) \approx Bx + [(1-a)/a][T/(T-\hat{s})]$. The estimated coefficient of .101 on this ratio variable implies that $[(1-a)/a] = .101$, or $a = .908$. The implication is that the market value of structures is underassessed by about 9 percent.

7. The empirical analysis of this case study has several limitations. First, it does not hold the quality of the land constant, except for its proximity to the Saturn plant. The lack of controls for other qualitative features of the land may bias the results, but the bias is of unknown sign and magnitude. Second, it focuses on whether or not the date of sale is after the Saturn announcement. If contracts were signed some time before the announcement but the sale was not completed until after the announcement, some of the postannouncement sale prices may reflect preannouncement economic conditions. Thus, the land price effects estimated here may understate the true effects of the Saturn plant on land values. I thank Robert Schwab for pointing out these two limitations of the case study.

8. The CPI rent index has been criticized for ignoring the depreciation of housing that inevitably occurs due to age (see Apgar 1987). Recently, the Bureau of Labor Statistics has begun correcting for depreciation when calculating the rental housing price index, although the index is uncorrected throughout the period of this study. This is not a problem because it is reasonable to assume that this depreciation rate is roughly constant across cities in the sample. Hence, the depreciation rate will be absorbed by the constant term in the regression. To put it another way, the results estimated here are based on observing how differences in metropolitan growth from the U.S. average are related to differences in housing inflation rates from the U.S. average. Adjusting the average housing inflation rate everywhere by the same amount will only affect the U.S. average, not the deviations of city inflation rates from the average.

9. There were other problems with traditional CPI measure of owner-occupied housing prices. These are reviewed by Gillingham (1980) and Gillingham and Lane (1982). While these problems are important in measuring the overall magnitude of housing price inflation, they seem less important for this study because many of the problems are unlikely to vary due to differences in city growth rates. For example, the use of nominal interest rates in calculating housing price indices will bias homeowner price indices by a similar amount in all cities.

10. The discussion here of the role of expected appreciation in determining the home value effects of growth is in response to some helpful comments by Robert Schwab on a first draft of this book. The role of expected appreciation in home value determination is discussed in a paper by Hamilton and Schwab (1985).

11. Table 5.4 shows effects for the optimal AIC specification. Long-run effects in the 8-lag specification, and their standard errors, are: shelter, .312 (.097); food, .154 (.038); transportation, .072 (.051); household utilities, .036 (.127); furnishings, .059 (.046); apparel, .164 (.059); medical care, .111 (.049); entertainment, .076 (.078); other goods and services, .126 (.047); overall CPI, .178 (.036). These long-run effects are quite similar to those estimated in the optimal lag specification.

12. The Personal Consumption Expenditure Bridge Matrix developed by the Bureau of Labor Statistics suggests a figure of around 50 percent for the local share. Forty-three percent of food and beverage consumption goes directly to the food products industry, and 7 percent is purchased indirectly (via the eating and drinking establishment sector) from the food products industry. (The PCE Bridge Matrix and BEA Input-Output tables count food dollars as going directly to the food products industry, rather than to retail trade, in cases, such as grocery stores, where the product is not altered by the store before sale. Purchases from eating and drinking establishments are considered to be purchased directly from the establishment, which in turn purchases food and beverage input which it alters.) According to the PCE Bridge Matrix, 44 percent of clothing and shoe expenditure goes to pay for retailers' margins, and 4 percent goes to pay for wholesalers' margins. The 1982 Census of Retail Trade suggests somewhat smaller local shares. Adding together food stores and eating and drinking places, 65 percent of the value of sales is accounted for by merchandise purchase, leaving 35 percent for a local share. In apparel trade, 60 percent of the value of sales is accounted for by the purchase of merchandise, leaving 40 percent for a local share. These figures can be reconciled if some of these merchandise purchases are in fact local merchandise considered by BLS to be part of the retailers' margin.

13. For example, suppose that local inputs are 50 percent of costs in the food and beverage category, local labor makes up 60 percent of local inputs, and local real estate makes up 20 percent of local inputs. Suppose further that local labor costs go up a bit faster than local prices, say by .25 percent for every 1 percent shock to employment. This might occur if wages go up by about the same amount as prices, but productivity declines a bit as lower-skilled workers are hired (see chapter 6). Also suppose that local real estate costs for business go up by .50 percent for every

1 percent employment shock; this is just a little more than the estimated price effect on homeownership prices. Then costs in the food and beverage industry would increase, due to a 1 percent employment shock, by .50(.60)(.25) + .50(.20)(.50) = .125 percent. This is just a bit below the estimated effect of growth on food and beverage prices. There is no need to drop the assumption that competition will force prices in the long run in the various local industries to increase by no more than industry costs.

14. These figures are calculated by dividing the chapter 4 estimates of effects on labor participation and employment *rates* by the average rates in the sample, .875 for labor force participation, and .946 for employment.

15. That is, because Earnings = $LFP * ER * H * W$, where LFP = labor force participation, ER is the employment rate, H is usual weekly hours, and W is the wage rate, the percent change in earnings is the sum of the percentage change in these four components.

16. For sources of this information on the ratio of earnings to income, see table 7.6 in chapter 7.

17. Again, for sources of this information, see table 7.6.

— 6 —
Effects of Local Job Growth on Real Wages

Growth, almost any kind, tightens the local labor market and leads to overtime, second earners in the household, and rising wage rates. (Wilbur Thompson, Professor Emeritus of Economics at Wayne State University and one of the founding fathers of urban economics, p. 287 in *Economic Development Quarterly*, August 1987)

Real Wage Definitions and Growth

Much of economics is concerned with the causes and effects of the prevailing market "real wage," by which economists mean the amount a worker is paid per some unit of time at work (e.g., dollars per hour), adjusted for the price of consumer goods. Based on the empirical findings in chapter 4 that faster local growth lowers unemployment, one might expect local growth to increase real wages. Increased labor demand, tight labor markets, and rising real wages would all seem to go together. But the situation is more complicated than that, in part because there are many possible definitions of what one might mean by the "real wage."

The simplest definition of the real wage level in some local labor market, such as a metropolitan area, is the average real wage level. This definition would be relevant if a researcher were seeking a real wage measure whose increase would be most closely linked to consumer demand for goods and services in the local area. But the definition fails to control for the types of occupations or individuals in the local area. Hence, this measure does not capture what an individual with given skills and occupation might be paid in the local area compared to some

137

national average, or what a firm with given labor requirements might need to pay in that area.

A second definition of the local real wage level is the real wage of a given occupation in the local area compared to the national average. Real wages of different occupations can be aggregated to some local average using occupational employment weights. This real wage definition measures the relative wage that an individual could expect in this local area if the individual is occupationally specialized. However, occupational advancement may be easier in some local areas than in others. The occupational real wage measure does not capture this dimension of the real wage opportunities offered by a particular area.

Finally, one can measure how real wages vary across local areas, holding individual skills constant, but not occupations. This measure allows for differences in occupational advancement possibilities across local areas, as well as differences in occupational rates of pay. While it captures the real wage differences between local areas for the average individual, it is less accurate for workers who are highly specialized in one particular occupation.

These diverse real wage measures would respond differently in the long run to an increase in local employment. Local employment shocks might permanently affect occupational advancement for the same reasons that they permanently affect local unemployment: hysteresis effects in local labor markets. As discussed in chapter 3, an increase in local employment may lead in the short run to some individuals getting jobs who otherwise would not be employed. This short-run effect increases these individuals' "human capital" (i.e., their job skills). Because human capital depreciates only slowly, the short-run effect on unemployment persists in the long run.

For similar reasons, employment shocks may have long-run effects on occupational advancement. In the short run, an increase in local employment allows some individuals to get promotions or to get a better job at another employer that they otherwise would not have obtained. These individuals acquire additional human capital, which may help them retain their higher occupational status in the long run. The increase in average human capital of the local labor force may lead to an average occupational upgrading of the local labor force in the long run. The long-run equilibrium of the local labor market will have been altered by its history, which is the essence of the hysteresis perspective on labor markets.

It is less likely, however, for a local employment shock to raise real wages for a given occupation. In response to an employment shock, employers are more likely to promote less-skilled individuals to avoid raising the occupation's real wage. An increase in occupational real wages would be needed to attract individuals of "normal" skill levels from outside the labor force or from other metropolitan areas. Raising the occupation's wage may be more costly than hiring less-skilled individuals, since employers would feel constrained by social norms to increase occupational wage rates for all employees, not just new hires. If the short-run response of employers to a tight local labor market is to hire less-skilled workers instead of increasing occupational real wages, there may even be some downward pressure on occupational real wages in the long run. The average long-run skill level of individuals in the occupation will be lower, and employers will have learned how to use a larger pool of individuals in that occupation.

Even if employers do raise real wages for a given occupation in response to an increase in local employment, the increase would not be expected to be permanent. The increase in occupational real wages would not be associated with any change in individuals' human capital, but would merely represent more wages for the same work. Hence, there would be no reason to expect this type of real wage change to persist once labor supply adjusts through in-migration to the higher labor demand.

These different types of real wage changes would have different distributional implications. A general increase in an occupation's real wages helps all workers in that occupation and hurts firms. An increase in average occupational advancement only helps the workers who actually receive promotions. Real wage increases associated with occupational advancement may not hurt firms if the promoted workers increase their productivity enough.

Previous Studies of Growth and Wages

Table 6.1 summarizes local growth effects on wages from various studies.[1] The two studies using real wages as a dependent variable (Rosen 1979; Gyourko and Tracy 1986) found that a 1 percent increase in local employment increases real wages by .2 to .5 of 1 percent. Most other studies use nominal wages as a dependent variable. Based on the chapter 5 results, local prices probably increase by .2 of 1 percent in response to a 1 percent growth shock. Assuming this price effect, three of the studies (Browne 1987; Topel 1986; and Graves 1980) imply real wage elasticities with respect to local growth of .2 to .4, or a .2 to .4 of 1 percent response to a 1 percent employment shock. The Roback (1982) and Treyz and Stevens (1985) studies imply real wage responses around zero. Both of these studies control for occupation, however, so their results may not be comparable to other studies.

The studies summarized suffer from five limitations. First, none simultaneously examines the effects of local growth on the different concepts of the local "real wage"—the real wage available to an individual in a given occupation, and the real wage available through occupational advancement for an individual with a given set of skills.

The other four limitations are similar to the limitations of the growth studies discussed in chapters 4 and 5, so the discussion in this chapter can be brief. The second limitation is the failure to clearly distinguish the short-run and long-run effects of growth. Each study includes but one growth variable. The coefficient on this variable is some unknown combination of short-run and long-run effects.

The third limitation is that the studies do not distinguish between growth due to demand shocks and growth in general. State and local economic development policies are presumed to increase business profitability in a local area, leading to increases in local labor demand which in turn may increase local real wages. But supply shocks—such as improvements in local amenities—may increase an area's population, leading to lower real wages which in turn may attract additional employment to the area. Overall job growth is due to both demand shocks and supply shocks, and the estimated effect of local growth on real wages

Table 6.1
Effects of Local Growth on Wages

Study	Geographic Units Used	Population or Employment Growth	Period Over Which Growth Calculated	Micro or Aggregate Data	Dependent Variable	Controls for Individual Characteristics or Occupation[a]	Estimated Percentage Effect of 1 Percent Growth on Wages
Browne (1987)	States	Employment	3 years, 6 years	Agg.	Pay per worker	No	.4
Topel (1986)	States	Employment	1 year	Micro	Avg. wkly. earnings	Indiv.	.5 to .6
Gyourko & Tracy (1986)	MSAs	Population	?	Micro	Real wages	Indiv.	.2
Treyz & Stevens (1985)	States	Employment	1 year	Micro	Wage rate	Indiv.; excludes occupation switchers	.2
Roback (1982)	MSAs	Population	10 years	Micro	Avg. wkly. earnings	Indiv.; includes 4 occupation classes	.2
Graves (1980)	MSAs	Population	10 years	Agg.	Mfg. wages	No	.4
Rosen (1979)	MSAs	Population	10 years	Micro	Real avg. weekly earnings	Indiv.; includes 6 occupation classes	.2 to .5

a. Reports whether study included as explanatory variables for wages, in addition to growth terms, some controls for individual characteristics or occupation.

may be less positive for all growth than for growth due to labor demand shocks.

The fourth limitation is that the studies do not examine how the effects of a growth shock vary with the initial level of growth. Phenomena such as downward wage rigidity imply that changes in annual employment growth from 2 percent to 3 percent would have a greater impact on local real wages than changes in growth from –3 percent to –2 percent.

Finally, most studies fail to examine how the real wage effects of growth vary across individuals.[2]

Model and Data Used in this Chapter

The models and data used in this chapter to examine real wage effects of local growth are outlined in table 6.2. The aggregate model for real wages is similar to the aggregate model used to examine local growth effects on unemployment rates and inflation. It examines how the employment growth of a metropolitan area affects the average real wages of different occupations in that metropolitan area. The model allows for a national time period effect on year-to-year changes in real wages. Including a time period effect in the model means that the estimation is focusing on how variations in a metropolitan area's growth from the U.S. average affect variations in a metropolitan area's occupational real wages from the U.S. trend in those wages.

The micro model for real wages is similar to the micro model used for unemployment and labor force participation in chapter 4. Several measures of an individual's real wages are assumed to depend on the individual's characteristics, general national trends, and shocks to the employment level of the metropolitan area in which the individual lives.

The real wage variables used capture several definitions of real wages. The aggregate real wage variables use data from the Area Wage Survey (AWS). These variables look at the change in real wage indices for three different set of occupations: skilled workers in manufacturing, unskilled workers in manufacturing, and office and clerical workers. Each index is a weighted average of a number of individual indices for detailed

Table 6.2
Models Used to Examine Effects of Local Growth on Real Wages

The aggregate model is of the form:

(6.1) $\Delta w_{mt} = B_0 + N_t + C(L)g_{mt} + V_{mt}$

where Δw_{mt} is the percentage change in average real wages in MSA m from year t-1 to year t, N_t is a set of dummy variables for the time period, g_{mt} is the growth rate of MSA m's nonagricultural employment from year t-1 to year t, and V_{mt} is the disturbance term. The $C(L)$ term before employment growth means that a series of lags in employment growth are also included in the equation, with each allowed to have its own coefficient. The micro model is of the form:

(6.2) $W_{imt} = B_0 + N_t + F_m + \mathbf{B}'\mathbf{X}_{imt} + C(L)E_{mt} + V_{imt}$

where W_{imt} is the average real wage rate for individual i in MSA m during year t, F_m is a set of dummy variables, one for each MSA m, E_{mt} is the natural logarithm of nonagricultural employment for MSA m during year t, and $\mathbf{X}_{imt}$ is a vector of demographic characteristics of the individual. The "levels" equation (6.2) can be derived from the "changes" equation (6.1). The inclusion of the MSA fixed effect implies that the micro equation is examining the effects of MSA job *growth*, not job *levels* (see appendix 4.2).

The estimation allows for up to eight lagged years in the employment term. Reported results are based on the lag-length that minimizes the Akaike Information Criterion (AIC), a standard model selection criteria. The aggregate data on real wages comes from the Area Wage Survey's data on changes in average real wages in three different types of occupations: skilled manufacturing workers, unskilled manufacturing workers, office and clerical workers. Real wage changes are calculated by subtracting out area inflation numbers, so only the 25 MSAs with local inflation numbers are used. The data run from 1972-73 to 1982-83.

The micro data on real wages is derived from the March Current Population Survey, 1980-87, and reflects individuals' average real wages during the year preceding each survey (i.e., the years covered are 1979 to 1986). Alternative micro real wage definitions are described in the text. Real wages are calculated by assuming a price index for each MSA of 100 in 1986, and using local inflation indices to get price indices for other years. The MSA fixed-effect should absorb overall differences in price levels across MSAs. Total micro sample size is 13,299.

Estimation was by OLS and by 2SLS, using as instruments: (1) "share effect" predicted growth and lagged share effect predicted growth for equation (6.1); (2) share effect predicted employment levels for equation (6.2). See appendix 4.2 for more details.

occupations. Thus, the aggregate real wage variables probably do a good job of measuring changes in occupational real wages in the metropolitan area. As discussed above, we would expect migration to prevent any long-run effect of local growth on these wage variables.

The micro model uses three measures of an individual's real wages. First, the overall real wage is measured as annual real earnings for the individual divided by the product of annual weeks worked and usual hours worked per week. This measure of real wages reflects both individuals' success in reaching high-paying occupations, and the rate of pay they receive in that occupation.

This overall real wage variable suffers from considerable measurement error. The product of weeks worked and usual weekly hours is an inexact measure of annual hours. A well-known statistical consequence of greater measurement error in a dependent variable (in this case, real wages) in any empirical study is that the estimates of the effects of the independent variables (such as shocks to metropolitan area employment in this case) on the dependent variable will be much more imprecise. However, measurement error in the dependent variable will not cause estimated effects to be biased; that is, on average the estimated effects would be expected to be equal to the "true" effects.

A second micro real wage variable is defined as the individual's occupational rank. Each occupation was assigned an occupational rank index, equal to the average real wage, over the entire 1979-86 period, of that occupation in the nation.[3] Each individual's occupational rank was defined as the occupational rank of his/her primary job during the year. Local growth will only affect an individual's occupational rank if it affects the probability of getting a job in a higher- or lower-paying occupation. As discussed above, there are some grounds for believing that local growth could have long-run effects on an individual's occupational rank, as growth will augment human capital in the short run and thus affect what occupations are possible for an individual of a given education, age, and race.

The occupational rank variable will be less subject to measurement error than the overall real wage variable. Because the occupational rank variable averages across workers in a given occupation, errors in estimating individual workers' real wages will cancel out. The lesser measurement error implies that growth effects on occupational rank can be estimated with greater precision than growth effects on overall real wages.

The third micro real wage variable, the wage differential variable, is defined as the difference between the overall real wage and the occupation rank variable. An individual could have a positive wage differential for at least three reasons. First, the individual's occupation might pay more in this local area than it does nationally. Second, the individual may be employed in a detailed occupational category, within one of the occupational groups used to define the occupational rank variable, that pays more nationally than other occupational categories within the broader occupational group. Third, the individual may be paid more than other individuals within that detailed occupational category. For example, whites may be paid more than blacks within the same occupational category due to discrimination. Hence, the effects of local growth on this wage differential variable may reflect occupational advancement (within specific occupational groups), changes in the local pay of an occupational group, or changes in the way that individual is paid compared to others in that occupation.

Like the overall real wage variable, the wage differential variable will be subject to considerable measurement error. Estimates of growth effects on the wage differential will be imprecise.

Because of the way in which these real wage variables are constructed, I emphasize the results for the AWS variables and the occupation rank variables. As pointed out above, these wage variables are measured with more precision than the wage differential variable and the overall real wage variable. Furthermore, the real wage concept being measured is more specific for the occupation rank and AWS variables. The AWS variables capture changes in average occupational wages in the MSA. The occupational rank variable captures changes in occupational advancement in the MSA. In contrast, the wage differential variable and overall real wage variable can change due to growth for any number of reasons.

As described in table 6.2, the model used in this study allows estimation of both short-run and long-run effects of growth. In addition, the model also examines whether demand-induced growth has different effects on real wages from those of growth in general. Finally, I also examine whether a growth shock has different effects at different initial levels of growth.[4]

New Estimates of the Effects of Growth
on Real Wages

Table 6.3 summarizes this study's estimates of the effects of overall job growth in a metropolitan area—whether caused by labor demand or labor supply shocks—on average real wages.[5] (Appendix 6.1 presents some additional detail on the results.) As can be seen in the table, the effects of overall local growth on the various real wage measures does not change much as we move from the short run to the long run.

For the occupational wage indices, there is no evidence of significant positive effects of local growth. Average occupational real wage rates for skilled workers actually drop significantly in the long run, by about .1 of 1 percent for a 1 percent employment shock.

In contrast, the table shows that individual real wages increase by about .26 of 1 percent for a 1 percent employment shock. How can this be reconciled with either zero or negative effects of increased local growth on real wages in a given occupation?

The table suggests that these two findings may be consistent because of the growth effects on occupational advancement. A portion of the positive growth effects on a given individual's real wages occurs because higher local growth is associated with individuals of given skills achieving a higher occupational rank. On average, a 1 percent employment shock leads to individuals moving up to an occupation that pays .1 of 1 percent more.

In contrast, the long-run effect of growth on individuals' wage differential from the national occupational mean is not statistically significantly different from zero. Even though the effect is statistically

Table 6.3

Estimated Percentage Effects of a 1 Percent Once-And-For-All Shock to Local Employment, Due to Demand or Supply Shocks, on Various Measures of Real Wages

Real Wage Measure Examined	Immediate Effect	Cumulative Effect After:			Long-Run Effect
		1 year	2 years	3 years . . .	
Aggregate Occupational Real Wages					
Skilled workers	-.13	.03	-.17	-.01	-.01
	(.07)	(.08)	(.08)	(.05)	(.05)
Unskilled workers	-.11				-.11
	(.05)				(.05)
Office and clerical workers	-.03				-.03
	(.04)				
Micro Measures of Real Wages					
Individual average real wages	.260				.260
	(.116)				(.116)
Occupational rank of workers	.101				.101
	(.041)				(.041)
Wage differential from national occupational mean	.159				.159
	(.113)				(.113)

NOTES: For each real wage measure, this table reports percentage effects of a 1 percent local employment increase, for the specification with a lag-length (in the employment variables) that minimizes the Akaike Information Criterion (AIC). Because this lag-length is chosen after testing lag-lengths up to eight years, the implication is that this estimated effect does not change significantly (in a statistical sense) from the AIC lag-length up to eight years (a "long-run" effect). As can be seen in the table, except for the skilled worker occupational wage variable, there is little evidence of any significant change in employment shock effects after the immediate effect has occurred. Standard errors are in parentheses below the estimated effects.

insignificant, the point estimate of the effect of growth on the wage differential variable is positive. However, as discussed above, this positive effect of growth on the wage differential variable could reflect occupational advancement within the occupational categories used to define the occupational rank.

The estimated effects of local growth on the micro real wage variables are particularly sensitive to the number of lagged employment terms that are included in the specification. The statistical criterion used to choose the optimal lag-length correctly suggests that there are no *statistically* significant changes in the effects of growth after the initial shock. However, the relatively large standard error in estimating the local growth effect on real wages means that this lack of statistically significant change with the inclusion of additional lags is perfectly consistent with a decline in the estimated effect as lags are added that is *substantively* large. For example, if eight lags in the metropolitan area employment variables are included, the estimated long-run effect of growth on real wages drops to .17 percent for a 1 percent employment shock, compared to the .26 percent estimate from the "optimal" lag-length specification. Most of this drop appears to be due to a decline in the point estimate of the effects of local growth on the wage differential variable; the point estimate of this effect drops almost in half in the eight-lag specification compared to the optimal specification.[6] This sensitivity of estimates of the micro real wage and wage differential equations may be due to the imprecision with which these real wage variables are measured.

Effects of demand-induced growth in metropolitan employment on average real wages were also estimated. For the occupational wage rate indices, demand-induced growth has no statistically significant different effects from growth in general. For the micro real wage variables, demand-induced growth does have statistically significantly different effects. The estimated effects of demand-induced growth on the micro real wage variables are presented in figures 6.1, 6.2, and 6.3.

These figures and table 6.3 show two main differences between the effects of demand-induced growth and overall growth. First, the short-run and long-run effects on occupational advancement are twice as large for demand-induced growth compared to growth in general.

Figure 6.1
Percentage Effects of Demand-Induced 1 Percent Once-and-for-All
Local Employment Shock on Real Wages, Micro Sample

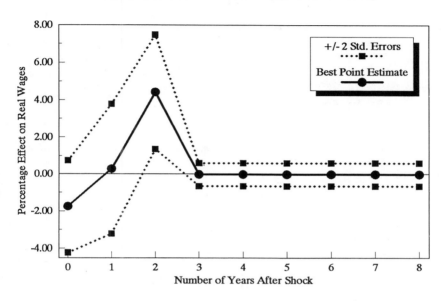

Estimates Underlying Figure

Cumulative Effect After:

Immediate effect = 0 years	1 year	2 years	Long-run effect = 3 years
−1.748	.272	.4.417	−.035
(1.241)	(1.751)	(1.526)	(.314)

NOTES: Estimates show cumulative percentage effect after *k* years of demand-induced, 1 percent permanent employment shock at year zero. Standard errors are in parentheses. Two standard errors to either side of point estimate are shown as dotted lines in figure. Long-run effect with eight lags is −.179 (.592).

Figure 6.2
Percentage Effects of Demand-Induced 1 Percent Once-and-for-All Local Employment Shock on "Occupational Rank"

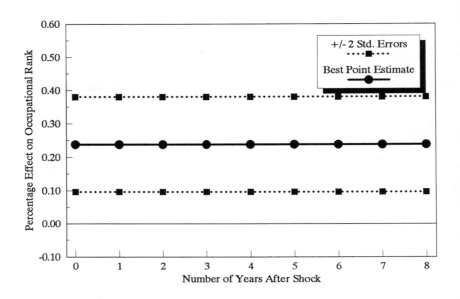

Estimates Underlying Figure

Cumulative Effect After:

	Long-run effect = 0 years
	.238
	(.071)

NOTES: Estimates show cumulative percentage effect after *k* years of demand-induced, 1 percent permanent employment shoch at year zero. Standard error is in parentheses. Two standard errors to either side of point estimate are shown as dotted lines in figure. Long-run effect with eight lags is .333 (.209).

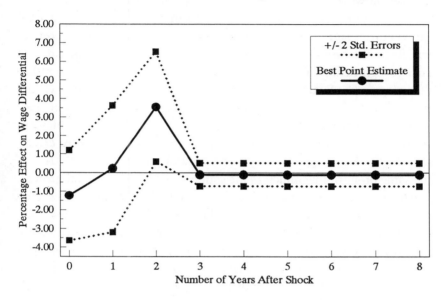

Figure 6.3
Percentage Effects of Demand-Induced 1 Percent Once-and-for-All
Local Employment Shock on Average "Wage Differential"
of Workers from National Mean Wage of Their Occupation

Estimates Underlying Figure

Cumulative Effect After:

Immediate effect = 0 years	1 year	2 years	Long-run effect = 3 years
−1.233	.219	3.550	−.110
(1.209)	(1.705)	(1.486)	(.305)

NOTES: Estimates show cumulative percentage effect after *k* years of demand-induced, 1 percent permanent employment shock at year zero. Standard errors are in parentheses. Two standard errors to either side of point estimate are shown as dotted lines in figure. Long-run effect with eight lags is −.513 (.579).

Second, the short-run effects on the wage differential variable and the overall real wage variable are significantly greater for demand-induced growth than for general growth. These estimates are quite imprecise, however.

Although the overall effects of demand-induced growth and general growth differ significantly for both the real wage and wage differential variables, the estimated long-run effects on these two variables do not change significantly when we focus on demand-induced growth rather than all growth. Examining only demand-induced growth increases the imprecision of estimates. The estimated long-run effects of demand-induced growth on the wage differential and real wage variables are so imprecisely estimated that it is impossible to rule out a zero effect, a modestly large negative effect, or a modestly large positive effect of the same order of magnitude as the estimated effects of general growth.

Although these estimates are more imprecise than we would like, they seem generally consistent with this book's perspective on how local growth affects local labor markets. Local growth may have short-run positive effects on the real wages of particular occupations. But such effects decay over time, presumably due to in-migration, and there is no strong evidence of positive effects of local growth on occupational real wages in the long run. Long-run effects of local growth on real wages occur because individuals advance to better-paying occupations, and remain in better-paying occupations in the long run, presumably due to the human capital they acquired in the short run.

Finally, whether the effect of growth shocks on real wages varies with the prevailing level of job growth in the metropolitan area is examined. The initial level of growth only seemed to be important for growth effects on the skilled worker real wage variable. For this variable, an increase in a metropolitan area's change in employment from –1 percent per year to zero growth was estimated to increase long-run real wages for skilled workers by .18 of 1 percent, while an increase in a metropolitan area's growth from 2 to 3 percent was estimated to reduce real wages for skilled workers by –.01 of 1 percent. The real wage effects of variations in growth were larger at low growth rates, contrary to expectations. Thus, the empirical results provide no evidence for downward rigidity of the real wage.

Growth Effects on Real Wages Across Different Groups

Table 6.4 reports how the long-run effects of job growth on real wages in a metropolitan area vary with education, age, and race. The table reports estimates of the effects of demand-induced growth because these results differ significantly from the effects of general growth.[7]

Table 6.4 indicates that growth has significantly greater percentage effects on real wages for blacks, less-educated workers, and younger workers. The greater percentage effects on these groups' real wages are due to greater effects on both the occupational rank and wage differential variables.[8]

A plausible story can be told to explain these variations across individuals. During a boom period, firms promote people who otherwise would not be promoted: workers with lower education, younger workers, and blacks. Credentials of all sorts are less important to promotion decisions. Given the chance, workers with fewer credentials are able to demonstrate their abilities and acquire additional human capital, thus increasing their chance of keeping this job or another job of similar occupational rank.[9]

These results seem broadly consistent with Topel's (1986) article, the only previous research that has looked at how local job growth affects the real wages of different types of individuals. Topel found that local growth shocks affected real wages the most for less-educated workers.[10]

Conclusion

This chapter's results suggest that increased employment in a metropolitan area does not increase the long-run real wages offered by different occupations. The wage paid by an employer for a specific occupation increases about the same amount as local prices. But increased area employment does help some individuals advance to better-paying occupations. In response to increased local labor demand, employers may relax their hiring standards, allowing jobs to be more quickly filled

Table 6.4
Demographic Variation in the Long-Run Effects on Real Wages of a Demand-Induced Shock That Increases MSA Employment by 1 Percent

Real Wage Measure	Percentage Effect for "Mean" Individual	Change in Percentage Effect Due to Standardized Increase In:		
		Education	Age	Black
Real wages	.442 (.222)	-.056 (.007)	-.048 (.007)	.117 (.028)
Occupational rank	.161 (.080)	-.035 (.003)	-.027 (.003)	.054 (.012)
Wage differential	.282 (.220)	-.022 (.008)	-.022 (.009)	.064 (.032)

NOTES: A standardized change is a one standard deviation change for education (3.0 years) and age (11.8 years), and a change from white to black. The results reported here for age are actually for experience (= age-education-6); hence, it should be remembered that the education variable change holds constant experience, not age. The mean individual has 13.0 years of education, 22.3 years of experience, and a probability of being black of 9.7 percent. Standard errors are in parentheses. As described in appendix 6.1, standard errors reported here are conditional on sample values of some variables and parameters. The percentage effects for a mean individual show the percentage effect of 1 percent growth on that measure of real wages for an individual with mean characteristics; for example, for an average individual, their occupational rank increases by .161 percent for a 1 percent shock to MSA employment. The change in that percentage effect with different demographic characteristics must be added to these "mean effects" to get the actual effects for individuals whose demographic characteristics differ from the average. For example, an individual with three more years of education than average would be expected to have their occupational rank increased by .126 percent (=.161-.035) due to a 1 percent job growth shock.

without an increase in real wages. Individuals are able to keep these better-paying jobs even in the long run. These effects are consistent with hysteresis theories of local labor markets, which suggest that better labor market conditions in the short run may allow an improvement in the average labor market skills of the population.

The positive effects of increased metropolitan employment on occupational advancement are strongest for blacks, less-educated, and younger workers. This suggests a relatively "progressive" pattern to the real wage effects of metropolitan job growth: the percentage increase in real wages due to occupational advancement is greatest for the groups with the lowest incomes.

NOTES

1. This summary excludes the many studies of local wages that do not include an employment growth or population growth term. Four good examples of such studies are the papers by Blomquist, Berger, and Hoehn (1988); Clark, Kahn and Ofek (1988); Henderson (1988); and Gyourko and Tracy (1986). The summary also excludes the many studies of local wages that take a Phillips curve approach, regressing local wage inflation on local unemployment. (These Phillips curve regional wage studies are discussed in the excellent review of the literature on regional labor markets by Isserman, Taylor, Gerking, and Schubert 1986.) From the perspective of this study, both unemployment and wage growth are endogenous variables that respond to faster local employment growth, and OLS estimation of Phillips curves may be misleading. In addition, the summary excludes studies of local wages that include unemployment as well as local growth as a wage determinant. (For examples, see studies by Freeman 1981; Howland 1988; Howland and Peterson 1988; and Levy 1982). Estimates of the wage effects of local growth, holding unemployment constant, are not comparable to estimates of the wage effects of local growth, allowing unemployment to endogenously adjust. Finally, the summary excludes the recent paper by Holzer and Montgomery (1989) that looks at sales growth, wage growth, and employment growth at the firm level, as this paper is a very preliminary analysis of their data, and the paper's authors request that it not be quoted as yet.
2. The exception is Topel (1986), who examines how local growth effects vary with education and age.
3. The average occupational real wage was calculated using the same pooled Current Population Survey sample that was used for the micro real wage empirical analysis.
4. One difference between the micro model in table 6.2 and the real wage models of most other studies is that the wage variables are expressed in absolute form, as dollars per hour rather than as the logarithm of dollars per hour. This is done largely because real wages can take on negative values for individuals with negative self-employment earnings. I included individuals with low or even negative implied real wages to avoid arbitrary exclusion restrictions. But this meant that a logarithm of the real wage variable cannot be used. However, all results in the text and the text tables are presented as percentage effects on real wages, calculated at the means of the sample. This allows easier comparison with other studies, and is more intuitive. Appendix 6.1 presents the original estimates of the effects on dollars earned per hour.

5. The OLS estimates are presented in summary tables, rather than graphs as in chapter 4, because the dynamics of real wage responses to growth do not appear to be particularly interesting in the OLS specification. Graphs tend to focus reader attention on the dynamics of how labor market and housing market variables adjust over time.

6. In OLS specifications with eight lags in employment, the long-run percentage effect of 1 percent growth (with the standard errors in parentheses) on the micro real wage measures is as follows: micro real wage, .165 percent (.151); occupational rank, .086 percent (.054); wage differential, .079 percent (.148).

7. The lag-length chosen for overall real wages is also used for the occupational rank and wage differential variables to ensure that the estimated variations across individuals for the occupational rank and wage differential variables add up to the variation across individuals for the overall real wage variable.

8. Table 6.4 presents calculations for how the percentage effects of growth on real wages varies with a one-unit "standardized change" in a particular individual characteristic. This standardized change is defined as a one "standard deviation" change in the education and age variables (3.0 years for education, 11.8 years for age), and a change from white to black for the race variable. This standardized change approach is used to get some sense of the relative size of the effects of the different characteristics; even though both the education and age variables are expressed in years, for example, there is a lot more natural variability in the age variable than in the education variable.

It should be noted that the significant negative effect of education and age on growth's percentage impact on overall real wages and the wage differential variable is sensitive to the exact specification used. These percentage effects are calculated at the mean of this sample for the real wage, and the mean estimate of the percentage effect of growth on that particular dependent variable. As noted above, this average percentage effect of growth varies quite a bit for the overall real wage and wage differential variables. If lower average percentage effects of growth are assumed, age and education do not have significant effects on the percentage impact of growth on these two variables. However, the effects of racial status for these two variables is robust to different specifications. Furthermore, the effects of age, education, and race on the percentage impact of growth on occupational rank are robust to different specifications.

9. The greater growth effects on the wage differential variable for blacks, less-educated, and younger workers might be interpreted as indicating that growth causes some reduction in wage discrimination against these individuals: their wage increases relative to the wage of educated older whites within the same occupation. But, as noted previously in the text, estimates using the wage differential variable as a dependent variable are subject to several interpretations. The wage differential variable could increase more for blacks, less-educated, and younger workers because faster local growth allows these individuals to advance to better occupations within the occupational categories used to define the occupational rank variable. Hence, the text discussion emphasizes the greater effects of local job growth on the occupational rank of blacks, younger workers, and less-educated workers.

10. Topel's estimates of how an individual's age altered the real wage effects of local growth were quite sensitive to the particular empirical specification used.

— 7 —
Effects of Economic Development Policy on Individual Earnings, Income Distribution, and Economic Efficiency

This chapter analyzes the overall effects of state and local economic development policy on the earnings and incomes of different types of individuals, taking into account all the different economic effects of local job growth—on unemployment, labor force participation, occupational advancement, and housing prices—and taking into account the costs of financing economic development policies as well as the benefits of these policies. To state and local policymakers, these effects of economic development policies on the overall well-being of an area's residents and landowners should be the "bottom line" in deciding whether the policies make sense.

Effects of Local Growth on Real Earnings

The effects of job growth in a metropolitan area on the annual real earnings of an individual are considered first. The empirical results from previous chapters already provide an indirect estimate of local growth effects on real earnings. As defined in this book, real earnings is the mathematical product of labor force participation, the employment rate, weekly hours, and the real wage. Because the percentage change in any mathematical product will approximately equal the sum of the percentage change in its components, the percentage effect of growth on real earnings should approximately equal the sum of the percentage growth effect on labor force participation, wage rates, and other components of real earnings. This chapter's direct estimates of real earnings effects of

157

growth provide a useful check on the study methodology. Also, direct estimation is the simplest way to determine the statistical uncertainty in estimated effects of growth on real earnings.[1]

Previous Research on Local Growth and Earnings

Only two previous studies have looked at local economic growth and earnings or income: a book by Bradbury, Downs, and Small (1982), and a paper by Salinas (1986). These studies are summarized in table 7.1. Both studies find some earnings effect of growth.

Each of these studies has important strengths compared to most other research reviewed in previous chapters on effects of local growth. Bradbury, Downs, and Small recognize that demand-induced job growth will have different earnings effects from growth in general. A local demand shock that increases profits will increase labor demand, and thus real earnings, resulting in a positive correlation between employment growth and real earnings. In contrast, a local labor supply shock will lower local real wages, thus attracting employment and resulting in a negative correlation between employment growth and real earnings. The estimated effects of all types of local employment growth on real earnings will be downward-biased estimates of the effects of demand-induced growth on real earnings.

The Bradbury, Downs, and Small approach to measuring demand-induced growth is similar to the approach used in this book. Specifically, they used the growth in demand for each metropolitan area's export industries to predict overall growth for the metropolitan area.[2]

The Salinas paper, unlike other studies of local growth effects, allows the effects to differ between slow-growth and fast-growth areas. She found increased local job growth had greater effects on a metropolitan area's proportion of low-income earners in slow-growth metropolitan areas than in fast-growth metropolitan areas.

But the Bradbury and colleagues and Salinas studies also have significant limitations. Like the studies reviewed in other chapters, these studies fail to distinguish between the short-run and long-run effects of growth. The coefficient on the single growth variable included in each study combines short-run and long-run effects of growth.

Table 7.1

Previous Research on Effects of Local Growth on Local Earnings Variables

Study	Geographic Units Used in Growth Analysis	Population or Employment Growth	Period Over Which Growth Calculated	Micro or Aggregate Data	Dependent Variable	Estimated Percentage Effect of 1 Percent Growth on Dependent Variable (Elasticity)
Salinas (1986)	MSAs	Employment	4 years	Aggregate	"Subemployment" rate: proportion earning less than 125% of poverty	-.15 drop in rate points in nongrowing cities
Bradbury, Downs & Small (1982)	MSAs	Employment	5 years	Aggregate	Per capita income	.2

NOTE: Bradbury, Downs & Small results are from their tables 5.4 and 5.6.

Furthermore, both studies only look at aggregate data on metropolitan areas. Hence, their studies cannot tell how growth effects vary across individuals.

Finally, neither study is able to adequately control for price changes in the metropolitan areas. Thus, the implication of the results for growth effects on real earnings is unclear. The dependent variable used by Salinas is the proportion of the metropolitan area's population that falls below 125 percent of the level of income used to define the national poverty line, which is based on average consumer prices in the nation. A poverty line based on a separate price index for each metropolitan area would be more appropriate and might yield different results. Bradbury, Downs, and Small use nominal *per capita* income in the metropolitan area as the dependent variable. They control for price change by including the change in the price index of the nearest metropolitan area for which such an index is available. Of the 121 metropolitan areas in their sample, only 33 have local price indices. Hence, it is unclear whether their results would hold up if they had been able to use better measures of local prices for all the metropolitan areas in their sample.

New Estimates of Local Growth Effects on Earnings

The methodology and data used here to estimate real earnings effects of local job growth are outlined in table 7.2. The methodology and data are similar to what was used in previous chapters, so the discussion can be brief.[3]

The data used are again on adult males from 1979 through 1986, taken from the Current Population Survey. The empirical analysis examines how job growth in a metropolitan area affects the annual real earnings of individual residents of the metropolitan area, where annual real earnings includes all the individual's dollar compensation from working during the year. Annual earnings differs from average wages during the preceding year in that wages are the average earnings per hour worked during the preceding year, while annual earnings do not control for hours worked.

Table 7.2
Methodology and Data Used in Model of Effects
of Local Growth on Real Earnings

Basic Model: The model used can be written as

$$(7.1) \quad Y_{imt} = B_0 + N_t + F_m + \mathbf{B}'\mathbf{X}_{imt} + C(L)E_{mt} + V_{imt}$$

where Y_{imt} is real earnings of individual i in MSA m at year t, N_t represents a set of dummy variables for the time period, F_m represents a set of dummy variables for the metropolitan area (MSA), $\mathbf{X}_{imt}$ is a set of individual characteristics thought to influence real earnings, $C(L)E_{mt}$ represents a set of coefficients times current and lagged values of the logarithm of average total nonagricultural employment in MSA m during year t, and V_{imt} is the disturbance term. The inclusion of the MSA fixed effect means that this equation is focusing on the effects of MSA job *growth*, not job *levels* (see appendix 4.2).

The equation is estimated both by ordinary least squares (OLS), and by using two-stage least squares (2SLS) to look at the effects of "demand-induced" growth. Some specifications also included interaction terms between the employment variables, and the education, age, and race of the individual; others included terms in growth squared. All equations were tested on a variety of possible lag-lengths in employment from zero to eight lagged years. The optimal lag-length, based on the Akaike Information Criterion (AIC), is reported in subsequent figures. This optimal lag-length means that the cumulative effect does not seem to vary after that.

The individual data come from the March 1980 through March 1987 CPS, and cover annual earnings for the years 1979 through 1986. Only individuals in the 25 MSAs with a local CPI index were used. Total sample size was 14,918 adult males, ages 25-64. Employment data come from the BLS 790 program and ES-202 program.

The methodology allows statistical tests to determine when the effect on earnings of a shock to a metropolitan area's employment stabilizes at some long-run effect. Also examined is whether the effects of demand-induced job growth in a metropolitan area differ from the average effects of all types of growth (either from shocks to labor demand or shocks to labor supply).

Figure 7.1 presents estimates of the average effects of all types of local growth, including both demand and supply shocks. A 1 percent permanent increase in the employment level of a metropolitan area is estimated to increase real earnings by 44/100 of 1 percent in the long run. The effect on real earnings is significantly greater in the short run.

Statistical tests indicated significant differences between the real earnings effects of demand-induced growth and overall growth.[4] Figure 7.2 presents estimates of the real earnings effects of demand-induced growth in employment in a metropolitan area. It shows that the short-run real earnings effects of demand-induced growth are significantly greater than the effects of overall growth. The estimated long-run effects of demand-induced growth on real earnings are virtually identical to the long-run effects of overall growth, but they are insignificantly different from zero because the standard error—which represents our statistical uncertainty about them—is relatively large.

Figure 7.2 raises some difficult issues about what inferences we are willing to make on the basis of these estimates and economic theory. In particular, do we conclude that there is no strong evidence of positive long-run effects of demand-induced local growth on real earnings because the estimated effects are not statistically significantly different from zero?

It is more reasonable to conclude that demand-induced growth does have long-run effects on real earnings. The statistical discussion above indicated that the estimated real earnings effects of overall growth are downward-biased estimates of the effects of demand-induced growth. Hence, the estimated long-run effect of overall growth on real earnings should be an underestimate of the true effect of demand-induced growth. The empirical estimates are consistent with this hypothesis. The estimated short-run effects of demand-induced growth are greater than the effects of overall growth, as expected. Furthermore, there is no

Figure 7.1
Estimated Cumulative Effects on Real Earnings
of Once-and-for-All 1 Percent Shock to Local Employment,
at Different Times After the Shock

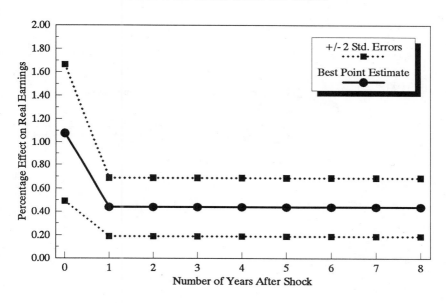

Estimated Cumulative Effects on Which Figure is Based:

Immediate effect = 0 years	Long-run effect = 1 year
1.077	.438
(.293)	(.125)

NOTES: Figure presents OLS estimates. Standard errors are in parentheses. Figure shows best point estimate, plus two standard errors to either side of point estimate. True effect has 95 percent probability of falling in that interval. Optimal lag-length, based on AIC is one year among all lag-lengths up to eight years. This optimality implies cumulative effect does not vary significantly from one year to eight years. Long-run effect in 8-lag model is .277 percent, with standard error of .157.

Figure 7.2
Estimated Cumulative Effects on Real Earnings of Once-and-for-All
1 Percent Demand Shock to Local Employment,
at Different Times After the Shock

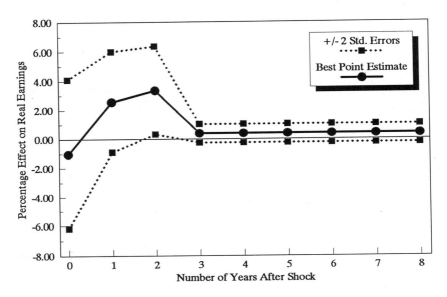

Estimated Cumulative Effects on Which Figure is Based

Cumulative Effect After:

Immediate effect = 0 years	1 year	2 years	Long-run effect = 3 years
−1.049	2.552	3.344	.382
(2.572)	(1.724)	(1.511)	(.322)

NOTES: Figure presents 2SLS estimates, using share effect "demand shock" variables as instruments. Standard errors in parentheses. Figure shows best point estimate, plus two standard errors. Three years is optimal lag-length according to AIC. With eight lags, estimated long-run effect is .382, with standard error of .617.

evidence that the long-run effects of demand-induced growth are significantly less than the long-run effects of overall growth.

The basic problem is that the statistical uncertainty in the estimates of the long-run effects of demand-induced growth is so great that we cannot make strong inferences on the basis of the estimates. Hence, we must rely on the estimated effects of overall growth to make any inferences. Estimated effects of overall growth do suggest that long-run effects of demand-induced metropolitan job growth on real earnings are significant, as demand-induced growth should have larger effects than overall growth.

Examination of how the effects of extra growth on real earnings varied with the initial level of growth found no evidence of any significant differences.

Consistency With Results of Previous Chapters

I now consider the relationship between these estimated real earnings effects and the estimates in previous chapters of the effects of local employment shocks on unemployment rates, labor force participation, weekly hours worked and real wages. As argued above, the percentage effect of employment shocks on real earnings should approximately equal the sum of the percentage effects of employment shocks on each of the real earnings components. Table 7.3 presents the estimated short-run and long-run percentage effects of local employment growth on real earnings and its components. The table indicates a rough consistency between the results of this chapter and previous chapters.

Table 7.3 shows that one-half to two-thirds of the long-run effects of local growth on real earnings are due to growth effects on labor market activity: unemployment rates, labor force participation, and hours worked per week. The remaining portion of the earnings effects is due to effects on real wages. Furthermore, a considerable portion of local growth effects on real wages is due to effects on occupational upgrading. In the long run, for the average individual, local growth increases real earnings by increasing work or providing better jobs, not by increasing real wages for the same job.

Table 7.3
Contribution of Various Components to Percentage Effect on Real Earnings of a 1 Percent Employment Shock

	Labor Force Participation Effect		Employment Rate Effect		Weekly Hours Effect		Occupational Upgrading Effect		Wage Differential Effect		Sum of Components	Direct Estimate of Real Earnings Effect
Long-Run Effects													
Overall growth estimates	.157	+	.070	+	.066	+	.101	+	.159	=	.553	.438
Demand shock estimates	.265	+	.103	+	.000	+	.238	+	(−.110)	=	.496	.382
Maximum Short-Run Effects													
Overall growth estimates	.157	+	.446	+	.248	+	.101	+	.159	=	1.111	1.077
Demand shock estimates	.265	+	.613	+	.000	+	.238	+	3.550	=	4.666	3.344

NOTES: Table reports percentage effects, at sample mean of each variable, of a 1 percent increase in employment in the metropolitan area. Thus, the long-run labor force participation effect of .157 percent for overall growth is equal to .137 change in labor force participation rate, reported in chapter 4, divided by mean labor force participation rate of 87.5. Long-run effects are for specification, for each component separately considered, that minimized the Akaike Information Criterion (AIC). Short-run effects are maximum effects in these "Optimal AIC" specifications. Hence, in each case the estimated effects may be after various lengths of time.

In the short run, the relative contribution of different components to local growth effects on real earnings is sensitive to whether one examines the effects of overall growth or demand-induced growth. In either case, effects of local growth on unemployment are clearly much more important in the short run than in the long run. But the importance of real wage effects varies quite a bit across the two sets of estimates. Estimates based on the effects of demand-induced growth indicate that real wage effects of local growth are extremely large in the short run, explaining most of their short-run effects on real earnings. The estimates based on the effects of overall growth do not indicate a very large role for real wage effects in the short run.

It is difficult to know which of these decompositions of the short-run effects of local growth on real earnings is closer to the truth. As pointed out in chapter 6 and in this chapter, the estimates of the short-run effects of demand-induced growth on real wages and real earnings are extremely imprecise, so the true short-run effects could differ quite a bit from the estimates reported in table 7.3. Furthermore, even if these large short-run effects of local growth on real wages are correct, they appear to disappear rapidly. Any real wage benefits of local growth for individuals who keep the same job are short-lived.

Effects of Local Growth on Earnings
By Demographic Group

Table 7.4 presents estimates of how the long-run real earnings effects of local employment shocks differ across demographic groups. These results show that the real earnings effects of an employment shock are significantly greater for less-educated workers and blacks. Real earnings effects of employment shocks are similar for different age groups, however.

Using results from previous chapters, table 7.4 breaks down what factors contribute to differences across demographic groups in the long-run real earnings effects of local employment shocks. Differences across demographic groups in percentage effects of employment shocks on real earnings should approximately equal the sum of the differences across

Table 7.4

Differences Across Individuals in the Long-Run Effects of Employment Shocks on Real Earnings: Overall Results and a Decomposition

Real Earnings Elasticity for Mean Household	Impact on Elasticity of Standardized Change in:		
	Education	Age	Black
.399 (.349)	-.065 (.008)	-.011 (.008)	.082 (.032)

Contribution of Different Factors to Differences Across Individuals in Real Earnings Effects

	Education	Age	Black
Labor market activity			
Labor force participation	.004 (.002)	.028 (.002)	.002 (.008)
Employment rate	-.005 (.001)	-.002 (.001)	-.011 (.004)
Weekly hours	-.002 (.002)	.003 (.002)	-.004 (.007)
(subtotal)	-.003	.029	-.013
Real wages			
Occupational rank	-.035 (.003)	-.027 (.003)	.054 (.012)
Wage differential	-.022 (.009)	-.022 (.009)	.064 (.032)
(subtotal)	-.057	-.049	.118

NOTES: All calculations in the table show impact of "standardized change" in a demographic characteristic on *percentage* effect of a 1 percent growth shock on a particular dependent variable. All calculations are for the "optimal" interaction specification; the optimal interaction specifications for all except the real earnings variable are discussed in previous chapters. The real earnings calculations are for the 4-lag specification with interaction terms, which minimizes the AIC. A "standardized change" in education and age is one standard deviation change for education (3.0 years) and age (11.8 years), standardized change in the race variable is from a value of zero (= white) to one (= black). The calculated elasticity impact of a standardized change in one of these demographic variables examines how the ratio of the absolute effect of a demand shock, divided by the expected value of the dependent variable, changes as the demographic characteristic is altered. For example, as education increases by 3.0 years, the absolute dollar effect of a growth shock on real earnings goes up (see appendix 7.1), but the expected value of real earnings goes up even more. Thus, the *percentage* impact of a 1 percent growth shock on real earnings, equal to the absolute dollar effect divided by real earnings, declines by .065 percent from its mean value of .399 percent. Standard errors are in parentheses. Standard error calculations are discussed in appendix 7.1 and appendix 6.1. Note that impacts of demographic variables on percentage effect of growth shock, for each component of real earnings, approximately sum to impact on percentage real earnings effect. Thus, for education, −.003 − .057 ≈ −.065.

demographic groups in the percentage effects of employment shocks on the components of real earnings. This equality appears to approximately hold in table 7.4.

Based on table 7.4, the greater real earnings gains from growth for blacks and the less-educated are due to greater effects of growth on their real wages. As discussed in chapter 4, local growth helps blacks and the less-educated to get jobs, but by no more than others. Growth's effects on labor market activity explain much of its real earnings effects for the average individual, but little of the differences in real earnings effects across individuals. But local growth helps the promotion prospects for blacks and the less-educated significantly more than it helps the promotion prospects for other groups.

Table 7.4 also shows that the similarity across age groups in real earnings effects of employment shocks conceals offsetting influences of age on how shocks affect labor market activity and real wages. Older workers' labor force participation is more affected by employment shocks than is true for younger workers. But younger workers' promotion possibilities are more affected by local employment shocks than is true for older workers. These differences are understandable. Compared to younger workers, older workers find it more socially acceptable—and financially feasible—to drop out of the labor force when the local economy is depressed. Compared to older workers, younger workers face more barriers to promotion due to inexperience, and their promotion prospects improve more when employers are forced to relax promotion standards in a booming, labor-short local economy.

A different perspective on how local employment shocks affect different demographic groups is provided by comparing these effects with alternative programs for increasing the real earnings of residents of economically depressed metropolitan areas. As discussed in chapter 4, the policy alternatives usually proposed are education and training programs and assistance for migration to more fortunate regions. These two alternatives have in common that the main beneficiaries are likely to be young. The real earnings effects of local employment shocks, however, do not vary much with age. Older workers in economically depressed metropolitan areas are benefited more by state and local economic development programs that promote growth, than by alternative policies proposed for helping people in depressed areas. Presumably, much of this special benefit for older workers occurs due to fewer plant closings or contractions in more rapidly growing areas. State and local economic development programs focused on existing plants, particularly those in distress, might be of the most assistance to older workers.

Effects of Economic Development Policy on Income Distribution

. . . Growth likely increases inequality within places through its effects on the distribution of rents. Increases in urban scale mean larger numbers of bidders for the same critically located land parcels (for example, the central business district or the site for a freeway intersection), inflating land prices relative to wages and other wealth sources. (Page 95 in *Urban Fortunes: The Political Economy of Place,* John Logan and Harvey Molotch, 1987)

The target population, the unemployed labor force, is not always the only—or even the main—beneficiary of new industry. A disproportionately large share of the increased purchasing power goes to the owners of immobile resources other than labor. Real estate owners, banks, retailers, and utilities are surer beneficiaries than are the unemployed coal miners or loggers who are less likely to get the jobs in the new plants than are new in-migrants, younger and with more appropriate skills. (Page 280 in Louis Winnick, "Place Prosperity vs. People Prosperity: Welfare Considerations in the Geographic Redistribution of Economic Activity," in *Essays in Urban Land Economics*, 1966)

I now turn from considering how the benefits of growth are distributed across demographic groups to how they are distributed across income and earnings groups. It is often argued that local economic growth will worsen the local income distribution. The rationale for this argument, well-stated by Logan and Molotch and by Winnick above, is that local growth will push up property values to a greater extent than it increases real wages or employment prospects for the bottom part of the income distribution.

The evidence compiled in this book enables us to test this hypothesis. Results from this and previous chapters imply a particular pattern of effects of local employment shocks on the income distribution. Individuals in low-income groups are disproportionately less-educated and black, and hence will tend to have greater percentage gains in real earnings from an employment shock. On the other hand, higher-income individuals are more likely to own homes and other property, and hence are more likely to gain property value appreciation benefits from local growth. Which effect dominates?

Local Growth and the Earnings Distribution

Table 7.5 presents calculations of growth effects on different quintiles of the male earnings distribution. I first calculated, for each individual in the real earnings sample (14,918 in all), the estimated real dollar effects of a 1 percent demand shock on their annual earnings, based on their education, race, and age. The sample was then ordered by annual real earnings and divided into quintiles. The average real earnings effect of a 1 percent demand shock in each quintile was divided by average real earnings in each quintile to obtain estimated percentage effects.

These percentage effects by current annual earnings quintile are shown in column (2) of table 7.5. The pattern of growth effects on earnings is extremely progressive. The lowest earnings quintile's percentage gain in earnings from growth is over 20 times as great as the percentage gain of the highest earnings quintile.

Like most analyses of distributional effects of policy, these calculations relate policy effects to current income. This approach might be criticized because this year's income will, on average, understate long-run expected annual income for low-current-income persons. Low-current-income persons will tend to have experienced temporary adverse

Table 7.5
Long-Run Effects of Local Labor Demand Shocks on the Earnings Distribution

Quintile	Share of Quintile in Total Sample Labor Earnings	Percentage Effect of 1 Percent Shock on Quintile Earnings	Share of Quintile in Total Sample Permanent Labor Earnings	Percentage Effect of 1 Percent Shock on Quintile Permanent Labor Earnings	Maximum Earnings Equivalent Gain for Property Value Increase
	(1)	(2)	(3)	(4)	(5)
1	1.7%	4.64	10.8%	.67	
2	11.7	.66	17.5	.43	
3	19.0	.42	19.9	.41	
4	25.7	.32	23.4	.36	
5	41.9	.21	28.4	.33	.21%(?)
Average		.41		.41	

NOTE: The average real earnings effects of growth are weighted averages, where the weights are each quintile's share in total earnings.

misfortunes. For similar reasons, high-current-income persons will tend to have current incomes that overstate their long-run expected annual income.

To help address this problem, I estimated for the real earnings sample a simple earnings equation predicting annual real earnings as a function of education, age, and race. (Appendix 7.2 presents these estimates.) Individuals in the sample were then ordered by these predicted real earnings, which can be seen as rough estimates of "permanent" real earnings, the long-run average earnings that individuals can generally expect to receive. The sample was then divided into quintiles. Estimates of the percentage effects of local growth on permanent real earnings were then obtained by dividing the average real dollar effect of growth on each quintile's earnings, by the average predicted permanent earnings of each quintile.

These percentage effects by permanent earnings quintile are shown in the fourth column of table 7.5. The pattern of effects revealed is still highly progressive. The estimated percentage effect of a local demand shock on the lowest permanent earnings quintile is twice the effect on the highest earnings quintile.

Which of these two sets of estimated percentage effects of growth on real earnings quintiles is "better"? First, it should be noted that these estimates are not as different as they appear, if one analyzes the pattern of effects by earnings relative to mean earnings. For example, the lowest permanent earnings quintile, and the second lowest current earnings quintile, both have average earnings of around half the average earnings for the sample. (Each of these quintile's share of earnings is slightly over 10 percent, while a quintile with average earnings would have an earnings share of 20 percent.) The percentage effects of earnings on these two quintiles are similar. This implies that the percentage effect of demand shocks on earnings varies in much the same way as earnings vary, using either current earnings or permanent earnings. What is different in the permanent earnings calculation is that the average earnings of low- and high-earnings quintiles are compressed towards the middle of the earnings distribution, and thus the differences in percentage effects across quintiles are muted.

Second, for comparison with other studies, the estimation using current earnings is more appropriate. Almost all studies of the distributional effects of taxes, transfers, or other policies use current income or earnings as a basis for calculating relative percentage effects.

Property Value Effects

Progressive effects of local job growth on annual earnings probably cannot be offset by the regressive distribution of the benefits from local growth effects on property values. The effects on property values are too small to substantially alter the net distributional effects of local job growth.

Consider the following extreme, unlikely assumptions, designed to maximize the regressive influence of property value effects of growth. Suppose that only males in the top earnings quintile owned any share of property. Assume further that their ownership stake in property assets in their metropolitan area amounted to 10 times their earnings, almost certainly higher than is realistic. At a 3 percent real discount rate, the annual earnings equivalent of this property value ownership would be 30 percent of earnings. The estimated effects in chapter 5 of a 1 percent growth shock on housing prices ranged from .25 percent to .70 percent in different specifications, with most estimates less than .50 percent. Suppose that the highest of these estimated housing price effects, .70 percent, actually represented the increase in the value of local property assets due to a growth shock. Then a 1 percent growth shock would raise the implicit income from property assets to the upper earnings quintile by .7 percent of their annual implicit income from this property, or by .21 percent of annual labor earnings (.21 = .30 times .7).

Even under these very extreme assumptions, the net gain to the highest earnings quintile from growth—including both property value and labor earnings effects—would still be less than the gain to the lowest earnings quintile from growth. In the real world, property ownership is more widespread across earnings classes, local property ownership is not so large in the highest earnings quintiles, and the effects of growth on property values is probably not as high as was assumed. Under these more realistic assumptions, property value effects are even less likely to alter the progressive effects of local growth on earnings.

Distributional Effects on Family Income vs. Male Earnings

Progressive effects of local growth on the male earnings distribution do not necessarily imply a progressive effect on the family income distribution. Distributional effects of growth on female earnings could be more progressive or regressive than distributional effects on male earnings. Classifying individuals by family income will reshuffle some lower-earnings males into higher-income quintiles, and some higher-earnings males into lower-income quintiles, which will tend to mute the differences in percentage effects across quintiles. Finally, lower-income quintiles receive a great deal of their income from transfers. Even if transfers are unchanged when the earnings of the lowest income quintile goes up, the percentage effect of growth on the income of the lowest income quintile will be less than the percentage effect on earnings; furthermore, we would expect some decline in means-tested transfers when earnings go up, as most transfers (e.g., welfare and food stamps) have some formula for reducing benefits as earnings increase.

Despite these many differences between family income distribution and individual male earnings distribution, local growth is likely to have progressive effects on the distribution of family income. This prediction can only be tested by further empirical investigation with a much different focus from this book. The main rationale for this prediction is that the effect of local growth on the distribution of male earnings is so strongly progressive that it seems highly unlikely that other factors could offset it.

Economic Development and Lower-Income Households

Even if local growth does turn out to have progressive effects on the distribution of family income, this finding would not mean that lower-income households always gain from state and local economic development policies. Local residents must pay the costs of economic development subsidies to firms. Hence, the exact distribution of these costs across different income groups is also important, and this depends on the method of financing. Because state and local taxes are generally believed by economists to be distributed regressively (i.e., the poor pay a greater percentage of their income in taxes than the rich), there is reason to be concerned that the net impact of these policies is regressive.

Under some methods of financing economic development, adverse net impacts on the poor are quite likely. For example, figures from the Congressional Budget Office suggest that "means-tested" transfer income (welfare, etc.) comprises 16 percent of the income of the lowest income quintile, and less than 0.5 percent of the income of other quintiles. Suppose a state or local government expands economic development subsidies, and finances this expansion by cutting real welfare benefits. Suppose further that the overall costs and earnings benefits from this economic development program are roughly in balance. Under these assumptions, the program will hurt the poorest households as a group. The poorest households pay all the cost of the program, and only receive a portion of the benefits, even though this portion is a greater percentage of their income.

Growth Effects on Individuals
vs. Income or Earnings Groups

Another important point is that these average effects of growth on different income or earnings groups conceal important differences within groups. It is quite likely that growth's effects vary more within income groups than across income groups. Unemployed individuals who happen to get a job due to growth gain. Unemployed renters who don't happen to get a job due to growth lose. Developers who own choice parcels of appropriately zoned land gain a great deal.

The argument that local growth tends to have progressive effects on the earnings and income distribution merely means that, on average, individuals and families who happen to be in lower earnings and income groups tend to gain more in percentage terms than individuals and families in more fortunate groups. Growth will still often have large costs for specific poor individuals and families and large benefits for specific wealthy individuals and families.

Net Efficiency Effects of Economic Development Policy

Income distribution effects are just one possible "bottom line" in deciding on the desirability of state and local economic development policy. Economists often argue that policymakers should pay more attention to the "efficiency effects" of policy, that is, the net balance of dollar benefits and costs summed over the relevant population. The argument is that if a policy is efficient—that is, has net benefits that are positive—adopting it makes sense because any undesirable distributional effects can be offset by other policies. From the perspective of state and local policymakers, the relevant population over which we should sum benefits and costs to obtain net "efficiency effects" is all current residents. I consider this state and local efficiency perspective here, and postpone an analysis of economic development policy from a national perspective to chapter 8.

Examining the net dollar benefits and costs of a specific state and local economic development program for a specific metropolitan area is obviously impossible for this book, due to lack of suitable data. The estimates reported, however, allow at least a rough estimate of the range of plausible values for benefits and costs that might be associated with an "average" economic development policy in an "average" metropolitan area.

This policy will have a number of effects on local residents and businesses. Local residents gain in real earnings and property values from an economic development program that successfully promotes growth. On the other hand, they must pay for the program in increased taxes or reductions in public services or transfers.[5] Furthermore, local residents will have a higher cost-of-living, which will erode the real value of the nonlabor component of their incomes. Local business may receive benefits in the form of extra profits from economic development subsidies, increased demand for their products due to growth, and possible agglomeration benefits from greater specialization in supplier markets in larger cities. Local businesses may also face increased wage costs if the wage increases caused by growth are not matched by higher real productivity. Local business will also face increased explicit or implicit costs of renting the land and structures they use in their operations. Fiscal benefits or costs of the growth may occur, depending on the balance of incremental tax revenue versus service demands from new development.

In addition, there are more intangible benefits and costs from economic development policy. Growth may have environmental and congestion costs, and may change the "character" of the community either in a positive or negative direction. Finally, the earnings benefits from growth may be partially or totally offset by the value of leisure foregone when individuals work more. In high-unemployment cities, the opportunity cost of leisure time could be argued to be close to zero. In high-unemployment cities, where obtaining a job is difficult, many unemployed individuals will place a very large dollar value on getting a job, in that they would be willing to accept very low wages. In low-unemployment cities, where obtaining a job is much easier, most residents who place a large value on getting a job will be able to find a job. The remaining unemployed will place a relatively high value on their leisure time. At the extreme, the unemployed worker's reservation wage—the lowest wage at which the worker would be willing to accept a job offer—may be as high as the market wage in low-unemployment cities. In that case, the increased employment probabilities and working time associated with growth would produce little net benefit to residents.[6]

What will not be included in this benefit-cost analysis is the effect of economic development in this metropolitan area on the residents of other areas. Positive effects of growth on the value of property owned by nonresidents will be ignored, along with potential damaging effects on other areas if faster growth here tends to reduce growth there. The national perspective on state and local economic development policies will be addressed in chapter 8.

Table 7.6 shows the assumptions made here to develop this metropolitan area benefit-cost analysis for an average development policy in an average metropolitan area. Where assumptions are needed, I consider a "central case" assumption based on the most likely estimates. I also consider a range of plausible assumptions that deviate from that central case assumption.

Table 7.6
Assumptions and Sources for Benefit-Cost Analysis
of "Average" Economic Development Program
for Hypothetical Average MSA

Assumption	Source
1. Earnings as percentage of personal income = 73.5 percent.	1988 figures from *1990 U.S. Statistical Abstract*, p. 432.
2. Asset value of local property as percentage of personal income = 263.6 percent.	Figures on net structure value in 1988 from pp. 101 and 102 of August 1990 *Survey of Current Business*, times 1.25, divided by personal income figures from p. 432 of 1990 *U.S. Statistical Abstract*. Multiplication by 1.25 is based on assumption that land is one-fifth of real estate value, structure value is four-fifths.
3. Flow value of explicit and implicit income from local property, to local residents, as percentage of personal income = minimum of 4.0 percent, maximum of 7.9 percent, central case of 5.9 percent.	Assumption of 3 percent real discount rate. 263.6 * .03 = 7.9 percent. Central case assumes 75 percent of property is locally owned, with range of 50 to 100 percent.
4. Long-run elasticity of MSA employment with respect to state and local business taxes = −.3 in central case (−.1 to −.6 is range of assumptions).	Review of literature in chapter 2.
5. Business share of state and local taxes = .34.	U.S. Advisory Commission on Intergovernmental Relations, *Interstate Tax Competition*, March 1981, p. 63. (UI included as tax; revised version of report appendix used.)
6. Average personal state and local taxes as percentage of personal income = 10.6 percent.	Figures on state and local tax receipts from *Survey of Current Business*, January 1990, p. 15, table 3.3, multiplied by personal share of .66 (= 1−business share).
7. Elasticity of real earnings with respect to employment growth = .44 ± .26.	OLS estimates from this chapter, ± 2 standard errors.

Table 7.6 (Continued)

Assumption	Source
8. Elasticity of property values with respect to employment growth = .45 ± .24.	OLS estimates from chapter 5 of growth impact on old BLS measure of owner-occupied housing prices, ± 2 standard errors.
9. Cost of foregone leisure = maximum value of 74 percent of earnings benefit.	Table 7.3: using long-run demand shock estimates, sum of employment shock effects on labor market activity, divided by sum of employment shock effects on all earnings components ((.265 + .103 + .000) / .496).
10. Effects of higher costs of living for local residents in reducing real value of nonearnings components of income = .20 ± (.06) times 26.5 percent of income that is nonearnings = .05 percent ± .02 percent.	Chapter 5 estimates of effects of growth shock on local CPI, ± 2 standard errors, and information on nonearnings share of income from p. 432 of *1990 U.S. Statistical Abstract*. Effects of increased CPI on real value of earnings already reflected in real earnings estimates.
11. Cost of extra wages to local businesses, not offset by productivity influences = maximum value of 24 percent of earnings benefit.	Table 7.3: using long-run overall growth estimates, sum of employment shock effects on real wages, divided by sum of employment shock effects on all earnings components ((.101 + .159) / .553) = .47. Assumption that no more than 50 percent of businesses are locally owned: 47 percent times .50 = 24 percent.
12. Implicit or explicit extra costs of land and buildings to locally owned business = minimum of 2.6 percent of property value benefit, maximum of 13.1 percent, central case of 7.8 percent.	Figures on private nonresidential value of structures, p. 463 of *1990 U.S. Statistical Abstract* = 26.1 percent of all structure value. Central case assumes 30 percent of all business property is locally owned. Minimum assumes 10 percent, maximum assumes 50 percent local ownership.

Based on these assumptions, table 7.7 presents the range of plausible estimates of annual benefits and costs of a program that leads to 1 percent extra employment for a metropolitan area in the long run. The range of plausible estimates is wide enough that it is impossible to say whether state and local economic development policies will generally benefit the residents of the targeted metropolitan area. This indeterminate conclusion is not surprising. If the programs quite clearly always had net benefits, we would expect a lot more money to be devoted to economic development than is currently the case. If the programs were obviously net losers, their enormous expansion in most states during the 1980s would have been unlikely.

Despite this uncertain conclusion about the "bottom-line" of economic development, table 7.7 is informative because it shows what factors and assumptions are most important in determining the net benefits of development policies. The net benefits appear to be most sensitive to the magnitude of real earnings effects, the program cost per job created, and the cost of forgone leisure. On the other hand, the exact magnitude of property value effects appears to be of lesser importance.

The sensitivity of net benefits to these three factors has important implications for both research and policy. For researchers, these findings indicate areas where more research would be most helpful in evaluating the net benefits of development policy.

For policymakers, these findings indicate areas where policy design may make the most difference in the overall benefits of the programs. Table 7.7 shows effects of an "average" policy in an "average" metropolitan area. Presumably, each metropolitan area and each chosen policy will differ in important ways from the average, with consequent difference in effects. For example, economic development policies in metropolitan areas where unemployment is high will tend to have lower reservation wages for the unemployed, increasing the probability of net benefits from the program for area residents.

In addition, table 7.7 suggests that state and local policymakers should focus a great deal of attention on the "cost-effectiveness" of economic development programs—the program cost per job created—as this may be crucial to whether the program should be adopted. This increases

Table 7.7
Long-Run Annual Benefits and Costs
of an "Average" Economic Development Program
Resulting in 1 Percent Employment Growth,
Stated as Percentage of MSA Annual Personal Income

Benefits	Value as Percent of MSA Income
Real earnings	.32 (.13 to .51)
Property income, both explicit and implicit	.03 (.01 to .05)
Benefits to locally owned businesses of subsidies, extra profits from growth	?
Sum of benefits	.35 plus ? (.14 to .56 plus ?)

Costs	Value as Percent of MSA Income
Tax costs to residents	.18 (.09 to .55)
Foregone leisure	Up to 74 percent of earnings benefits (Max. = .38)
Effect of higher local cost-of-living in reducing real value of residents' nonlabor income	.05 (.03 to .07)
Environmental/congestion costs	?
Costs to locally owned business of higher wages, not offset by productivity improvements	Up to 24 percent of earnings benefit (Max. = .12)
Costs to locally owned businesses of higher rental prices of land and structures	.00 (.00 to .01)
Sum of costs	.23 percent plus ? (.12 plus up to 1.13 plus)

Other Factors	
Fiscal benefits or costs	?
Change in character of community	?
Net efficiency effects	?

NOTES: Parentheses show plausible range of estimated benefits and costs. See table 7.6 for specific assumptions and sources behind these figures. The table assumes: typical estimated growth effects from this study on earnings and property values, with the range given by two standard errors to either side; tax elasticities of business employment of −.1 to −.6 (−.3 for central case); maximum value of foregone leisure that exactly offsets all earnings effects caused by more work rather than more wages. All figures are recalibrated as percent of personal income from whatever units they initially were in. Maximum values for foregone leisure and wage costs are based on earnings benefit of .51 percent.

the attractiveness of "new wave" economic development programs—programs focused on small business, entrepreneurship, and improved technology—which claim to be more cost-effective than traditional economic development programs of financial subsidies to branch plants. In addition, the sensitivity of net local benefits to program costs per job created indicates that there are potentially great advantages from more selective economic development subsidy programs that seek to focus subsidies on the few firms whose location and employment choices are most likely to be affected, rather than simply cutting business taxes across-the-board.

Finally, the earnings effects of local economic growth probably vary quite a bit, depending on the nature of the growth and the nature of the local labor market. Because this book is an initial study of economic development and the local labor market, the focus has deliberately been narrowed to the basic issue of how aggregate employment demand in local areas affects average economic outcomes. A more sophisticated and difficult analysis would recognize that the types of jobs and the skills of existing residents also make a difference. Specifically, faster local growth is more likely to increase employment probabilities of current residents and less likely to simply lead to in-migration, if the new jobs require skills that current unemployed residents either already have or can easily obtain. The empirical estimates only directly indicate that overall local labor demand has important long-run effects on labor market outcomes for a region's residents. However, it is a plausible inference that specific types of local labor demand also have important long-run effects. If this is so, state and local policymakers should focus more attention on trying to increase the types of jobs that will provide the greatest employment and upgrading benefits for current residents.

Conclusion

The bottom line is that real earnings effects of faster local growth are significant. These effects are greater in percentage terms for blacks and less-educated workers. As a result, lower-earnings males gain far more in percentage terms from local growth than higher-earnings males. The pattern of these earnings effects is so progressive that it seems likely that overall effects of local growth on the income distribution, including other sources of family income and the property value effects of growth, are at least modestly progressive.

Furthermore, it is easy to make plausible assumptions under which state and local economic development policies promoting faster local growth will have net benefits for an area. Even when the costs of economic development programs are considered, the local area may well gain.

This optimistic view of state and local economic development policy as both efficient and progressive depends on a specific set of circumstances. In particular, it is most accurate for a high-unemployment area that uses relatively cost-effective economic development incentives, finances these programs in a manner that is at least roughly proportional to income, and attracts jobs that are accessible to the area's unemployed. Changing any of these assumptions makes it less likely that the area's poor will benefit from economic development.

Thus, the results in this chapter could also be used to develop a relatively pessimistic view of state and local economic development policy. In an area with low unemployment, the benefits of more jobs will be relatively small. If the area uses economic development programs that are relatively costly per job created, the net benefits of economic development for the area could easily be strongly negative.

Furthermore, just looking at the aggregate well-being of the poor, or of other groups, ignores the particular gains and losses of specific individuals. Even under the optimistic view, even with an efficient, progressive economic development policy, specific poor individuals will no doubt lose significantly from the policy, due to increases in the cost-of-living and taxes that, in their particular case, are not counterbalanced by labor market or property market gains.

Finally, all of the analysis in this chapter has taken a local perspective: what are the distributional and efficiency effects of state and local economic development policy from the perspective of the local area in which the policy is implemented? We should also consider the national perspective. The next chapter turns to that issue.

NOTES

1. That is, because $RE = 52* LFP * ER * HRS * RW$, $d\ln RE/dX = d\ln LFP/dX + d\ln ER/dX + d\ln HRS/dX + d\ln RW/dX$, where RE is real earnings, LFP is the proportion of weeks in the labor force during the year, ER is the ratio of weeks employed to weeks in the labor force, HRS is the average hours worked per week when employed, RW is the real wage per hour, and X is some variable such as job growth. But knowledge of the variance of the estimates of each of the right-hand side derivatives does not tell us the variance in the left-hand side derivative of this equation, except in the unlikely event that these estimates are uncorrelated. The easiest way to estimate the variance of the left-hand side derivative is to directly estimate the derivative.

2. That is, they used the share component of a shift-share analysis to predict overall growth.

3. Appendix 7.1 presents the results in more detail.

4. See appendix 7.1 to this chapter for statistical tests of differences between the effects on real earnings of overall growth and demand-induced growth.

5. There is unlikely to be a "Laffer curve" for regional economic development programs; that is, the budgetary effects of these programs are unlikely to offset their initial budgetary cost. Based on the literature review in chapter 2, the effects of a state or metropolitan area business tax rate reduction on job growth are not strong enough to prevent business tax revenue from declining. Furthermore, additional business growth will require additional services. Finally, household in-migration probably imposes fiscal costs. Thus, any regional economic development program will have a net budgetary cost, considering both the explicit budgetary cost of the program and the net fiscal effects of growth.

6. The rationale for this variation across metropolitan areas in the value of providing jobs for the unemployed is explored in much greater detail in chapter 8 and appendix 8.1.

— 8 —
Is State and Local
Economic Development Policy
a Zero-Sum Game?

When seen from a national perspective, economic development policy makers are involved in a zero sum game. When one state wins by convincing a firm to locate within its boundaries, the other 49 states lose. (Barry M. Rubin and C. Kurt Zorn, "Sensible State and Local Economic Development" in *Public Administration Review*, March/April 1985, p. 334)

It would be best if states would get together and declare an end to the rampant bidding war [for business investment, especially foreign investment]. The Massachusetts legislature has proposed a moratorium on incentives, but only a state with such low unemployment can afford to push for one. Poorer states are unlikely to sign such a pact and will continue to do everything they can, within their budget constraints, to entice more investment. There is perhaps no way to stop it without federal intervention, unless the federal government taxes the incentives given to localities, to make incentives less valuable to firms and diminish the mad scramble a little. (Page 250 in Norman Glickman and Douglas Woodward, *The New Competitors*, 1989)

Previous chapters show that economic development policies may benefit the state or metropolitan area that adopts them. But does the nation benefit?

The zero-sum game argument against economic development is that development policies only redistribute jobs among state or local areas. The number of jobs in the nation is unchanged, and the efficiency of the national economy is unaffected. The gains of the unemployed in one local area are offset by the losses of the unemployed in other local areas. Furthermore, state and local competition for jobs results in generally lower business taxes, making the national distribution of income less fair.

The easiest defense of economic development policies is that some of these policies—such as research and development subsidies and assistance to entrepreneurs—may increase the productivity of the economy. A more difficult issue is whether economic development policies aimed at increasing local job growth result in national benefits.

I will argue in this chapter that state and local competition for jobs does provide benefits for the nation, admitting at the outset that the empirical evidence for or against this argument is sparse. The argument rests more on logic than on the weight of the empirical evidence.

The zero-sum game argument against state and local competition for jobs can be addressed from several perspectives. First, even if overall national job growth is unaffected by this competition, will this competition redistribute jobs among local areas in a pattern that offers any benefits for the nation?

Second, will state and local competition for jobs affect overall national job growth?

Third, what implication does state and local competition for jobs have for the national distribution of income?

Arguments that the economic development competition for jobs might offer some national benefits have previously been made by Blair, Fichtenbaum, and Swaney (1984) and Rinehart and Laird (1972). My argument provides more specifics about the different benefits and costs of state and local competition for jobs. It is also distinctive in discussing some of the empirical evidence for and against the national benefits of state and local competition for jobs.

The Easy Argument:
Encouraging Productivity is not a Zero-Sum Game

Wealth is our capacity to produce goods and services that we value. Economic development is the process of innovation through which we increase the capacity of individuals and organizations

> to create wealth. . . . The relocation of a factory from the frostbelt
> to the sunbelt will not count as additional wealth from the national
> point of view—it is simply a zero sum game. . . . The emphasis
> in this book is upon those policies that are not zero sum games.
> (Pp. 12-13, in *The Wealth of States,* Roger Vaughan, Robert
> Pollard and Barbara Dyer, 1985)

Many of the newer, more interventionist economic development
policies—which I labeled "new wave" economic development policies
in chapter 1—have broader goals than creating jobs. New wave policies
include: encouraging more applied research projects between state
universities and businesses; encouraging existing state businesses to
modernize; providing information and training on how to be an en-
trepreneur, or on how to export products.

New wave policies have diverse goals, but many aim, in one way
or another, at increasing the productivity of the economy of some local
area. With more knowledge about technology, exporting, or sound
business practices, businesses can produce more highly valued products
with the resources they have available.[1]

New wave policies to increase business knowledge cost money, of
course. In order for social productivity to increase as a result of these
policies, the value in greater business productivity of greater business
knowledge must exceed the costs of providing the knowledge. For this
to be the case, private knowledge markets must, for some reason, have
operated imperfectly prior to the government intervention. One can think
of a number of reasons why valuable business knowledge and information might not be optimally provided by the private market. For example, firms might distrust private consultants claiming to provide valuable
information. In addition, acquiring information can be expensive, and
firms might have difficulty obtaining the financing needed. Finally, some
types of business knowledge acquisition, such as high technology
research, may have spillover benefits for other firms that are not taken
into account by firms in making their investment decision. Based on
these problems with private markets in information and knowledge, the
case that government intervention might improve matters is plausible.

New wave policies that successfully improve the productivity of a local area will also improve the productivity of the nation. State and local competition to improve productivity will impose costs on some local areas. While more productive areas will grow, less productive areas will decline. But the net result of this process is that overall productivity goes up. The nation will be able to obtain more valued goods and services at a lower cost.

This defense of state and local economic development policies is not totally satisfactory, however. First, although the case for government programs to improve business knowledge and information is plausible in theory, empirical evidence for the efficacy of these policies is lacking, as discussed in chapter 2. We need better evaluations of whether these new wave economic development policies actually achieve their goals.

Second, as mentioned in chapter 1, most state and local economic development resources today are not devoted to new wave policies, but to tax and other business subsidies intended to increase local job growth. If we want to evaluate the national benefits of state and local economic development policy, we must consider the national implications of state and local competition for jobs.

Is Redistributing Jobs a Zero-Sum Game?

I first analyze the national benefits of state and local competition for jobs under the assumption that the competition has no effect on national job growth.[2] The competition for jobs results in some redistribution of jobs across local areas. Is this redistribution likely to provide any national benefits, and if so, under what conditions?

To answer these questions, I first ask whether the benefits of additional jobs are likely to vary in different local labor markets, such as different metropolitan areas. The empirical results in this book might be interpreted as indicating that the benefits of job growth are unvarying across local areas. The results in chapter 4, for example, indicate that extra job growth has similar effects on unemployment and labor force participation in different metropolitan areas, regardless of their initial rate of job growth. The benefits of a reduction in unemployment, however, are probably much greater in high-unemployment local areas compared to low-unemployment areas. Some of the theoretical reasons behind this position are outlined in appendix 8.1; the intuition behind this theory will be presented here in the text.

The basic reason for the diverse benefits of reducing unemployment in high- versus low-unemployment areas is that the average characteristics of the unemployed will differ between areas. Suppose that at current market wages, there is excess labor supply. Individuals willing to supply labor will differ, however, in the lowest wage at which they are willing to work, which economists call the "reservation wage" of the individual. Some individuals may place a great value on getting a job, and their reservation wages are quite low. Reservation wages could be low for any of a number of reasons. Some individuals with low reservation wages may have no other source of income. Others may have strong moral beliefs about the importance of having a job.

In the same local labor market, some individuals may place a low value on getting a job: their reservation wages are high. Some of these individuals may have other sources of income, from other family members or from financial assets. Others may feel they have valuable uses of their time other than wage labor, such as taking care of their children.

In a local labor market with excess labor supply, what types of individuals are most likely to get and keep the scarce jobs that are available? The most reasonable assumption is that those individuals with the lowest reservation wages will be most likely to get the available jobs. They are likely to wait longer in line for job interviews and search more vigorously for job openings, and they are less likely to quit a job once they obtain one.[3]

Under these assumptions, consider now two local labor markets that differ only in that one has a lower demand for labor, and hence higher unemployment, than the other. Assume that the two local labor markets have a similar distribution of individuals across different reservation wages.

In the local labor market with low labor demand, only individuals with very low reservation wages will obtain jobs. The remaining unemployed will include many individuals with quite low reservation wages. An additional job in this high-unemployment local area will go to an individual whose reservation wage is relatively low, and hence the benefit of this job—the wage paid minus the reservation wage— will be large. A loss of a job in this high-unemployment area will be suffered by an individual with an extremely low reservation wage, and hence the social cost of this lost job—the lost wage minus the reservation wage—will be large.

In contrast, in the local labor market with high labor demand, many individuals with relatively high reservation wages will obtain jobs. The remaining individuals will mostly be individuals with even higher reservation wages. An additional job in this low-unemployment local area will likely go to an individual whose reservation wage is relatively high, and hence the benefits of this job will be small. A loss of a job in this low-unemployment area will likely be suffered by an employed individual with a relatively high reservation wage, and hence the social cost of this lost job will tend to be small.[4]

The net national benefits of increasing job growth in one local area and reducing job growth in other areas thus depend on the relative unemployment rate of the local area that enjoys increased job growth. If the area has a higher-than-average unemployment rate, the benefits of reducing unemployment in that local area are likely to exceed the costs that result from increasing unemployment in other areas. If the area has a lower-than-average unemployment rate, the benefits of reducing unemployment in that local area are likely to fall short of the social costs from increasing unemployment in other areas. From a national perspective, we should applaud economic development policies to increase job growth when these policies are pursued by high-unemployment local areas, and deplore economic development policies to increase jobs when they are pursued by low-unemployment areas.

Reservation Wages and Local Unemployment

We would like to have empirical evidence on whether the average reservation wages of the unemployed are lower in high-unemployment local labor markets. Unfortunately, although a number of studies have surveyed the unemployed to determine their reservation wages, the issue of whether stated reservation wages vary with local unemployment has received little attention.

Only one study has examined how reservation wages vary with the local unemployment rate. This study by Jones (1989) finds that for every 1 percent increase in the local unemployment rate, the average reservation wage of the unemployed is reduced by 1.2 percent to 1.6 percent.[5]

This estimated effect of local unemployment on reservation wages seems small, but it would result in significant differences in the net benefits of additional jobs in different local labor markets. The social benefit of an additional job is the wage paid minus the reservation wage. Suppose that the average reservation wage of the unemployed is about 90 percent of market wages; this is consistent with data presented by Jones, as well as with a number of reservation wage studies summarized by Gordon (1973).[6] Then the benefit of an additional job in the average local labor market is 10 percent of the wages paid. Consider a local area whose unemployment rate is 5 percent above average. Based on the results in Jones, reservation wages in such a local area may be as much as 8 percent lower than in the average area, or only 82 percent of average wages. The benefits of an additional job in this high-unemployment local area will be 18 percent of the wages paid, 80 percent greater than the benefits of an additional job in an average local area.

In addition, several studies show that reservation wages decrease the longer an individual is unemployed (Kasper 1969; Stephenson 1976; Fishe 1982; Kiefer and Neumann 1979). Local labor markets with high unemployment would be expected to cause a longer duration of unemployment for the average individual, which would tend to decrease average reservation wages.

Which Areas Pursue Economic Development?

Economic development efforts in high-unemployment local labor markets may produce some benefits for the nation. But are high-unemployment local areas more likely than the average area to adopt and expand economic development programs?

The political rewards for expanding economic development programs in high-unemployment local areas are stronger than in the average area. Many unemployed individuals in these high-unemployment areas—and their relatives and friends—would perceive large employment benefits from attracting jobs to the area. In contrast, in low-unemployment local areas, the unemployed are fewer and perceive lower employment benefits from obtaining a job.

State and local governments may not always be responsive to all their constituents, however. Governments in low-unemployment areas may push particular development projects in order to benefit a few landowners. Governments in high-unemployment areas may reject development opportunities in order to keep wages down for existing employers. William Winter, former Governor of Mississippi, tells stories of how, in his early political career as an economic developer in rural Mississippi, he was informed that his Chamber of Commerce employers did not want him to pursue a particular industrial prospect from the North, as it would ruin the local "labor climate." Hence, whether state and local governments respond to their unemployment situation in deciding on economic development policies cannot be determined by theoretical analysis. We have to examine what governments actually do.[7]

The available evidence is scant, but it indicates that the most needy jurisdictions play the economic development game the most. Marianne Clarke (1986) of the National Governors Association surveyed state governments in 1985, asking why their particular state had expanded its economic development programs. According to Clarke, "many states identified two factors that helped make economic development a priority issue for their state government in the past five years. The first was the nature and extent of the 1981-82 recession. The second was the changing structure of the U.S. economy, resulting in plant closings and worker dislocation. . . . Twenty-seven states responded specifically that the 1981-82 recession had been the key factor resulting in change in their development policy'' (p. 11).

There also are three empirical analyses of what types of state and local governments tend to adopt more economic development programs.[8] Rubin and Rubin (1987) analyzed a 1986 survey of 178 small cities in Illinois. They found that cities with lower median income, higher poverty, or higher unemployment made greater use of a wider variety of economic development incentives. Bowman (1987b) analyzed a 1986 nationwide survey, sponsored by the National League of Cities, of 322 cities. She found that the most economically distressed cities, as measured by the official criteria used by the U.S. Department of Housing and Urban Development in the now defunct "UDAG" program, were more likely to use more economic development programs and incentives, and were more likely to use them extensively. Luger (1987) found that states with higher past unemployment tend to be more active in industrial recruitment and other economic development programs.

Despite this empirical evidence, some informed observers do not feel that state and local competition for jobs helps areas with high unemployment. For example, according to John Levy, an urban planner at Virginia Tech who has written extensively on economic development, "Whether there are net equity gains from the sum of all local economic development activity is an open question. It is unlikely that more needy places generally outcompete less needy places for new industry" (Levy 1990, p. 157).

The quotation from Levy combines two separate issues. We should distinguish between the economic development effects of having a system of quasi-independent state and local governments that provide public services, and the effects of giving state and local governments the discretion to use special economic development subsidies for particular business expansion decisions.

The overall U.S. system of quasi-independent state and local governments may harm the economic development prospects of poorer areas. This harm is more likely the more we assign responsibility for government programs that redistribute income—such as welfare and social service programs—to lower levels of government. Governments in poorer local areas may then find themselves burdened with heavy redistribution responsibilities. As a result, governments in poorer local areas may be forced to have higher business taxes and lower public services than other areas.

Giving state and local governments the discretion to adopt flexible economic development programs, however, may help poorer areas. With this discretion, state and local governments can target economic development subsidies on the business expansion decisions that offer the greatest employment benefits and for which the subsidies are most likely to affect the decision. With high overall tax rates, state and local governments in poorer areas are most likely to need this flexibility. Furthermore, they are most likely to use this flexibility, due to political pressure from their unemployed and underemployed.

The problems caused by inadequate federal support for redistributional programs should not be confused with the issue of whether state and local competition for jobs helps poorer areas. Most public finance economists, whether conservative or liberal, would agree that income redistribution programs should be a federal responsibility. If the federal government fails to assume this responsibility, as is true at the present time, economic development problems and other problems for poor areas result. Allowing discretionary economic development programs may actually help poorer areas, however, and alleviate some of the problems from inadequate federal support for redistributional programs.

Does State and Local Competition
Increase National Growth?

The argument that merely redistributing jobs among states and local areas—with national job growth fixed—yields national benefits is subtle. State and local competition for jobs would certainly have more obvious national benefits, from the perspective of politicians and the public, if the competition increased national growth. Does it do so?

At the outset, some misconceptions about branch plants, small business, and national job growth should be clarified. Whether economic development programs target branch plant attraction or small business start-ups does not necessarily have much to do with whether the programs increase national job growth. It may seem obvious that a branch plant has to locate in one area or another, while small business start-ups or expansions represent new jobs. But encouraging some small businesses to start-up or expand must mean less sales for some other business. Overall national job growth may be unaffected. Furthermore, competition for branch plants may improve the national business climate enough that corporations decide to increase the total number of new branch plants.

Whether national growth is affected by state and local competition for jobs depends on what national pattern of subsidies and taxes results from this competition, and how markets respond to the pattern of subsidies and taxes. One effect of this competition is higher subsidies for business throughout the nation. Economic development subsidies may appear to be for new capital investment, as the most important economic development subsidy is property tax abatement. Subsidies are typically not automatic, however, but are under the discretionary control of state and local governments, who are interested in using this discretion to award subsidies to the businesses that create the most new jobs. Hence, economic development subsidies for business are probably best viewed as subsidies for increased business labor demand.[9]

To analyze the national effects of state and local competition in providing these labor demand subsidies, it is simplest to consider the effects of a uniform national subsidy for business labor demand. Such a nationwide subsidy will increase national employment if the nation suffers from chronic involuntary unemployment. A high level of national involuntary unemployment could persist in the long run, even at business cycle peaks, if wages for some reason fail to adjust downward enough to allow labor demand to equal labor supply. The best recent theory of why wages will tend to be "too high"—that is, too high to allow labor markets to clear—is efficiency wage theory. This theory assumes that higher wages increase labor productivity, because better-paid workers will feel more fairly treated and will be more motivated to want to keep their job. As a result, businesses will maximize profits by increasing wages above the market-clearing wage level, even though there would be plenty of unemployed workers available at lower wages.

With above market-clearing wages, national labor demand is less than national labor supply, resulting in chronic involuntary unemployment. In any market, the actual amount traded can never be greater than the lesser of market demand or market supply. In the case of above market-clearing wages, national employment will be constrained to be equal to national labor demand, while the supply of labor will not be a constraint. Hence, economic development subsidies for increased business labor demand will relax this constraint, and allow national employment to expand. The employment subsidies make it profitable for businesses to increase employment even if efficiency wage considerations prevent wages from adjusting downward. Furthermore, as employment increases, aggregate national income and product demand will expand sufficiently to buy the products produced by these additional workers.

Of course, these economic development subsidies must be paid for by some sector of the economy. But if the financing of economic development programs is properly designed, it need not impede the employment expansion resulting from the subsidies. For example, if households pay for the economic development subsidies, this may result in some adverse effects on labor supply. But in a labor market with chronic involuntary unemployment, labor supply is not a constraint on the level of employment, and these reductions in labor supply will not reduce employment.

In the real world competition for jobs, as mentioned above, economic development subsidies for increased labor demand will not be uniform nationally, but will tend to be higher in areas with higher unemployment. This geographic variation only strengthens the argument for positive effects of the competition on national job growth. Higher labor demand subsidies in high-unemployment areas encourage the expansion of employment, because in high-unemployment areas labor demand is the key constraint on employment and product demand. The increased jobs in high-unemployment areas result in enough added product demand that national employment can increase. On the other hand, areas with full employment will not offer extensive economic development subsidies for labor demand. Subsidies in such areas would not increase national employment much, as local labor demand in these areas is not the key constraint on employment; any incentive effects of subsidies on increasing local labor demand would tend to be offset by the reduced labor supply caused by the financing of the subsidies, and the market wage will adjust so that local employment is not much changed.

The concentration of economic development subsidies in high-unemployment areas may also tend to increase national employment by reducing inflationary pressures associated with a given rate of average national unemployment.[10] Economists have usually assumed that the effect of a 1 percent change in unemployment on the inflation rate will depend on the level of the unemployment rate. At high-unemployment rates, small decreases in unemployment will only modestly increase inflation, and small increases in unemployment will only modestly decrease inflation; as unemployment gets lower and lower, the same size small decrease in unemployment will cause larger and larger increases in inflation.

Hence, encouraging national job growth in high-unemployment areas will tend to result in less inflationary pressures than encouraging uniform national job growth in all local areas, including low-unemployment areas. This allows the nation to sustain higher employment levels and lower unemployment rates without igniting an inflationary spiral.

All the above arguments for job competition's beneficial effects on national employment are theoretical. There is little empirical evidence available to support—or refute—these theoretical arguments. My point here is not to prove that economic development competition will increase national employment, but to simply suggest that an increase in national employment is quite plausible. The usual assumption that the competition only reshuffles jobs among local areas is not clearly supported by logic or empirical data.

Does State and Local Competition
Affect the National Income Distribution?

Despite the potential national benefits of state and local competition for jobs, a plausible argument could be made that this competition has regressive effects on the national income distribution: the rich gain and the poor lose. State and local competition for jobs probably reduces net taxes on business and increases household taxes. The beneficiaries would appear to be business owners, who disproportionately come from upper-income groups. The losers would appear to be lower- and middle-income groups; this appears particularly likely because state and local household taxes, such as income taxes, sales taxes, and property taxes, are often believed to be distributed in a mildly regressive fashion, and increases in state and local household taxes would be assumed to have a regressive effect on the income distribution.

Some progressive effects of the state and local job competition may help offset the regressive effects.[11] State and local job competition will help reduce unemployment, particularly in high-unemployment areas. The unemployed who get jobs will tend to come from families with lower incomes than the national average for all families. The unemployed in high-unemployment areas will tend to have lower reservation wages. Individuals with lower reservation wages, other things equal, are more likely to come from lower-income families. As shown in chapter 7, blacks and less-educated individuals, who tend to have lower incomes than average, will gain the most in occupational upgrading and real earnings from economic development.

Even if the net national distributional effects of state and local job competition are regressive, national policymakers should try to offset the effects rather than try to eliminate competition. I argue above that state and local job competition has beneficial effects on national economic efficiency. Any undesirable regressive effects can be offset by making the federal tax system more progressive. The desirable increase in efficiency from state and local job competition can be achieved without increasing the regressivity of the national income distribution, if appropriate federal tax policy adjustments are made.

If increasing the progressivity of the federal tax system is politically infeasible, the best national policy concerning state and local job competition is a more difficult issue. But if political feasibility is a key issue, one could also question whether national restrictions on state and local economic development policies are feasible. It might be politically easier to increase the progressivity of the federal tax system than to prevent state and local governments from promoting their economic growth.

Conclusion

Can the nation benefit from state and local economic development policies? My answer is a tentative yes. State and local economic development competition may increase productivity, redistribute jobs towards the high-unemployment areas that need jobs the most, and increase national employment by using previously unemployed labor. Some empirical evidence supports these propositions, although the evidence is sparse.

A key empirical issue is whether this competition actually encourages economic growth in areas with high unemployment. Current empirical evidence is consistent with the belief that it does. If new empirical evidence showed that the economic development competition failed to help high-unemployment areas, the case for federal intervention would be stronger. Federal support for greater economic development of high-unemployment areas—and, if politically feasible, federal efforts to discourage employment growth in low-unemployment areas—would become a much more desirable and important policy to achieve economic efficiency.

NOTES

1. Some new wave programs, as outlined in chapter 1, provide capital as well as knowledge to firms. This may also increase productivity if business projects offering good returns are discriminated against for some reason by our existing capital market structure. However, the argument that knowledge and information markets are imperfect and can be improved upon by policy seems stronger than the argument that government policy can correct for capital market failures. Bartik (1990) discusses these issues in more detail.

2. The argument here and in following sections of this chapter focuses on state and local competition for jobs in order to achieve employment benefits. Many of the same arguments could also be made about state and local competition for jobs in order to achieve fiscal benefits. This competition will tend to reallocate jobs towards local areas where the fiscal benefits are greatest, just as competition for employment benefits reallocates jobs towards areas where the employment benefits are greatest. National job growth may go up as a result of lower average fiscal burdens on business, and as a result of reallocation of business activity towards areas where public service costs and environmental costs of additional business activity are lower. Finally, any undesirable national distributional implications of this competition for fiscal benefits can be offset by changes in federal tax policy. These arguments about competition for fiscal benefits are not presented in the text for two reasons: this book mainly focuses on employment benefits of state and local economic development policies; and the arguments are so closely parallel that discussing both types of competition appears superfluous.

3. My assumption here differs from what has sometimes been assumed by other authors. Gramlich (1981), for example, in his book on benefit-cost analysis, assumes that scarce jobs will be rationed randomly among all individuals willing to work at any wage at or below the market wage. I believe it more plausible to assume that one's eagerness to work—as measured by the reservation wage—has at least some correlation with one's probability of finding and keeping a job.

4. Of course, there is considerable randomness in the short run in who gains and loses jobs due to economic change. I would not expect the labor market to always allocate more jobs to those unemployed individuals with the lowest reservation wages, and allocate layoffs to those employed individuals with the highest reservation wages. But over time, as individuals quit and are fired, and search for available job openings, there will be some tendency to reallocate jobs towards individuals with lower reservation wages.

5. A study by Kiefer and Neumann (1979) claims that reservation wages tend to increase as the local unemployment rate increases. However, this study does not directly examine how reservation wages vary with local unemployment. Rather, Kiefer and Neumann use actual accepted wages to infer how reservation wages vary with local unemployment, based on a complex model of worker search behavior. Their conclusion may be sensitive to their maintained model.

6. Gordon (1973), in his table 1 on p. 148, summarizes six studies of average reservation wages. These reservation wages vary from 71.8 percent to 97.9 percent of the previous wage of the individual. The simple average percentage ratio of reservation wages to previous wages, considering all six studies, is 85.6 percent. Jones (1989) reports that reservation wages averaged 10 percent below previous wages. I should also note that the social benefit of an additional job should be adjusted upwards to reflect unemployment insurance, welfare, or other financial transfers that tend to increase the reservation wage, but cost the government money. These reduced government transfers could either be considered to increase the social benefits of reducing unemployment, or could be considered a fiscal benefit of additional jobs.

7. The text does not discuss the Tiebout literature (Tiebout 1956) on intergovernmental competition. Some recent articles in this literature have discussed government competition to attract business (Oates and Schwab 1988a, 1988b; Wildasin 1989, 1986; McLure 1986; Wilson 1985, 1986; Kenyon 1988). Most of this literature focuses on problems of government competition for business when governments are constrained in the types of taxes they can use. For example, if governments have to use uniform property taxes, and this results in business property taxes exceeding the costs of supplying business with public services, then government competition for business will lead to property taxes and public services that are too low and environmental regulations on business that are too lax. Local governments reduce taxes and regulations in order to obtain the fiscal benefits from more business activity; but benefits gained by one local government are lost to others, so they are not true social benefits, and should not play a role in optimal government decisions. However, I would argue that in the current competition for business, state and local governments have so many different tax abatement and subsidy programs available that they can, if they wish, fine-tune their incentives to each particular firm. There are no effective constraints on state and local government tax and subsidy policy towards individual businesses. If they wish, state and local governments can set taxes and economic development subsidies for each business expansion decision so as to exactly equal the net perceived additional benefits for the local area that result from that expansion, including the employment benefits, as well as the public service and environmental costs it might cause. If all state and local governments follow this "optimal subsidy" policy, then a local area competing for business imposes no net external costs on other areas. Attracting jobs to one area does reduce employment benefits in others, but it also reduces subsidy costs in those other areas. In an "optimal subsidy" world, these employment benefits and subsidy costs will be equal. The more important issue is whether state and local governments will, in practice, consider the employment benefits of business expansion in deciding on economic development policy. It is this issue that is addressed in the text.

8. Two other studies (Grady 1987; Reese 1991) fail to find a positive relationship between jurisdiction need and jurisdiction involvement in economic development. Unfortunately, methodological problems with the studies prevent them from revealing whether a more needy jurisdiction adopts more aggressive economic development programs than less needy jurisdictions. Grady's study examined the average correlation, for the five time periods from 1974-75 to 1978-79, between two measures of changes in state economic conditions (the percent change in manufacturing employment; the percent change in the state's relative unemployment rate) and the percentage change in the state's use of economic development incentives. He found no evidence that a change to more distressed economic conditions was positively correlated with increases in economic development incentives.

Unfortunately, at least from the perspective of this chapter, Grady's analysis does not control for national time trends in incentives. For the purposes of this chapter, what we want to know is whether states that are more distressed than the average tend to adopt more economic development incentives than the average. We want to abstract from general national trends in economic development incentives and focus on the geographic distribution of those incentives. During the 1974 to 1979 time period, there was a general national trend towards more use of incentives, while the national economy was improving. These national trends will tend to cause a negative correlation between economic distress and incentives, obscuring the possible positive correlation between geographic variations in economic distress and geographic variations in incentives. An analysis better suited to the purposes of this chapter would regress the change in economic development incentives for each state on the change in economic conditions in the state, with national time period effects included as control variables.

Reese's study uses a regression model to explain the variations across Michigan cities in the dollar volume of property tax abatements granted from 1974 to 1983. She finds that holding other variables constant, higher median income cities granted a greater total dollar volume of abatements. Unfortunately, among her control variables are "dollars of new development" and "percent of new development abated," which appear, not surprisingly, to explain much of the variation in total dollars of abatements; after all the natural logarithm of tax abatements granted for new development (a large portion of total tax abatements) will exactly equal, by definition, the sum of the logarithm of dollars of new development and the logarithm of abated new development as a percent of total new development. It is difficult to know how to interpret a positive effect of median income on total abatements holding the percent of new development abated constant. The percent of new development given abatements is one of the key policy variables a more needy jurisdiction might directly use to promote economic development. Total dollars abated is only indirectly a policy variable. Perhaps higher income cities tend to have more rehabilitation and expansion of existing facilities, and have more opportunity to grant abatements.

9. In some cases, state and local governments appear to be interested in creating "good jobs" through economic development subsidies. "Good jobs" appear in some cases to be jobs that pay well relative to the skills required, such as auto industry jobs, and in other cases appear to be any type of high-paying jobs in nonpolluting industries, such as high technology jobs. There may well be national benefits to these state and local "industrial policies" that target particular types of industrial growth. As discussed in Bartik (1990), encouraging jobs with high "efficiency wage premia"—high pay relative to the skills required—may offer efficiency benefits for the national economy. High technology jobs may offer research externality benefits for the national economy. I focus in the text on the national benefits of general subsidies for job creation because the majority of state and local governments today do not focus much attention on particular industries in their pursuit of economic development.

10. The potential for improving the inflation/unemployment tradeoff through microeconomic labor demand policies has previously been discussed in papers by Baily and Tobin (1977, 1978) and Nichols (1982). These papers focus on the potential gains from reallocating employment towards

204 Is State and Local Economic Development Policy a Zero-Sum Game?

low-wage occupations or industries. But many of their arguments would also apply to reallocating employment towards high-unemployment local areas.

11. The text considers possible offsets in a world where labor markets do not clear, and hence the real wage rate does not necessarily change due to an expansion of employment caused by heightened labor demand. In a full employment world, business subsidies for labor demand may increase profit rates, which may encourage additional savings and investment. This additional savings and investment may increase labor demand, thus increasing real wages. Some of the initial benefits to business of the subsidies are shifted to workers.

— 9 —
Conclusion
People and Places

Summary of Major Findings

This book's findings fall into four major areas: the effects of state and local policies on growth; the labor market and land market effects of local growth; the distributional effects of local growth; and the national implications of economic development competition among state and local governments.

State and Local Policies Affect Local Growth

The review of previous research suggests that state and local policies can have significant effects on local growth. A state and local business tax reduction of 10 percent, without reducing public services to business, probably increases business activity in a state or metropolitan area in the long run by 2.5 percent. Improved state and local public services to business can increase growth. Some evidence suggests that increasing state and local taxes to finance improved business services will have a net positive effect on local economic growth.

Local Growth Has Long-Run Labor Market Effects

The book's empirical estimates show that faster local growth not only raises housing prices, but also has significant long-run favorable effects on labor markets. An increase of 1 percent in local employment reduces the long-run local unemployment rate by around .1 percent, raises the long-run local labor force participation rate by .1 percent, and allows individuals to get and keep promotions to occupations with .2 percent greater wages per hour. Average annual real earnings increase in the long run by around .4 percent.

205

The theoretical explanation for these effects is provided by hysteresis theories of local labor markets, which suggest that better short-run performance of a local labor market helps improve its long-run performance. A positive job growth shock allows current area residents to acquire valuable employment experience. This experience enhances their long-run labor market success.

Faster Local Growth Helps Blacks and Less-Educated Individuals

The empirical estimates indicate that faster local growth has stronger effects on the annual real earnings of blacks (20 percent greater effect than the average) and on less-educated individuals (15 percent greater effect for someone with three less years of schooling). Growth effects do not vary much with the age of the individual. Somewhat surprisingly, the greater effects of local growth on blacks and less-educated individuals are mostly due to greater effects on their occupational advancement, not greater effects on their unemployment or labor force participation.

The greater effects on blacks and less-educated individuals are large enough that local economic development policies probably have progressive effects on the distribution of nontransfer income. However, state and local economic development policies can hurt lower-income groups if the cost per job created is too high, or if they are financed in a highly regressive manner.

State and Local Economic Development Policy Is Not a Zero-Sum Game

The competition for economic development among state and local governments probably enhances the efficiency of the U.S. economy. Because the most aggressive policies will be pursued by depressed areas that need growth the most, the economic development competition geographically redistributes economic activity towards depressed areas, which is economically efficient. Furthermore, widespread economic development subsidies may encourage an expansion of national employment, leading to a lower average national unemployment rate. Finally, many state and local economic development policies have the potential for enhancing the productivity and innovativeness of private business.

The economic development competition may redistribute national income towards wealthy business owners. This undesirable distributional effect should be offset by making the federal tax system more progressive.

Implications for Public Policy

This book's findings have three broader implications for policy: state and local economic development policy can work; labor demand policies matter; and the fate of particular places deserves attention from national policymakers.

Two Cheers for State and Local
Economic Development Policy

This book provides empirical evidence that state and local economic development policies can achieve their goal of significantly helping local workers and the local unemployed. State and local policies can have large effects on local growth, and local growth has important long-run effects on individuals' job prospects.

These important empirical findings do not justify an unqualified endorsement of all state and local economic development programs. While economic development policies have significant effects on local growth, and local growth has significant effects on local labor markets, these effects are not so large that labor market benefits will always exceed the costs of the programs. The likely benefits and costs of economic development policy in a typical local area are closely balanced. Net benefits are most likely to be positive for high-unemployment local areas, where the benefits of more jobs are the greatest. For average unemployment areas, the desirability of aggressively pursuing economic development is likely to depend on designing programs with a low cost per job created.

New wave economic development programs, which encourage technology innovation, entrepreneurship, and modernization, offer the promise of creating local economic growth at a relatively low cost. Unfortunately, while there is substantial evidence on the local growth effects of state and local taxes, and significant evidence on the local growth effects of state and local public services, we have little reliable evidence on whether these newer economic development programs work. The logic underlying new wave programs makes sense, but the lack of empirical evidence on their efficacy suggests that policymakers should proceed with caution.

Labor Demand Matters

While the book examines the effects of shifts in local labor demand, these results have implications for the probable effects of national labor demand shifts. Shifts in national labor demand probably have greater effects on individual's labor market success than shifts in local labor demand. National labor demand shifts would not be offset as much by in-migration supply responses.

One policy implication is that short-run macroeconomic policies to control inflation by increasing unemployment may have more negative long-run effects on the labor market than is commonly understood. Restrictive macro policy, by increasing unemployment in the short run, may increase the long-run unemployment rate and reduce long-run real earnings. These adverse effects may be particularly severe for blacks and less-educated individuals.

Another implication is that policymakers should give renewed attention to dealing with structural unemployment through labor demand as well as labor supply policies. In the 1980s, policymakers stressed job training and education as the way to deal with the employment problems of the poor. We might want to give renewed consideration to wage subsidies, public service employment, and other policies that attempt to increase the demand for the labor of the poor.

Places and National Policy

The most important finding of this book is that what happens to the economy of a metropolitan area has significant effects on individuals' economic futures. The fate of a particular place matters because it affects the fate of people. Places, therefore, should play a role in national policy. National policymakers should at least consider how policies adopted for other purposes affect the economic development of particular states, metropolitan areas, rural labor market areas, or other "places" that have some separate labor market identity. An ideal national policy would also consider how to best revive the economy of particular places suffering from persistent poverty and unemployment.

Place-oriented policies are controversial. One concern is that place-oriented policies will constrain geographic mobility, which in turn will constrain upward social and economic mobility. James Fallows, national correspondent for *Atlantic* magazine, and former chief speechwriter for President Carter, argues that "American society works best when people are in flux" (Fallows 1989, p. 111). Part of this flux, in Fallows' view, is geographic mobility, and his book describes several cases in which individuals' geographic mobility led to economic success.

Helping economically distressed places is argued to discourage the needed geographic out-migration from these places. For example, the President's Commission for a National Agenda for the Eighties (1980) argued that "urban programs aimed solely at ameliorating poverty where it occurs may not help either the locality or the individual if the net result is to shackle distressed people to distressed places" (P. 56). More recently, a *Business Week* article highlighted the views of Alice Rivlin, former director of the Congressional Budget Office: "Brookings Institution economist Alice Rivlin questions the usefulness of both liberal 'improve the ghetto' efforts and the conservative enterprise zone idea. Instead, Rivlin argues, 'we ought to come to a positive policy about moving poor people out of cities, where everything's so bad' " (September 25, 1989, p. 152).

Another concern is that focusing on places is divisive and leads to poor national policy. The U.S. is a diverse country. Policies focusing on one distressed area, or even distressed areas in general, arouse enormous political opposition. As a result, place-oriented federal policies have often been distorted to spread some money to every Congressional district, or to the areas represented by powerful senators and congressmen. Quoting the President's Commission for a National Agenda for the Eighties again, "Federal policies that marry a place orientation with a formula allocative mechanism almost dictate that funds will be diluted to the disadvantage of the most distressed people and the most distressed places. Funds end up being available to people and places that have relatively less need. The moral authority undergirding national goals can often become eclipsed by more localized agendas" (p. 76).[1]

These criticisms do not, in my view, fatally undermine the case for national policymakers paying some attention to the fate of particular places. The political infeasibility of place-oriented policies is often exaggerated. Historically, federal programs that target geographic aid to particular places, while politically required to spread their largesse around to some extent, still have retained some targeting on distressed areas. Furthermore, there are federal policies that could usefully help distressed places while avoiding an explicit geographic redistribution of economic activity. For example, funding better evaluations of economic development programs need not be geographically divisive. Providing wage subsidies to firms hiring unemployed individuals will tend to help distressed areas, because that is where the unemployed live, yet this policy does not involve explicitly promoting one area over another.

In addition, there is no necessary contradiction between the argument for helping distressed places and the argument that geographic mobility has great benefits. Promoting economic development in distressed places can help the resident unemployed. Eliminating barriers to geographic mobility, such as housing market discrimination, can also help the poor and the unemployed.

Economic development policies and mobility policies can even be seen as complementary. Assisting individuals in moving may be of greatest benefit to those individuals who are younger and relatively well-educated. Providing jobs in distressed areas will help less-educated, older individuals. We should not elevate the virtues of geographic mobility so much that we forget the needs of those who have strong and valuable ties to their homes.

Ultimately, places are important because they are important to individuals. Most individuals are attached by both financial and psychological moving costs to their home areas. As Adam Smith put the matter over 200 years ago, "a man is of all sorts of luggage the most difficult to be transported."[2] As this book has argued, because of the ties of people to places, policies to improve local economies can have long-lasting effects upon individual well-being.

NOTES

1. This quotation from page 76 of the Commission report is taken from Roger Bolton's paper, "Place Prosperity vs. People Prosperity Revisited," presented at the November 1989 meetings of the Regional Science Association (Bolton 1989b).
2. *Wealth of Nations,* Book I, chapter 8.

Appendix 2.1
The Elasticity of State or Local Business Activity With Respect to Local Cost Variables Should Be Roughly Proportional to the Variable's Share in Costs

I assume initially that the percentage change in an area's business output due to some profit change will be a multiple of the percentage change in average profits in the area.

It is then straightforward to show that the percentage change in output due to a percentage change in some area cost variable (the elasticity of business output with respect to the cost variable) will be proportional to the variable's share in business costs. Suppose that net profits (including both pure economic profits and normal profits) for a representative firm at a location can be written as:

(1) Profits $= R - \mathbf{P}'\mathbf{X} - T(\mathbf{X})$,

where R is revenues (R equals price of output, which I assume is fixed nationally, times output), $\mathbf{P}$ is a vector of input prices, $\mathbf{X}$ is a vector of inputs, and T is total state and local taxes, which may depend on the firm's input usage. Then the elasticity of profits with respect to price variable P_i and taxes T will be given[1] by the following equations:

(2) $d\ln(\text{Profits})/d\ln P_i = P_i \bullet X_i /(\text{Profits}) = (P_i \bullet X_i /C)(\text{Pure Profits/Profits})(C/\text{Pure Profits})$;

(3) $d\ln(\text{Profits})/d\ln T = T/\text{Profits} = (T/C)(\text{Pure Profits/Profits})(C/\text{Pure Profits})$.

C is the total cost of all inputs; X_i is the ith input. The ratio of costs to pure profits is constant as input prices vary for all homogeneous production functions (Lau 1978). The Pure Profits/Profits ratio is approximately a constant for small changes in prices and taxes, and will be exactly a constant for a Cobb-Douglas production function. Thus, the elasticity of profits with respect to local prices or taxes will be approximately proportional to the cost share of the particular input or tax. Hence, if the elasticity of local business output with respect to profits is assumed to be a constant, the elasticity of local business output with respect to some local cost variable will be approximately proportional to that variable's cost share.

Let us consider the initial assumption that the elasticity of local business output with respect to local profits is a constant. This assumption holds if all local output came from identical competitive firms. For a given homogeneous production function, the ratio of revenue to pure profits is a constant. If capital's share is roughly constant, then the ratio of revenue to total profits (pure profits

213

plus normal profits) will also be a constant. With a fixed national price of output, the elasticity of the representative firm's output with respect to its profits will be a constant.

A constant long-run elasticity of local output with respect to expected local profits may also hold if all local growth occurs as a result of discrete investment decisions.[2] Firm death rates and contraction rates are roughly the same in all areas. Most differences in area growth rates are due to differences in branch plant openings, small business start-ups, and plant expansion decisions. In that case, business activity in an area at time t will be equal to:

(4) $A_t = A_{t-1} + G_t - dA_{t-1}$,

where A is business activity, G is some multiple of the number of discrete investment/location decisions made in favor of this location, and d is some multiple of the death rate for firms. If d is a constant, then the long-run equilibrium business activity level will be

(5) $A^* = G/d$.

Hence, the elasticity of long-run business activity with respect to area profits will equal the long-run elasticity of new investment decisions in favor of this location with respect to area profits. Several papers (Bartik 1985, 1989a) have shown that the elasticity of the number of start-ups with respect to average profits will be a constant if the disturbance term (equal to unobserved factors that affect profits) enters in a log-linear fashion into the profit equation and follows a Weibull distribution. The disturbance term is quite likely to be a log-linear addition to the log profit equation if the disturbance is composed of unobserved area prices or other characteristics that affect profits.[3]

Even if these assumptions do not hold, we could assume that any regression is implicitly estimating the average relationship that holds in the sample between long-run local business output and average profits in the area. The elasticity of local output with respect to some local cost variable will then still equal some sample-specific constant times the cost share of that variable.

Finally, suppose we are concerned with the effects of local taxes or other costs on local employment—or some other type of factor demand—rather than local output. The elasticity of local employment with respect to a local cost variable will be the sum of the elasticity of the employment/output ratio with respect to that cost variable plus the elasticity of local output with respect to that cost variable, or

(6) $d\ln E/d\ln P_i = d\ln(E/Y)/d\ln P_i + d\ln Y/d\ln P_i$,

where Y is output and E is employment. Even if the second term is approximately proportional to the input variable's cost share, the first term will depend on the substitution possibilities provided by the production function.

However, if the output elasticity with respect to profits is large enough, then differences in substitution will not make much of a difference. Consider, the example of a Cobb-Douglas production function with two factors of production, capital and labor. The Cobb-Douglas production function allows for more substitution possibilities than is probably true for most real world production functions, so we are considering an extreme case.

Chapter 2 indicates that the elasticity of state or local business activity with respect to state and local taxes is probably −.25 or even more negative. A consistent elasticity of business activity with respect to wages would be about 14 times as great (because labor's cost share is about 14 times the cost share of state and local taxes), or about −3.50. For a Cobb-Douglas production function, the elasticity of the labor-output ratio with respect to wages will be equal to minus the capital share of output (probably around −.34).[4] Hence, the elasticity of employment with respect to wages would be only slightly greater in absolute value than the elasticity of business activity with respect to wages, about −3.84 (= −3.50 −.34). The general lesson is that despite substitution possibilities, it is quite plausible that the elasticity of any business factor usage in an area with respect to any local cost variable will be approximately proportional to the variable's share in costs.

Of course, if local business output is less responsive to taxes and other costs than is assumed above, substitution effects would loom larger. But we could also assume less substitution possibilities in the production function, and substitution effects would be less important.

NOTES

1. These elasticity derivatives follow by applying the envelope theorem when taking the derivative of maximum profits with respect to a factor price or tax.
2. To accentuate the rigidity of this alternative model, I assume that output is not chosen. For simplicity, I assume all establishments are the same size.
3. For example, if we assume a Cobb-Douglas production function, but assume that some unobserved price varies randomly across areas and firms, then the logarithm of this unobserved price variable would be a linear addition to a log-linear profit function. It is more difficult to determine whether the Weibull distributional assumption is reasonable.
4. These numbers are derived from Commerce Department figures on Gross State Product for 1986. Specifically, .66 equals total compensation divided by total national Gross State Product less proprietors' income.

Appendix 2.2
Studies of Effects of State and Local Taxes on Business Activity

Study	Business Activity Measure	Tax Measure	Fixed Effect Controls	Public Service Controls	Significant Tax Effects	Long-Run Tax Elasticity
		INTERMETROPOLITAN OR INTERSTATE STUDIES				
Coughlin, Terza & Arromdee (1991)	No. of manufacturing direct investments, by state, 1981-83	State and local taxes per capita	Existing activity	Some specifications	No	In 2 specifications tried, elasticity varied as follows: -.27; -.16 (Avg. is -.21)
Eberts (1991)	No. of new plant openings by MSA & industry, 1976-78	"Taxes"	Existing activity	Yes	Yes	.18 for all firms, .34 for small firms, -.20 for large firms
Mullen & Williams (1991)	Average growth rate of Gross State Product, 1969-86	Average state and local tax rates as percentage of GSP; Marginal tax rate calculated by examining how taxes vary with GSP	No	Yes	Yes	-.14
Beeson & Montgomery (1990)	MSA employment growth, 1980-88	Effective business tax rate, sales and income tax rate	No	Yes	Yes	?

Study	Dependent variable / data	Tax variable	Control 1	Control 2	Control 3	Result
Crihfield (1990)	Percentage change in MSA output, 1963-77 by manufacturing industry	State and MSA taxes per $ of income, property tax rate	Yes	Yes	Yes	-.88
Luce (1990a)	Shift effect in employment for individual manufacturing industries for 38 MSAs, 1972-77, 1977-82	ACIR tax effort index	Lagged activity	Yes	Yes	-.15
McConnell & Schwab (1990)	New auto branch plants in county, 1973-82	Wheaton effective business tax rate for state, property tax rate for county	Existing activity, regional dummies	Yes	Yes	-1.4
Mehay & Solnick (1990)	State employment, pooled time series cross-section data from 1976 to 1985	State and local taxes and fees per $1000 of personal income	?	Yes	See notes	See notes
Mofidi & Stone (1990)	Change in manufacturing employment & investment, 1967-72, 1972-77, 1977-82, by state, pooled time series cross-section	Taxes as percentage of personal income	Yes	Yes	Yes	See notes
Munnell (1990)	State employment growth rate, 1970-88	State and local taxes as a percent of personal income	No	Yes	Yes	-.66

Appendix 2.2 (continued)

Study	Business Activity Measure	Tax Measure	Fixed Effect Controls	Public Service Controls	Significant Tax Effects	Long-Run Tax Elasticity
O'hUallacháin & Satterthwaite (1990)	MSA 1977-84 employment growth by industry	Wheaton corporate tax variable	No	Yes	No	?
Reynolds & Maki (1990)	New autonomous and branch plant establishments per 10,000 residents 1982-84, for 382 labor market areas in U.S., by various industry classifications	Taxes per capita, 1972	No	Unclear	Unclear	Positive effect for autonomous births in manufacturing and local industries; negative effect for branch plants over all industries, dropped from other specifications
Woodward (1990)	Number of new Japanese branch plants by state, 1980-89	Effective corporate income tax rate, presence of unitary tax	Regional dummies	Only index of state industrial development programs (counted as no)	No	-.14

Bartik (1989a)	State small business start rate by industry, 1976-78, 1980-82, pooled time-series cross-section.	Effective business rates for many taxes	Yes	Yes	Yes	-.73
Bauer & Cromwell (1989)	No. of new firm births divided by existing employment, 259 MSAs, 1980-82	Effective state corporate tax rate	No	No	Yes	-.61
Carroll & Wasylenko (1989)	Percentage employment change by industry for each state, 1981-87	State and local taxes as percentage of income	No	Yes	Yes	-.39 for total employment, -1.25 for manufacturing
Crihfield (1989)	Percentage change in aggregate MSA labor demand, 1963-77, by manufacturing industries	State and MSA taxes per $ of income, effective county property tax rate	Yes	Yes	Yes	-.77
Deich (1989)	Number of small business starts and branch plant starts	Effective corporate income tax rate and property tax rate	No	Yes	Yes	.13 for small business, .02 for branch plants (Avg. = .07)
Duffy-Deno & Eberts (1989)	Per capita personal income level, 28 MSAs, each year from 1980-84, pooled cross-section time series	State & local tax revenue divided by state and local tax capacity (from ACIR)	No	Yes	Yes	-.27

Appendix 2.2 (continued)

Study	Business Activity Measure	Tax Measure	Fixed Effect Controls	Public Service Controls	Significant Tax Effects	Long-Run Tax Elasticity
Friedman, Gerlowski & Silberman (1989)	No. of foreign manufacturing branch plant openings, by state, 1977-86	Effective corporate income and property tax rates	No	No	No	Elasticities can't be calculated; not counted in avg. calculations
Papke (1989a)	State GSP in 4 industries, 1975-82, pooled cross-section time-series	Effective tax rate from AFTAX model	Yes	No	No	-.74 for apparel, -.19 for furniture and fixtures, .13 for printing and publishing, -.32 for electric and electronic equipment (weighted avg., using GSP as weights, is -.15) -.49 for communication equipment; -.13 for furniture; -.05 for apparel; .08

Study	Dependent variable	Tax variable				Results
Papke (1989b, 1986)	Number of new plant births, by state, 1975-82, by industry, pooled cross-section time series	Effective tax rate from AFTAX model	Yes	Yes	Yes	for publishing; .23 for electronic components (Avg. = -.07)
Testa (1989)	Percent change in total manufacturing and nonmanufacturing employment, 1976-85, and manufacturing output, 1976-82	Percent change in per capita state and local taxes	No ?	Yes ?	Yes	-.35 for total employment, -.93 for manufacturing, -.02 for nonmanufacturing, .04 for manufacturing output (-.35 used in average calc.)
Wasylenko (1988)	Percentage employment change by industry for each state, 1980-85	State and local taxes as % of income	No	Yes	Yes	-.13 for total employment, -.90 for mfg.
Canto & Webb (1987)	Annual percentage change in state per capita personal income, separate time-series analysis of each state, 1957-77	Percentage change in state and local tax burden per $1000 of personal income	Yes	No	Yes	Average elasticity of -.35 over all 48 states
Doeringer, Terkla & Topakian (1987)	Percentage growth in state employment, 1970-80	Nominal corporate tax rate	No	No	No	-.16

Appendix 2.2 (continued)

Study	Business Activity Measure	Tax Measure	Fixed Effect Controls	Public Service Controls	Significant Tax Effects	Long-Run Tax Elasticity
Gyourko (1987a)	Labor intensity of MSA manufacturing base, 1972 and 1977	Property taxes, payroll taxes, corporation income taxes	Regional dummies	No	Yes	Elasticity not comparable; property taxes tend to increase labor intensity of mfg.
Luce (1987)	Absolute change in # of high-tech jobs, by MSA, 1972-77, 1977-82	ACIR tax effort	Existing activity	No	No	-.82 for 1972-77, 1.18 for 1977-82 (Avg. = .18)
McGuire & Wasylenko (1987)	Percentage employment change by industry for each state, 1973-77, 1977-84	Personal taxes, sales taxes, corporate tax rate, effective property tax rate	No	Yes	No	Units unclear; generally insignificant results (Avg. assumed to be zero)
Nakosteen & Zimmer (1987)	Probability of manufacturing firm locating out of state, 1970-80	State corporate income taxes divided by state employment	See notes	Yes	No	-.76 (wrong sign & insignificant)
Papke (1987)	New capital expenditure in state per production worker, by industry, for 1978	Effective tax rate for representative firm, using AFTAX model	No	Yes	Yes	-.17

Study	Description	Tax Measure				Result
Quan & Beck (1987)	State manufacturing employment relative to the national average, annual data from 1974-83, pooled cross-section time series	Polynomial distributed lag in state and local taxes as % of personal income relative to national average	No	Yes	Yes	-.95 for Northeast states, -.20 for Sunbelt states (-.58 used as average)
Schmenner, Huber & Cook (1987)	New branch plants, and new branch plants that say they want low taxes	Nominal corporate rate, property tax % of personal income	No	Yes	Yes	-.50 for all plants; -3.09 for plants desiring low taxes
Benson & Johnson (1986)	Per capita manufacturing investment in state as share of U.S., 1966-78, pooled time-series cross-section	Total taxes as % of personal income relative to U.S.	Yes	No	Yes	-1.02
Harris (1986)	Formation rate of high technology establishments, low technology establishments, and high technology branches in various MSAs, 1976-80	Index of local taxes	Sometimes	No	Yes	.12 for high tech branch formations, -.31 for all high tech est., -.49 for non-high tech est. (Avg. est. result is -.40)

Appendix 2.2 (continued)

Study	Business Activity Measure	Tax Measure	Fixed Effect Controls	Public Service Controls	Significant Tax Effects	Long-Run Tax Elasticity
Place (1986)	Annual state employment growth, 1972-84, pooled cross-section time series	State revenue per capita	No	Yes	No	Units unclear; sign varies across specifications; usually insignificant (Avg. = 0)
Wheat (1986)	Percent growth in state manufacturing employment, 1963-77	Total corporate income taxes divided by manufacturing value-added	No	No	No	Wrong sign, magnitude unreported (Avg. = 0)
Bartik (1985)	Number of new Fortune 500 branch plants choosing the state, 1972-78	Effective corporate tax rate, property tax rate, UI tax rate, workers' compensation tax rate	Regional dummies, existing activity	Yes	Yes	-.45
Helms (1985)	State personal income, pooled cross-section time series from 1965 to 1979	Property tax, other taxes as % of personal income	Yes	Yes	Yes	-.39
	Number of new foreign plant start-ups in 3 industries (drugs,	Weighted average of				Significantly negative for drugs, significantly positive for motor vehicles

Study	Measure of economic activity	Tax measure				Results
Luger & Shetty (1985)	machinery, motor vehicles), 1979, 1981-83	Wheaton business tax measure and personal tax rate	Existing business activity	No	Yes	(not included in average calculations)
Summers and Luce (1985)	Metropolitan employment growth rate by industry, pooled over all manufacturing, 1967-77, 1977-83	MSA tax effort index from ACIR	No	No	Yes	-.10 for 1967-77, .05 for 1977-83 (Avg. = -.03)
Wasylenko & McGuire (1985)	Percent growth in total state employment, and by major industry, 1973-80	Tax effort, effective corporate and personal income taxes	Existing business activity	Yes	Yes	-.85 for total employment, -1.54 for manufacturing employment
Armington, Harris & Odle (1984)	No. of business formations per 1000 workers and employment growth in MSAs, 1976-80, for high-tech industries, other manufacturing and business services, and other industries, overall and divided into small firms and large firms	ACIR tax capacity index	No	No	Yes	Formation rate/employment growth results for high-tech: -.25/-.89; for other mfg.; -.50/-.22; for small firm high-tech: -.34/.38; for large firm high-tech:-.10/-1.05; small firm low-tech: -.52/-.26; large firm low-tech: -.40/-.16 (Avg. mfg. employment growth result = -.55)

Appendix 2.2 (continued)

Study	Business Activity Measure	Tax Measure	Fixed Effect Controls	Public Service Controls	Significant Tax Effects	Long-Run Tax Elasticity
Gyourko (1984)	New manufacturing capital investment per dollar of value added, 42 cities, 1969-78, pooled cross-section time series	Nominal state corporate tax rate, nominal local corporate tax rate, local income tax rate, effective property tax rate	Regional dummies	Yes	Marginally significant	Not calculable (not included in average calculation)
Steinnes (1984)	State employment change in manufacturing, two-year intervals from 1973-75 to 1977-79, pooled cross-section time series	Average tax bills for hypothetical firms	Yes	No	Yes	Elasticity not calculable (average assumed to equal zero.)
Yandle (1984)	Percentage change in real value added in manufacturing, by state, 1963-67, 1967-72, 1972-77	Total state and local taxes per $1000 of income	No	No	Marginally significant for 1963-67	-.03
Carlton (1983)	Probability of new branch location & plant size in various MSAs, for various industries, 1967-71	Effective property tax rate, average of corporate and personal income tax rate	No	No	No	.17 for plastics, zero for other industries (.06 used as average)

Study	Dependent variable / data	Tax variable				Result
Garofalo & Malhotra (1983)	Responsiveness of long-run optimal state manufacturing capital stock, based on estimated cost functions, pooled cross-section time series	Cost of capital term incorporates property tax rates and state corporate tax rates	No	No	Yes ?	-.02
Newman (1983)	Relative percentage growth in employment by state, for 2-digit manufacturing industries, 1957-65 and 1965-73, pooled cross-section time series	Maximum marginal corporate rate, lagged 10 years	Yes	No	Yes	-.26; more negative for more capital-intensive industries but not significantly so
Plaut & Pluta (1983)	Percent change in state manufacturing value added, employment and capital, 1967-72 and 1972-77	Business climate index, tax effort index, corporate income tax, sales tax, property tax, personal income tax	No	Yes	Yes	Units unclear (dropped from average calculations)
Bradbury, Downs & Small (1982)	MSA employment change, 1960-70, 1970-75	MSA local taxes per capita	No	?	Yes	-.13 for 1960-70, dropped from 1970-75 (-.07 used as average)
Graham (1982)	Number of small high-tech firms formed, 266 MSAs, in 1975	Taxes on hypothetical corporation	Existing # of small high-tech firms	No	No	Dropped from reported equation (assumed zero for use in average calculations)

Appendix 2.2 (continued)

Study	Business Activity Measure	Tax Measure	Fixed Effect Controls	Public Service Controls	Significant Tax Effects	Long-Run Tax Elasticity
Hodge (1981)	Gross investment rate in 4 industries, 42 MSAs, 1963-75, pooled cross-section time series	Effective property tax rate, nominal corporate tax rate	Regional dummies, existing business activity	No	Yes	-.60 for furniture, .54 for plastics and rubber, -.65 for apparel, .24 for electronics (-.15 used as average)
Kieschnick (1981 or 1983)	State share of investment, for 13 manufacturing industries, 1977	State & local taxes paid by hypothetical corporation	Existing activity	No	Yes	See notes in appendix
Vedder (1981)	State per capita income growth, 1970-79	Change in state and local taxes as % of personal income, 1967-77	?	No	Yes	Full results not reported
Browne, Mieszkowski & Styron (1980)	Net per capita investment in manufacturing, 1959-76 in state, and net per capita investment by industry, pooled cross-section time series	Personal taxes as a % of personal income	No	No	No	Report weak negative relationship but not actual coefficient (assumed avg. is 0)
	Percent change in state	State and local taxes as % of income; corporate				Units unclear

Dye (1980)	employment, income, and manufacturing value added, 1972-76	income tax rate; income tax as % of income; sales tax as % of income	No	Yes	?	(not counted in average calculations)
Carlton (1979)	Number of new single establishment plants, and number of new branch plants, in 28 to 42 MSAs, in 3 industries, 1967-71 and 1972-75, pooled cross-section time series for single establishment plants	Effective property tax rate; weighted average of corporate and personal tax rates	Existing activity	No	No	Births/branch results for plastics: -.02/-.70; for communication equipment: .33/-.82; for electronic components: .25/.13 (Avg. = -.14)
Romans & Subrahmanyam (1979)	Percent change in income, % change in employment, by state, 1964-74	ACIR measures of business tax effort, personal tax effort; average marginal personal income tax rate	Regional growth	No	Yes	.27 for income, .04 for employment (.04 used in average calculations)
INTRAMETROPOLITAN STUDIES						
Luce (1990b)	1980 employment in community	Effective property tax rate, wage tax rate	Lagged activity	Yes	Yes	-1.95
Gyourko (1987b)	No. of new manufacturing firms in Philadelphia MSA by zip code areas, 1980-83	Effective property tax rate	Lagged activity	Yes	Sometimes marginally significant	Not calculable; usually negative (not included in average calculations)

Appendix 2.2 (continued)

Study	Business Activity Measure	Tax Measure	Fixed Effect Controls	Public Service Controls	Significant Tax Effects	Long-Run Tax Elasticity
Summers and Luce (1987)	Percent change in share of MSA employment in central city, 1970-80	Relative central city to MSA tax effort	Lagged activity	Yes	Yes	Means not calculable (not included in avg. calculations)
McHone (1986)	Manufacturing employment per capita by community in Philadelphia MSA, 1970	Property taxes per employee for manufacturing	No	Yes	Yes	-.79
McGuire (1985)	Building permit value of all new firms and additions to firms, by community, in Minneapolis-St. Paul MSA, 1976-79	Effective property tax rate	No	No	Yes	-1.59
	Manufacturing	Ratio of central			Marginally sig-	Elasticity not calculable, neg. for mfg. & construction, pos. for total employment but always insignificant.

231

		city to suburban effective property tax rates	Lagged gradient included		nificant for manufacturing	(not included in average calculation)
Mills & Price (1984)	employment density gradients, 1970	city to suburban effective property tax rates	included	No	nificant for manufacturing	(not included in average calculation)
Schneider (1984)	Percent of manufacturing establishments in MSA, 1977, for 645 suburbs in 44 MSAs	Property tax rate	1972 # of establishments	Yes	Marginally	Units unclear (not included in average calculations)
Charney (1983)	Number of relocating manufacturing firms in each zip code of Detroit MSA, 1970-75	Effective property tax rate	Existing activity	Yes	Yes	-2.52
Bradbury, Downs & Small (1982)	City employment growth relative to MSA, 1960-70	City - MSA taxes per capita?	No	Yes	No	Dropped from final equation (average assumed equal to zero)
Grubb (1982)	Share of MSA manufacturing employment in central city, 1967	Relative central city to MSA average property tax rate	Lagged activity	Yes	No	Dropped from presented equation (Avg. = 0)
Church (1981)	Percent of manufacturing capital expenditures in urban area for central cities and identified suburbs 11 central cities and 89 of their suburbs, 1971	Property tax rate	No	Yes	Yes	Units unclear (not included in average calculations)

232

Appendix 2.2 (continued)

Study	Business Activity Measure	Tax Measure	Fixed Effect Controls	Public Service Controls	Significant Tax Effects	Long-Run Tax Elasticity
Fox (1981)	Amount of industrial land in suburban Cleveland communities, 1969	Effective property tax rate	No	Yes	Yes	-4.43
Erickson & Wasylenko (1980)	Proportion of manufacturing firms relocating from Milwaukee to suburbs that choose a particular suburb, 1964-74	Effective property tax rate	Lagged activity	Yes	No	.62
Wasylenko (1980)	Proportion of manufacturing firms relocating from Milwaukee to suburbs that choose a particular suburb, 1964-74	Effective property tax rate	Lagged activity	Yes	Yes	-2.70
MIXED INTRA- AND INTER-AREA STUDIES						
Palumbo, Sacks & Wasylenko (1990)	Overall city and overall suburban employment growth, analyzed separately, for 66 MSAs, 1970-80	Per capita taxes, 1977	No	Yes	Marginally	.31 for city taxes, -.72 for suburban taxes

233

Study	Description	Tax variable				Result
Inman (1987)	Philadelphia share of national jobs, annual observations, 1964-83, 1969-85, time series analysis	Philadelphia wage tax rate	No	No	Yes	-.15 in one specification, -.21 in other specification
Mills (1983)	Percent growth in central city and overall suburban employment, 115 MSAs, 1970-80	State and local taxes per capita in 1970	No	No	No	Elasticity not calculable, but some effects seem important
Church (1981)	Manufacturing capital expenditures per capita in 1967, for 11 cities and their 89 suburbs with available data	Property tax rate	No	Yes	Yes	Units unclear
Grieson (1980)	Philadelphia share of national jobs, annual observations, 1965-75, time series analysis	Distributed lag in Philadelphia wage tax rate	No	No	Yes	-.30 for all manufacturing and services, -.36 for manufacturing
INTRASTATE STUDIES						
Fox & Murray (1990)	Entry of new firms, by county, in Tennessee, each year from 1980 through 1986, pooled cross-section time series	Sales tax rate, hotel tax rate, business gross receipts tax, effective property tax rate	No	Yes	Yes	-.16

Appendix 2.2 (continued)

Study	Business Activity Measure	Tax Measure	Fixed Effect Controls	Public Service Controls	Significant Tax Effects	Long-Run Tax Elasticity
Woodward (1990)	Probability of Japanese plant choosing a county within a state, given that it chose state	Property taxes per capita	Existing activity	Only dummy for inter-state highway and median years of schooling	No	-.09 and -.15 in all-county regressions
Sander (1989)	Percentage growth in Illinois county employment, 1980-86	Property taxes and other local taxes per capita	No	Yes	Yes	-.81
Glickman & Woodward (1987)	Probability of foreign plant choosing a particular county within the state, given that it chose the state, 1979-83	Property taxes per capita relative to state average	No	No	No	-.12
White (1986)	Percent growth in manufacturing employ-ment, California counties, 1977-81	Change in effective property tax rate, 1977-81	Yes	No	No	-1.85

Howland (1985)	Number of new firms and new employment by county, within New Jersey, Maryland, Virginia, D.C., in machine tools and electronic components industry	Effective property tax rate, availability of property tax abatements	No	No	No	Not calculable from available information

GENERAL NOTES TO TABLE

A study is considered to fully control for fixed effects either by explicitly including state or MSA fixed effects, or by estimating a model in first differences. Partial controls for state or local fixed effects are provided by including regional dummies, or by including current levels of business activity in the state or local area. Tax effect significance column reports whether any of the tax variables included in the study were significant and had expected signs. Any tax variables that were insignificant or had unexpected signs are mentioned in notes to each study. The tax elasticity reports implied long-run percentage effect on total state or local business activity of a 1 percent reduction in all taxes, holding all else constant. This tax elasticity is calculated by summing over all tax variables included in the study that would be affected by a 1 percent uniform reduction in all state and local taxes. Whether tax variable is statistically significant or insignificant is ignored; tax variables that would not change with 1 percent across-the-board tax reduction are not included in calculation summation.

For studies in which the dependent variable was in the form of gross new capital investment, new branches, or new small businesses, the effect of taxes, as percent of the average value of the dependent variable in the study's sample, was used as a proxy for the long-run effect of taxes on local business activity. This assumption will be true if all gross new activity responds the same as the dependent variable being considered to taxes, and death rates are roughly constant. For example, suppose

(1) $N_t = N_{t-1} + G_t - D_t$,

where N_t is local business activity in year t, G is new activity, D is deaths of existing activity. Suppose further that deaths are a constant fraction f of existing business activity in year t-1. Then in long-run equilibrium, where N is constant over time, equation (1) after substitution and some manipulation becomes

(2) $N^* = G_t/f$,

where N^* is the equilibrium level of N. Hence, a given percentage effect of taxes on gross new activity will imply the same long-run percentage effect of taxes on total local business activity.

For studies in which the dependent variable was some measure of the net change in local business activity over some time period, I first calculated the effect of taxes as a percentage of the average level of local business activity in the sample. This percentage effect was then adjusted using information from Helms' (1985) study on how quickly state business activity adjusts to a new equilibrium. Helms indicates that state business activity adjusts annually by 8.9 percent of the difference between current state business activity and the long-run equilibrium level of state business activity. Based on this assumption, the relationship between the long-run effect and the effect after T years will be

$$(3) \quad B^* = B_T / (1 - (.9104)^T),$$

where B^* is the long-run effect, and B_T is the effect after T years. Each study's percentage effect after T years was multiplied by $1/(1-(.9104)^T)$ to get an estimated long-run effect. The actual adjustment made is described in the notes for each study.

The table only reports each study's estimates of tax effects on total business activity and manufacturing business activity. If a study reported estimates from several specifications, I used the author's preferred specification for my calculations. Where no specification was clearly preferred, I averaged estimates across all reported specifications. (Two exceptions to this rule are the studies by Helms (1985) and Mehay and Solnick (1990); see notes on these studies for details.) The elasticities used in the calculations summarized in table 2.3 are for the business activity variable that is most closely related to total business activity.

If a tax variable was excluded by the author from all reported specifications, I generally assumed its effect was zero for the calculations of the averages reported in table 2.3. The exception was cases where the author clearly stated that the tax variable had a negative effect when included. These cases were excluded from the table 2.3 calculations of average elasticities.

Most studies rely on cross-section evidence on determinants of economic growth or activity in different areas, although separate cross-section analyses may be done for different time periods. Studies restricted to one area's economic growth rely on time series evidence by default, and are identified as time series analyses under business activity measure. Studies that pool both time-series and cross-sectional variation in one estimating equation are identified in the summary of the business activity measure.

Statistical significance was judged on a 5 percent one-tail test. "Marginal" statistical significance means significance at a 10 percent level for a one-tail test.

NOTES ON SPECIFIC STUDIES

These notes on specific studies seek to explain how the long-run tax elasticity numbers for each study, reported in the last column of this appendix's tax table, are derived from the estimates actually reported by each study.

Armington, Harris and Odle (1984): I report the tax results from their tables B-15 through B-18. Employment growth elasticities are adjusted to long-run elasticities by being multiplied by $1/(1-(.9104)^4)$; see general notes above for rationalization. Results are statistically insignificant at 10 percent level for: high-tech business formations; low-tech employment growth; other industries' employment growth; small firm high-tech formations and growth; large firm high-tech formations; small and large firm low-tech employment growth. It should be noted that the technical skills variable included in all of these researchers' regressions, defined as percent of labor force, that is, scientists, professionals, or technical, may proxy for existing business activity for high tech industries.

Bartik (1985): Results used to calculate elasticity come from specification 3 in table 2 of Bartik's paper that includes 8 regional dummies. The reported elasticity considers an equal percentage increase in corporate, property, UI, and workers' compensation tax rates. The corporate tax rate coefficient is significantly negative at the 1 percent level, the property tax rate coefficient is significantly negative at the 10 percent level, the UI tax rate coefficient is negative but insignificant, and the workers' compensation rate coefficient is positive and significant.

Bartik (1989a): Study includes separate effective rates for business property taxes, corporate income taxes, personal income taxes, sales taxes, and specific tax breaks for small business. All results reported in text tables are taken from "changes" specification, except for environmental regulation results. The –.73 figure in the tax table is the sum of the elasticity for property taxes, corporate taxes, income taxes, and sales taxes in the "changes" specification. Only property taxes and corporate income taxes have significant effects. Sales tax is marginally significant.

Bauer and Cromwell (1989): Results reported in tax table are derived from column (3) of their table 2. Elasticity with respect to their tax variable is derived by using information they provide. The mean of their tax variable is .403.

Beeson and Montgomery (1990): Study does not report units in sufficient detail to determine magnitude of tax effect. Their business tax variable, adopted from Bania and Calkins (1988), appears to be similar to Wheaton's. The business tax elasticity is significantly negative, while the sales and income tax elasticity is significantly positive.

Benson and Johnson (1986): The long-run elasticity reported here is taken from their table I. It should be noted that most of the negative impact of taxes on investment in their model is a lagged effect, occurring after two or three years. Benson and Johnson also have a previous paper, using the same data set, that estimates a long-run tax effect of –.77. The models are identical except that the latter paper apparently corrects for heteroskedasticity. I do not include the former study in this official list of business location studies, as I assume that Benson and Johnson regard the latter set of estimates as better.

Bradbury, Downs and Small (1982): Mean for MSA local taxes per capita is inferred from their table 5.10. Inter-area results for 1960-70 come from their table 6.8 to be $277. Resulting elasticity is multiplied by $1/(1-(.9104))$[10] to get long-run elasticity. It is unclear whether public service controls were tested at some point in the estimating equations; if they were, they were dropped from the final equations that were presented.

Browne, Mieszkowski and Styron (1980): Authors report a weak negative relationship between tax variable and net manufacturing investment, but this variable is statistically insignificant and hence excluded from the final equation that is reported in their article.

Canto and Webb (1987): Results reported in this appendix are unweighted averages of their tax coefficients, multiplied by .1105, the mean value of their tax variable in the units they use. I treat this as long-run effect because this is essentially a time series analysis of each state. This analysis will tend to force the coefficient on the contemporaneous change in taxes to reflect long-run as well as short-run effects. The extent to which the coefficient reflects long-run vs. short-run effects is unknown. Canto and Webb only report single equation estimates. They report that using instruments led to similar results, but do not provide further details on the instruments used. Estimated tax effect is significant at the 5 percent (one-tail test) level in 35 of the 48 states, and significant at the 10 percent level in 8 of the remaining 13 states.

Carlton (1979): Results reported here rely on Carlton's footnote that tax elasticities can be derived for average observation by multiplying his reported property tax coefficient by .03, and his reported income tax coefficient by −.05. All of Carlton's tax coefficients are statistically insignificant.

Carlton (1983): Elasticity estimate for plastics is for new plant probabilities, and is equal to estimated coefficient divided by N parameter.

Charney (1983): Charney also finds that local income tax rate does not have significant effect, either statistically or substantively. But local income tax is only imposed by Detroit and three other jurisdictions in MSA.

Church (1981): I assume mean property tax rate of 2.0 in Church's sample. Church's study is cited twice in this table. His results when the dependent variable is the jurisdiction's share of total urban manufacturing capital expenditures reflect business location patterns within an MSA. His results when the dependent variable is the jurisdiction's absolute level of manufacturing capital expenditures per capita reflect business location patterns both within and across MSAs.

Coughlin, Terza and Arromdee (1991): I use the results from their 1991 REStat paper rather than results from their July 1989 working paper. The July 1989 paper does get significantly negative tax effects of somewhat higher absolute magnitude (−.26 rather than −.21). The earlier paper uses minimum chi-square conditional logit estimation, which authors appear to prefer, rather than maximum likelihood estimates of the final REStat paper.

Crihfield (1989): All elasticities reported here for Crihfield's 1989 study use his equation (1), and the coefficients on the changes variables (representing, in his model, the 1977 coefficient) rather than the initial level coefficients (representing, in his model, the changes between the 1963 and 1977 coefficients). Reported elasticities sum his tax variables, and then multiply by 1.37 (= $1/(1-(.9104)^{14})$) to get implied long-run effect from his 14-year effects. Crihfield treats wages as endogenous, and apparently uses changes in apartment rental rates, local real personal income, state income tax revenue, state direct expenditures, MSA government direct expenditures, and social security payments by MSA, as instruments. The exogeneity of these instruments is questionable.

Crihfield (1990): I use Crihfield's Model 1 to calculate elasticities. His estimated elasticities are multiplied by $1/[1-(.9104)^{14}] = 1.367$ to get long-run effects. Crihfield's wage elasticities for manufacturing value added are excluded from wage table in text, as he does not control for product price. Hence, his estimated wage elasticities combine effect on real value added with effect on output price.

Deich (1990): The elasticities can be calculated directly from Deich's table 3 and table 4, and his footnote 4. The Deich figures used in constructing all text tables are the simple average of his small business and branch plant elasticities. I use only his results for all manufacturing industries. I use Deich's results from the NTA meetings rather than results from his dissertation as the NTA meeting results are more readily accessible. His dissertation results are generally similar, even though the specifications are somewhat different.

Doeringer, Terkla and Topakian (1987): Long-run tax elasticities reported here multiply authors' reported tax elasticity in table 2.2 by $1/(1-(.9104)^{10})$.

Duffy-Deno and Eberts (1989): Reported elasticity in this appendix table is taken directly from 2SLS results reported in table 1 of their paper. I interpret this coefficient as long-run elasticity because dependent variable in their study is the personal income level of the MSA, and the tax variable does not change over time. Hence, the coefficient on their tax variable will depend on the average relationship that prevails between personal income levels and tax levels. This average relationship should approximate the long-run relationship between these two variables.

Dye (1980): Dye only reports limited set of regression results, apparently the product of many different specifications. In one reported specification, overall tax burden is apparently negative and significant, while corporate tax rate is positive and significant (table 3, value added dependent variable). But units used are not given.

Eberts (1991): Study does not describe tax data, but states that both tax variable and dependent variable (firm openings) are measured in log form, so estimated coefficients are elasticities. –.20 elasticity is for large firms headquartered outside state; elasticity for large firms headquartered inside state is –.16. The large firm elasticities are significantly negative at 5 percent level of significance, one-tail test.

Eberts and Stone (1988): The results reported in this appendix come from their table 3.7. Eberts and Stone experiment to find optimal lag-length for wage effects on employment, so I assume that their estimated sum of wage coefficients is significant. Their tax effect is based on a two-and-one-half-year lagged tax variable. I assume the long-run tax effect is $1/[1-(.9104)^{2.5}] = 4.78$ times their estimated elasticity.

Erickson and Wasylenko (1980): Data and variables are same as Wasylenko (1980), but communities are included even if zero new business activity or existing business activity. My calculated elasticity for manufacturing is based on assumption that average property tax rate in Milwaukee suburbs in 1969 was 3 percent, as stated in paper. Estimated positive effect is statistically insignificant.

Fox (1981): Fox treats the tax rate as endogenous. But the exogeneity of some of his instruments may be questioned; for example, population is used as an instrument, but it would seem that a community's population might have some effect on industrial land demand.

Fox and Murray (1990): Elasticity estimates reported in this appendix table come from their results for all industries, all firm size classes. Firms with 20 to 49 employees seem more sensitive to taxes than other firm size classes.

Friedman, Gerlowski and Silberman (1989): Paper does not report mean of dependent variable, so elasticities cannot be calculated. In overall regression, corporate and property taxes have estimated negative effect, but effect is not significant.

Garofalo and Malhotra (1983): Tax elasticities reported here are based on average results reported in their table 2 for own-price elasticity of capital for full U.S. sample. In addition, it was assumed that state and local taxes on manufacturing are 8.3 percent of business profits, based on Wheaton (1983), which implies that a 1 percent change in overall state and local taxes on businesses will change the user price of capital by .083 percent. Hence, the tax elasticity in my table equals Garofalo and Malhotra's table 2 figure of –.2865 times .083.

It should be noted that Garofalo and Malhotra's estimates rest on a very different methodology from most other studies of state and local business activity, and most of these differences will tend to reduce the effect of state and local business taxes. They estimate a pooled time-series cross-section cost function for manufacturing using annual data for states from 1974 through 1978 as the unit of observation. Cost shares for capital, labor, and energy in each state and year are used as dependent variables, and the state prices of capital, energy, and labor as independent variables. Cross-equation restrictions are imposed based on production theory. Because they do not include a time period dummy, but only a time trend variable, the estimates will to some extent reflect the effects of prices on the national capital stock, which presumably will be less than the effects of a given state's prices on its own capital stock. That is, the estimated responsiveness of state cost shares to state capital prices will depend to some extent on how states, on average, change their cost shares as national interest rates change. In addition, their cost function estimation procedure appears to assume that long-run equilibrium was achieved in all years and all states from 1974 through 1978. This assumption will lead to estimated long-run responses that actually represent short-run responses. Finally, their estimates impose cross-equation restrictions that may lower the estimated capital price effects. We know from other work that wage effects on business location are often low compared to tax effects, based on the relative cost share of labor and taxes. It is possible that relatively low wage effects may contaminate their estimated effects of capital prices.

Glickman and Woodward (1987): Interstate portion of the tax table excludes this study because their tax variable is defined as percentage of state taxes derived from corporate income tax. This variable will not increase with an across-the-board increase in state and local taxes, the thought experiment being conducted in this table. However, their empirical results do indicate a significant negative effect of this variable on domestic employment growth from 1974-83, but not on the growth of foreign-owned employment. For intrastate portion of the tax table, Glickman and Woodward results are derived from their table 23. Their coefficient, like all multinomial logit coefficients, reflects effect on log of odds. But in their case, the average probability of selection is .5, because they deliberately randomly chose a county within each state without foreign plants for each county within the state that has foreign plants. It is straightforward to show that $d\ln P/d\ln X = d\ln(P/(1-P)d\ln X)$ times $(1-P)$, where P is the probability of selection. At the mean probability of .50 in the sample,$(1-P)$ equals .50, and their coefficients must be multiplied by .50 to give percentage effects of a variable on new business locations.

Graham (1982): Graham's study investigates several independent variables that measure the presence and size of research universities in the MSA, which could be viewed as a rough measure of public service quality.

Grieson (1980): Grieson states that four-year lag works better than longer lags, so I assume that his stated elasticities in table 1 are actually long-run elasticities. I use the elasticities from column (9) of his table 1.

Grubb (1982): Grubb does find that higher relative central city expenditure, compared to the MSA as a whole, on what he calls "necessary spending" (highways, police, fire, sewerage, sanitation, and utilities) has a statistically significant negative effect on the suburbanization of manufacturing employment. Higher relative central city expenditures on what he calls "amenity-related" services (spending on parks and recreation and libraries) has a statistically significant negative effect on the suburbanization of retail employment. The reported regression also includes the property tax base per capita of the central city relative to its MSA. The relative central city to MSA property tax rate is dropped from the reported regression, and its sign and size are not reported.

Gyourko (1984): Gyourko gets some clearly significant negative tax effects, but only in specifications that omit regional dummies. State corporate tax rate and local payroll tax rate have negative coefficients when regional dummies are added, with state corporate tax rate coefficient marginally significant (r-statistic is 1.56). But property tax rate and local corporate tax rate have positive coefficients, although insignificant. If we assume a mean property tax rate of 2 percent, mean local corporate and payroll tax rates of .5 percent, and a mean nominal state corporate tax rate of 6 percent, sum of the tax coefficients would be negative (−.10) in Gyourko's table 13 in the specification with regional dummies. However, elasticity cannot be calculated because Gyourko does not present mean values of the dependent variables.

Gyourko (1987a): Gyourko also finds that higher wages significantly reduce labor intensity of a city's manufacturing base, while payroll taxes and corporate taxes have insignificant effects. Thirty cities are included in the sample for each of two years.

Gyourko (1987b): Gyourko finds negative effects of property taxes on new manufacturing firm density in his analysis of all five Pennsylvania counties in Philadelphia MSA. Property tax effects appear to be larger in absolute value when examining choice of a given zip code within a given suburban county. Effects of property tax on new service firm density tend to be positive, but insignificant. In addition, effect of property tax on overall zip code employment change is positive, although insignificant.

241

Harris (1986): Results in the tax table are based on elasticities reported by Harris in her tables 8.1a and 8.3. The elasticities for tax effects on high technology formation rates are not statistically significant at 5 percent (one-tail test), but are at 10 percent. Harris includes an existing activity variable in the equation for all high technology formations.

Helms (1985): Effects reported here are long-run effects from his fixed-effects IVC specification. Elasticity presented is long-run percentage change in personal income for a given percentage reduction in property taxes and other taxes, financed by increase in user fees. Mean values of property tax, other tax, and user fees as percentage of personal income, needed to do this calculation, are taken from *Governmental Finances in 1981-82*. Elasticity here differs from effects emphasized by Helms' table. Helms shows effects of all fiscal variables when welfare changes are used to keep government budget constraint satisfied. The long-run elasticity of personal income with respect to equal percentage increases in property taxes and other taxes, when the revenue is used to increase welfare spending, is −2.12. But welfare spending is likely to have its own independent effect on business growth, and is also highly endogenous. Hence, Helms' estimates as presented are not pure tax effects; he mentions this, but it is sometimes forgotten in reviews of his study. User fees seem more likely to have little effect on business location, and to be more exogenous than welfare spending. Helms' IVC estimates use instruments for transfers and budget deficit, but instruments are questionable: the other fiscal variables, and the fraction of the population aged 5-17 and over 65.

Hodge (1981): All results reported here come from specification A in Hodge's tables, which includes the most control variables. Because dependent variable is gross investment, the estimated elasticities in Hodge's study are treated in tax table as long-run elasticities. My summary of Hodge's results uses specification A for all of his industries.

Howland (1985): Howland's study of the number of new firms and employment by county in three states and Washington, D.C., is really a study of the intrastate distribution of economic activity, because of the inclusion of state dummy variables. She finds some negative tax effects, and positive tax abatement effects, but none that are statistically significant. Her wage elasticities tend to be very large and negative: −2.52 for electronic components, and −4.11 for machine tools. As an intrastate study, these wage elasticities were not included in table 2.6 in text.

Inman (1987): In calculating elasticity, I assume that Philadelphia's usual share of national jobs is about .00742, based on ES-202 data. In addition, I assume a usual wage tax rate of .02. −.15 is elasticity calculated for their County Business Patterns equation, −.21 is elasticity calculated for the Employment and Earnings-based equation. I do not attempt to adjust these elasticities to long-run elasticities, as it is unclear the extent to which estimated coefficients measure long-run versus short-run responses.

Kieschnick (1981 or 1983): Of the 13 industries, tax variable is dropped from reported results for 6 industries. The procedure for dropping variables was to exclude all variables with level of significance of less than .50. The tax variable is negative in five out of the remaining seven industries, but is only significantly negative in the rubber industry. Unweighted mean elasticity for these seven industries is −.07. For purposes of calculating the averages used in the text table, I treat Kieschnick as having estimated an average elasticity of zero.

Luce (1987): Results reported here are based on table B.5.2 in Luce (1987), and use means reported in table B.5.3. Luce elasticities are adjusted to long-run elasticities by being multiplied by $2.67 = 1/(1-(.9104)^5)$.

Luce (1990a): The elasticities used here are calculated as the average of Luce's results for 1972-77 and 1977-82 for all industries. The elasticities are calculated as a percentage of the simple average of high-tech and low-tech employment in the typical MSA. All calculated elasticities are multiplied by $1/[1-(.9104)^5]$ to convert to long-run effects of taxes. Significant negative tax effects are for high tech in 1977-82 time period.

Luce (1990b): For Luce study I calculate long-run elasticities for total employment allowing both employment and labor force adjustment. That is, his simultaneous equations are solved for employment, with employment and labor force variables assumed equal to last year's level. For the wage tax, I calculate the elasticity at a wage tax of 1.175 percent, which is employment-weighted mean (I assume all 339 suburban communities have wage tax of .19 percent, true weighted average wage tax would be greater than this if larger suburbs tend to have larger wage tax) for Philadelphia MSA, based on Luce's table 1. Long-run elasticity with labor force held constant is -1.87, only slightly less than allowing labor force adjustment. Because Luce uses 1970 explanatory variables to explain 1980 employment, his estimates may understate long-run elasticities; some adjustment to 1970 explanatory variables has already taken place in 1970.

Luger and Shetty (1985): Luger and Shetty do not present sufficient descriptive statistics to determine magnitude of their estimated tax effects.

McConnell and Schwab (1990): Result reported here is sum of average elasticity with respect to Wheaton tax variable and county property tax from their specifications 2, 3, and 4; their first specification does not include public service controls or region controls. Most of the effect is caused by Wheaton variable, which is statistically significant; county property tax rate variable, which appears to be nominal rate, is right sign but statistically insignificant. McConnell and Schwab include education variable in specification 2, welfare in specification 3 and regional dummies in specification 4. Results reported in public service table are from specifications 3 and 4, and results reported for unionization are from specification 4.

McGuire (1985): McGuire's results are sensitive to specification used. Results reported here are average elasticity over three reported specifications in table 1. Results change based on how one treats population density variables. However, in most specifications, property taxes are negative and in some cases significant.

McHone (1986): McHone treats taxes as endogenous. But his use of population density as an exogenous instrument may be questioned, as we would expect the community population density to potentially have some direct effect on industrial land demand.

Mehay and Solnick (1990): Mehay and Solnick's results, as presented, do not allow for calculation of the effects of across-the-board tax increases used to increase some "neutral" fiscal category. Hence, their results are not included in the summary table in the text. All their results show the effects of tax increases used to finance increases in welfare spending. But, as argued in text and in discussion of Helms' (1985) paper above, current welfare spending in a state is likely to be highly endogenous; in addition, welfare spending may have direct effects on business location. In addition, their Parks model estimates, which they prefer, imply extremely large elasticities that deserve further exploration before being used in this type of policy analysis. The Parks model controls for serial correlation in the dependent variable and contemporaneous correlation of the residuals across observations. But the model does not control for fixed effects of states. Their Parks model estimates imply a long-run employment elasticity with respect to taxes of (-242) ($=$ mean of tax variable of about $154 times coefficient of $-.011$ divided by $(1-.993)$), and similarly large long-run personal income elasticities with respect to state and local taxes. In addition, the coefficient on the lagged dependent variable implies that the economy adjusts by 1 percent or less between its long-run equilibrium position and its current position each year. This seems very low. The model that they don't prefer, the "covariance" or fixed-effects model, implies lower tax effects and a quicker adjustment to long-run equilibrium. The tax coefficient in the personal income fixed-effects model—the model most similar to the model estimated by Helms—implies a long-run tax elasticity of -4.85. This is similar to the Helms' elasticity when tax revenues are used to increase welfare spending. However, the endogeneity of welfare spending and possible direct effects of welfare spending on business location suggest that this elasticity should not be considered directly comparable to the elasticities estimated in other studies.

Mills (1983): Mills examines central city employment change (suburban employment change), both holding constant suburban (central city) employment change, and allowing it to endogenously adjust. The regressions holding constant employment change in the remainder of the MSA are in some respects similar to intermetropolitan area studies, in that any tax effects mostly reflect substitution across MSAs. Because only taxes in the central city (suburbs) are considered, however, this type of study is not closely comparable to other inter-MSA studies. Mills does not report means, but for some of the simulations he examines, taxes do appear to have important effects, although not as important as for other variables.

Mills and Price (1984): t-statistic on tax term in manufacturing and construction employment density gradient equation is -1.34, so this variable is significant at 9 percent (one-tail test) level.

Mofidi and Stone (1990): Mofidi and Stone elasticities are not used in the summary table in the text because they show effect of taxes when used to finance welfare spending. This combines two separate effects. Their implied long-run elasticity would be around -1.32 for manufacturing employment and -2.59 for manufacturing investment. (This adjusts their numbers by $[1/(1-.9104)^5]$, as they examine five-year intervals, and assumes a mean of 10 for their tax variable, taxes as percentage of personal income.) Hence, their results strengthen the case for some state and local tax effect on regional growth.

Mullen and Williams (1991): I use very preliminary results from a Mullen and Williams' draft. Mullen and Williams' specification is unusual in that it includes both the average state level of average and marginal tax rates, and the growth of public capital. Because their dependent variable is growth over a 17-year period, all their tax estimates are multiplied by $1/1-(.9104)^{17} = 1.254$ to get long-run estimates.

Munnell (1990): To calculate tax elasticities, I assume that Munnell's tax variable has typical value of around 10 percent of personal income, based on information in Munnell's table 11 and appendix B. I use Munnell's results for 1970-88 employment change in states, as these results are closer to long-run estimates than her results for 1970-80 and 1980-88. Using these results for 1970-80 or 1980-88 would yield somewhat greater implied long run elasticities. The tax elasticity for the 1970-88 regression is multiplied by $1.2264 = 1/[1-(.9104)^{18}]$ to yield a long-run elasticity.

Nakosteen and Zimmer (1987): All results reported use estimates for their equation (6). Their results are hard to interpret because they hold constant state employment growth from 1970 to 1980 in explaining out-migration of firms from 1970 to 1980. Perhaps results are best interpreted as showing differences between relocating firm's behavior and "average" firm's behavior. It is unclear whether their model holds omitted state characteristics constant, as they include both levels of state characteristics and changes in state characteristics in model explaining changes in some firms' behavior.

Newman (1983): Estimated elasticity in table uses tax coefficient from "fully constrained" model reported in table 3. This tax coefficient of -.136 is multiplied by $1.89 = 1/(1-(.9104)^8)$ to convert the eight-year effect estimated into a long-run effect.

O'hUallacháin and Satterthwaite (1990): This study estimated equations for many industries, but eliminated variables from the final reported specifications if they fell below a certain significance level. Corporate taxes only appeared in 4 of the 38 regressions, and was only significantly negative once, less than would be expected by chance. I chose to report this as the absence of any significantly negative tax effects.

Palumbo, Sacks and Wasylenko (1990): Elasticities presented in the tax table use means in authors' table 1, and correct for fact that their dependent variable is in absolute percentage form rather than logarithmic form. That is, their coefficient of −.09 for suburban taxes in employment equation is multiplied by the mean suburban tax of 311.8, and then divided by 100. This short-run coefficient is then multiplied by $1/(1-(-.9104)^{10})$ to get long-run elasticities. Their city tax effect is not significant, and their suburban tax coefficient is significant at about a 13 percent level of significance, under a two-tail test. Their study combines features of inter-area and intra-area studies because city or suburban employment growth can change for one of two reasons: employment growth shifting to the rest of the MSA; or employment growth shifting to other MSAs.

Papke (1986, 1989b): Results reported in table come from Papke's fixed-effects specification. All but the publishing elasticity are statistically significant. Calculated elasticities assume that state and local taxes average 10 percent of profits, and that a 10 percent change in taxes (= 1 percent of profits) would, after federal tax offsets, change the effective tax rate variable by 0.5 percent. Papke's effective tax rate variable comes from AFTAX model that simulates taxes for representative firms in different states. Her model includes 22 states, and uses as data observations on the number of births in each year from 1975 through 1982. The wage rate elasticities in the wage rate table are at the mean wage rate in each industry.

Papke (1987): Tax table elasticities assume state and local taxes are 10 percent of profits, with 50 percent federal tax deduction (accurate for 1978 period of study). Hence, 10 percent changes in state and local taxes would yield .1 percent change in rate of return at mean rate of about 12 percent, which would yield a 1.7 percent decline in investment per worker (.0169 = .1/12 times Papke's reported elasticity with respect to AFTAX of 2.024). Note that Papke's is one of few studies to use instruments for wages and energy prices. The exogeneity of the instruments used, however, might be questioned (state unemployment rate, lagged energy price, unionization rate). Papke's 1987 results were previously summarized in Papke and Papke (1986).

Papke (1989a): My calculation assumes that state and local taxes are 10 percent of profits, and are deductible against an approximately 50 percent federal tax rate. Hence, a 1 percent change in state and local taxes will change Papke's effective tax rate variable by 0.05 rate points. Papke's regression examines annual industry gross state product (GSP), for each year from 1975 to 1982. The regression includes a dummy variable for the state. Hence, this regression is equivalent to differencing all variables from state means. It is difficult to determine whether these estimated elasticities represent long-run or short-run elasticities. To avoid overstating these elasticities, I simply treat them as long-run elasticities. All calculations use Papke's regressions with log of industry GSP as dependent variables.

Place (1986): The analysis is two-stage least squares with real revenue and expenditures per capita treated as endogenous. The instrument is personal income per capita, whose exogeneity is questionable. Results show negative effect of this revenue variable on total employment growth and a positive effect on private employment growth, although neither variable is statistically significant. When additional controls for how revenue is raised are included, total revenue per capita becomes positive and significant. The units used are unclear.

Plaut and Pluta (1983): Because of the ways in which the tax variables are defined, and because the units used are unclear, the overall effect of a 1 percent tax reduction cannot be calculated based on Plaut and Pluta's reported results. The Alexander Grant and Fantus business climate indices used include taxes as one component; Plaut and Pluta further transform these indices using principal components, and it is impossible to determine how a 1 percent tax reduction would affect their variables. Personal income tax variable also is transformed by principal components, which makes it difficult to determine how it would be affected by 1 percent across-the-board tax reduction. Also, Plaut and Pluta do not report means or units used for other tax variables. Judging from reported beta statistics in their tables and their description of variables, it appears that tax effort is measured as an index, with a national mean of 1.0, and the other tax variables are measured in percentage terms. Assume that mean corporate taxes as percent of payroll are around 2 percent, sales tax as a percent of sales is about 4 percent and mean property taxes are about 2 percent in this sample. Then the implied elasticity for an equal percentage change in these four variables is .11 for real value added, $-.08$ for employment, and .09 for real capital stock. These elasticities are for a five-year period, and would be about 1.7 times as high in the long run if we adjust using the Helms' adjustment parameters (see general notes above for details). However, it is unclear how this calculation would be affected by the business climate variable and personal income tax variables. In particular, the "beta coefficient" on the business climate variable is fairly large and has the expected sign. The effects of tax reductions via this variable might be large enough to make all the implied overall tax elasticities negative for a uniform percentage change in all state and local taxes. Of their 18 tax variable coefficients (6 variables times 3 specifications), 3 are significant at the 10 percent level or better with the expected sign (business climate twice, tax effort once), 1 is significant at the 20 percent level (tax effort), and property tax coefficients are always significant with a positive sign.

Quan and Beck (1987): The segmentation of states by Quan and Beck into Northeast subsample (15 states) and Sunbelt subsample (17 states) could be considered an implicit way of controlling for omitted fixed effects of regions. Although Quan and Beck state that they base their model on the Helms' partial adjustment model of annual state business activity, the equation they actually report does not include lags in state employment. However, they do include eight-lagged years of their state tax variable. Because this is a polynomial distributed lag, all effects after eight years are implicitly set to zero. Therefore, I treat their estimate of the sum over all lags of the tax effect as a long-run effect. The elasticities are calculated with the assumption that state and local taxes are about .10 of personal income.

Reynolds and Maki (1990): Reynolds and Maki use SPSS "stepwise regression" procedures to decide on final specification. Sign and size of coefficients on omitted variables are not reported. Some of the control variables chosen may contribute to lack of significance of 1972 tax and spending variables. For example, they include 1980 unemployment rates and income per worker; some of the effects of 1972 tax and spending variables may be absorbed by these 1980 variables.

Romans and Subrahmanyam (1979): Reported results come from line 4 of their table II-A, and line 3 of table II-B. Calculations assume mean of 7.3 percent for average marginal tax rate, 100 for ACIR tax effort indices, and calculation increases all these rates by equal percentage amount. Only result on average marginal tax rate is negative and significant; business and personal tax efforts are positive, with business tax effort often significantly positive. Overall tax effect would be negative for states with very progressive tax systems. Elasticities are adjusted to long-run value by multiplying by $1/(1-(.9104)^{10})$.

Sander (1989): Sander's tax results seem to be robust to restricting the sample only to downstate Illinois. Such a restriction is a very rough test for whether the tax results are due to unobserved region effects. The long-run elasticity reported here in the table is calculated by using Sander's reported means and multiplying the short-run elasticity by $1/(1-(.9104)^9)$ to convert it to a long-run elasticity.

Schmenner, Huber and Cook (1987): Calculations of tax elasticities assume .042 as average property tax revenues per dollar of income (from ACIR figures), and 5 percent as typical top state corporate tax rate. Elasticities reported are combined elasticities for two stages of decision process. Elasticities reported are elasticities of probabilities $d\ln P/d\ln x$ = (reported effect in study)$(1-P)$(mean of X), where P is probability. $1-P$ is assumed to equal 1 for choice of states to seriously consider, .719 for second stage (3.56 is average number of alternatives at second stage, and $1-1/3.56 = .719$). The reported tax elasticities for all plants use paper's reported proportions of .58 for firms pursuing product plant strategies, .40 for firms pursuing low taxes. Text tax tables use Schmenner's "Panel C" estimates, which include all interaction terms. Because of interaction terms, statistical significance of tax effects is difficult to determine, but it seems reasonable to assume elasticities for firms desiring low taxes are probably significant; the differences in behavior of these firms from other firms is certainly significant. All Schmenner, Huber and Cook results reported in tables in other appendices to chapter 2 use Panel A estimates because they are simpler to interpret.

Schneider (1984): Schneider regresses the number of manufacturing establishments in each suburb in 1977 on each suburb's 1972 number, an MSA dummy, and other variables. The MSA dummy's inclusion means that Schneider is essentially looking at the change in the suburb's number of establishments relative to the MSA. Thus, this study is an intrametropolitan study. The effective tax rate variable has a t-statistic of 1.56, which is significant at the 6 percent (one-tail test) level.

Steinnes (1984): Steinnes finds that adding lagged dependent variables or using a specification with all variables defined as changes, makes a big difference to the results. Income and property taxes appear to have negative effects on manufacturing employment, while the sales tax has positive effects.

Summers and Luce (1985): Because of units used, actual Summers and Luce coefficients can be treated as elasticities. These short-run elasticities were multiplied by $1/(1-(.9104)^{10})$ for the 1967-77 regression, and by $1/(1-(.9104)^6)$ for the 1977-83 regression, to get long-run elasticities. The positive coefficient on tax effort in the 1977-83 regression is not significant. Summers and Luce also found significant negative effects of tax effort on service sector growth.

Summers and Luce (1987): Cited results come from table B.4.2.

Testa (1989): I appreciate Bill Testa's help in interpreting the coefficients in his paper. As defined in the paper, all dependent variables measure the change in employment or output as a proportion of the base. Tax growth per capita is indexed so that the mean value of per capita state and local tax levels is 100. Hence, Testa coefficients are multiplied by $100 * 1/(1-(.9104)^9)$ to get long-run elasticities reported in table. The manufacturing employment and output elasticities also include equal percentage increases in UI taxes, which have a mean of .0106 in Testa's study. It is a little difficult to determine whether Testa's specification controls for fixed effects, as independent variables are defined both as changes and as levels. Testa's results are also described in Testa and Davila (1989), along with some results using other definitions of the UI tax variable.

Vedder (1981): Vedder relates changes in per capita income to changes in taxes, but then includes other variables measuring the level of state characteristics. It is not clear whether this model controls for unobserved state fixed effects or not.

Various state reports by Wasylenko and his colleagues (McGuire and Wasylenko 1987; Wasylenko 1988; Wasylenko and Carroll 1989): These results come from a summary paper written by Robert Carroll and Michael Wasylenko, "The Shifting Fate of Fiscal Variables and Their Effect on Economic Development," 1989. I assume that average value of taxes as a percent of personal income is 10.0 for these elasticity calculations. Estimated elasticities from their table 3 are multiplied by $1/(1-(.9104)^5)$ to get long-run elasticities. Estimated elasticities from their table 4 are multiplied by $1/(1-(.9104)^6)$ to get long-run elasticities.

Wasylenko (1980): Data and variables are same as Erickson and Wasylenko (1980), but communities with zero new and existing business activity are dropped from sample on the assumption that they zone out new business activity. Calculated elasticity is based on assumption that average property tax rate in Milwaukee suburbs in 1969 was 3 percent, as stated in Erickson and Wasylenko's paper. Property tax effects are larger for wholesale trade, smaller for retail trade, finance, services.

Wasylenko and McGuire (1985): Reported tax elasticities sum effects for tax effort and effective corporate and personal tax rates. Sales tax is excluded from calculation because, due to its definition (percentage of general revenue from sales tax), this variable would not change with across-the-board tax change. Calculation of elasticities assumes mean of 100 for tax effort, 3.3 for effective personal income tax rate, and 4.45 for effective corporate income tax rate. Conversion to long-run effects is done by multiplying estimated elasticities by $2.08 = 1/(1-(.9104)7)$. The tax effort variable is defined as the change from 1967 to 1977, while other tax variables are defined in levels terms. This makes it somewhat difficult to decide whether specification controls for state fixed effects or not. Percentage change in tax effort is the only tax variable significant in the total employment and manufacturing employment regressions.

Wheat (1986): Table's assertion that tax variable coefficient is wrong sign and insignificant is based on Wheat's statement that this was the case when tax variable added to basic model; results with tax variable included are not actually presented by Wheat.

White (1986): White's estimated tax coefficients are only one-third their standard errors, so her results do not give great support to any hypothesis about the effects of taxes.

Woodward (1990): State tax elasticities presented here are for Woodward's regressions that include regional dummies. Woodward prefers these specifications, and the regional dummies are significant. Corporate tax rate has a positive, but a statistically insignificant, effect in specification that omits regional dummies.

Yandle (1984): t-statistic for Yandle's tax variable for 1963-67 is -1.336. Same variable is positive and significant for 1967-72, negative and not significant for 1972-77. Based on conversations with the author, it appears that both the tax and dependent variable were measured in the same units. That is, if the dependent variable was measured in percentage terms, the tax variable was measured in percentage terms. This implies a mean value of the tax variable of about 15.35 percent. Using this mean, the average long-run elasticity for all three time-period regressions run by Yandle is $-.03$.

Appendix 2.3

Studies of Effects of Public Services on Business Location

Study	Types Included	Positive Significant	Positive Not Significant	Negative Not Significant	Negative Significant
Coughlin, Terza & Arromdee (1991)	Highway miles per square mile, rail-roads per square mile, # of airports per square mile	Highways Railroads Airports			
Mullen & Williams (1991)	Public capital stock growth rate (from Munnell 1990)	X			
Crihfield (1990)	State capital outlays, MSA capital outlays		Local		State
Jones (1990)	Per capita spending on police/fire; education; highways; health & hospitals; welfare	Police/fire		Health	Welfare
		Other variables' coefficients depend on time period examined.			
Luce (1990a)	Education, welfare, health, and high-way spending as percent of personal income, for 1972-77, 1977-82 periods	Education-72	Health-72 Education-77 Health-77	Welfare-72 Highways-77 Welfare-77	Highways-72

			Education	Welfare	
McConnell & Schwab (1990)	Education, welfare				
Mofidi & Stone (1990)	Health, education, highways, other spending, UI benefits, other transfers as percentage of personal income; (E) indicates employment dependent variable; (I) indicates investment dependent variable	Health (E) Education (E) Highways (E) Other (E)	Health (I) Education (I) Highways (I) Other (I)	UI (I)	UI (E) Welfare (E) Welfare (I)
Munnell (1990)	Public capital stock		Positive and significant.		
O'hUallacháin & Satterthwaite (1990)	Local government spending, educational percentage	Insignificant in overwhelming majority of industries studied.			
Reynolds & Maki (1990)	Education, highways, welfare, health spending per capita	Significance unclear; counted as insignificant for public service results. Welfare spending tends to be significant for branch plants.			

250

Appendix 2.3 (continued)

Study	Types Included	Positive Significant	Positive Not Significant	Negative Not Significant	Negative Significant
Bartik (1989a)	Per capita spending on education, police, fire, higher education, welfare, highway density	Fire	Education Highways	Police Higher education	Welfare
Carroll & Wasylenko (1989)	Higher education spending, other spending as % of income		Higher education	Other spending	
Crihfield (1989)	State capital outlays per $ of income; SMSA capital outlays per $ of income		SMSA		State
Deich (1989)	Police and fire spending per capita	Positive and significant for both small business and branch plants.			
Duffy-Deno & Eberts (1989)	Public capital stock	X			
McGuire & Wasylenko (from Carroll & Wasylenko, 1989)	Welfare, highways, higher education, education spending per capita		Higher education Education Welfare	Highways Education Welfare	Highways

Study	Variable	Classification
Testa (1989)	Education expense per pupil	X
Wasylenko (from Carroll & Wasylenko, 1989)	State and local expenditures as % of income	X
Nakosteen & Zimmer (1987)	Education spending per capita	Education
Papke (1987)	Combined police/fire per capita	Police/Fire
Quan & Beck (1987)	Per capita spending on local education, higher education, other nonwelfare spending	Local education; Higher education; Other; Other
Schmenner, Huber & Cook (1987)	Spending per $ of personal income	Spending; Higher education; Local education
Benson & Johnson (1986)	Welfare share of state spending	X

252

Appendix 2.3 (continued)

Study	Types Included	Positive Significant	Positive Not Significant	Negative Not Significant	Negative Significant
Papke (1986, 1989b)	Police and fire spending per capita, in 5 industries	Publishing	Furniture Communication equipment	Apparel	Electronic components
Place (1986)	Total per capita spending on high-ways, sewers, public welfare, education	Total	Highways	Sewers, Education	Welfare
Bartik (1985)	Highway miles per square mile	X			
Helms (1985)	Expenditures as % of personal income, for health, highways, local schools, higher education, other	Health Highways Schools Higher education			
Wasylenko & McGuire (1985)	State and local education spending as % of income, state and local welfare spending as % of income	Education	Welfare		

Study	Variable		
Gyourko (1984)	Total state and local spending per capita	X	
Plaut & Pluta (1983)	Combined index of education expenditures and total expenditures as % of personal income; welfare expenditures as % of personal income		Education/total index positive and significant for two out of three dependent variables used, welfare positive and significant for one out of three
Romans & Subrahmanyam (1979)	Transfer to revenue ratio	X	

NOTES ON STUDIES

Jones (1990): This study includes no tax variables, but does include public service variables. Jones examines the percentage change in state business activity (using various measures) for each of the four 5-year periods from 1964 to 1984, as a fraction of per capita spending in various categories. Focusing on his results for the percentage change in employment, the police and fire coefficients tend to be positive and significant; welfare tends to be negative and significant; health and hospitals negative but insignificant; and education and highways results are quite sensitive to the time period. These results are summarized in the table.

Appendix 2.4
Studies of Wage Effects on Business Location

Study	Negative and Significant Wage Effect?	Elasticity
Coughlin, Terza & Arromdee (1991)	Yes	For 2 specifications with taxes: –4.40; –4.39 (Average is –4.39)
Eberts (1991)	Yes	?
Crihfield (1990)	No	.77 (This elasticity is not included in calculation of mean elasticity for text summary table, as dependent variable is growth in nominal value added. Crihfield's elasticity is positively biased by expected positive elasticity of product price with respect to wages)
Luce (1990a)	Marginally significant (*t*-statistic = –1.58)	Average long-run elasticity = –.43
McConnell & Schwab (1990)	No	Average elasticity is .19 in their specifications 2, 3, and 4. (Mean wage is $4.94— private communication with Schwab)
Mehay & Solnick (1990)	No	–.34 (Used Parks model for employment; LR defined as 50 years)
Munnell (1990)	Yes	–2.47 (Assumes average wage of around $8.00)
O'hUallacháin & Satterthwaite (1990)	Yes in 10 out of 37 industries	?

Appendix 2.4 (continued)

Study	Negative and Significant Wage Effect?	Elasticity
Woodward (1990)	No	−.26
Bartik (1989a)	No	−.12
Bauer & Cromwell (1989)	Yes	−.51
Crihfield (1989)	Yes	−3.16
Deich (1989)	Yes, for both small business and branch starts	−1.77 for small business −.29 for branch plants (average = −1.03)
Friedman, Gerlowski & Silberman (1989)	Yes	?
Papke (1989a)	Yes, in 2 out of 4 industries	−1.00 for apparel, −.17 for furniture, .42 for printing, .66 for electric equipment; weighted average, using industry GSP as weights, is .27
Testa (1989)	Yes	−1.41 for manufacturing employment; −2.22 for manufacturing output; −.06 for nonmanufacturing employment; −.06 for total employment
Eberts & Stone (1988)	Yes	−.58
Doeringer, Terkla & Topakian (1987)	No	−.05
Glickman & Woodward (1987)	Yes	? Significantly negative for domestic employment growth, not for foreign employment growth in their Table 21

Appendix 2.4 (continued)

Study	Negative and Significant Wage Effect?	Elasticity
Gyourko (1987b)	Yes	Increase in wage reduces labor intensity of MSA manufacturing; elasticity not comparable
Luce (1987)	No	.18
Papke (1987)	No	?
Schmenner, Huber & Cook (1987)	Yes	?
Benson & Johnson (1986)	Yes	−.39
Harris (1986)	No	−1.08 for formation of high-tech establishments, −.91 for other manufacturing (−1.00 average)
Papke (1986, 1989b)	Yes	−.78 for furniture −.36 for publishing −.13 for communication equipment −.12 for apparel .41 for electronic components (−.20 average)
Place (1986)	Yes	?
Bartik (1985)	Yes	−.88
Helms (1985)	No	−.27
Luger & Shetty (1985)	Yes	−1.76 for industrial machinery −3.00 for pharmaceuticals −4.44 for motor vehicles (−3.07 average)
Wasylenko & McGuire (1985)	Yes	−.98 for total employment −.69 for manufacturing employment

Appendix 2.4 (continued)

Study	Negative and Significant Wage Effect?	Elasticity
Armington, Harris & Odle (1984)	Yes	Formation/employment growth results for high tech: −.96/-2.11; for other manufacturing: −1.10/-.41; for other industries: −.61/-.57 (average employment result is −1.03)
Gyourko (1984)	No	.78
Yandle (1984)	Yes	?
Carlton (1983)	No	?
Garofalo & Malhotra (1983)	?	.45
Plaut & Pluta (1983)	No	?
Graham (1982)	No	?
Hodge (1981)	Yes	−1.92 for furniture, −.38 for rubber, 1.55 for apparel, −.46 for electronics (−.30 used as average)
Kieschnick (1981)	Yes	In 13 industries, negative and significant in 1; mean elasticity over all 13 (counting industry where dropped as zero) is 1.66
Browne, Mieszkowski & Syron (1980)	Yes	?

Appendix 2.4 (continued)

Study	Negative and Significant Wage Effect?	Elasticity
		−1.46/−.92 for plastics births/ branch plants; −1.22/.21 for communication equipment births/branches; −1.07/−.42 for electronic components births/branches
Carlton (1979)	Yes	(−.81 average)
Romans & Subrahmanyam (1979)	No	?

NOTES: This table summarizes results for the wage variable in various inter-area business location studies since 1979. More details on the studies can be found in appendix 2.2. All results in this table use the same specifications examined in the appendix 2.2 table. All wage elasticities were adjusted to long-run levels where necessary using procedures identical to appendix 2.2. Wage elasticities were only calculated for studies that used the logarithm of wages as an independent variable, or for which mean of wage variable was readily available.

Appendix 2.5
Studies of Effects of Unionization on Business Activity

Study	Expected Sign and Significant Coefficient on Unionization, Work Stoppage or RTW Variable?	Expected Sign and Significant Coefficient on Unionization or Stoppage Variable?	Long-Run % Effect on Business Activity of 1% Increase in % Unionized	Wage Variable Included
	(1)	(2)	(3)	(4)
Coughlin, Terza & Arromdee (1991)	No	No	3.3 (Assumed mean unionization = 20%)	Yes
Eberts (1991)	Yes	Yes	−.20 (Assumed mean unionization = 20%)	Yes
Crihfield (1990)	No	No	.01	Yes
McConnell & Schwab (1990)	No	No	−1.32	Yes
Mofidi & Stone (1990)	No	No	2.14 for net investment, .50 for employment (average is 1.32)	No
Woodward (1990)	Yes	Yes	−8.67	Yes
Bartik (1989a)	No	No	−.11	Yes
Crihfield (1989)	No	No	.01	Yes
Deich (1989)	Yes, for branches, no for small business	Yes, for branches, no for small business	−.23 for branches −.10 for small business (avg. = −.16)	Yes

260

Appendix 2.5 (continued)

Study	Expected Sign and Significant Coefficient on union- ization, Work Stop- page of RTW Variable?	Expected Sign and Significant Coefficient on Unioni- ization or Stoppage Variable?	Long-Run % Effect on Business Activity of 1% Increase in % Unionized	Wage Variable Included
	(1)	(2)	(3)	(4)
Duffy-Deno & Eberts (1989)	No	No	.17	No
Doeringer, Terkla & Topakian (1987)	Yes	Yes	?	Yes
Glickman & Woodward (1987)	Yes	?	?	Yes
Heywood and Deich (1987)	Yes	Yes	−.96 for over- all state union- ization; −.45 for industry-specific unionization	No
Luce (1987)	No	No	−.01	Yes
Nakosteen & Zimmer (1987)	No	?	?	No
Schmenner, Huber & Cook (1987)	Yes	Yes	2.4	Yes
Place (1986)	No	?	?	Yes
Wheat (1986)	Yes	Yes	?	No
Bartik (1985)	Yes	Yes	−3.28	Yes
Helms (1985)	Yes	Yes	−2.23	Yes

Appendix 2.5 (continued)

Study	Expected Sign and Significant Coefficient on Union- ization, Work Stop- page or RTW Variable?	Expected Sign and Significant Coefficient on Unioni- zation or Stoppage Variable?	Long-Run % Effect on Business Activity of 1% Increase in % Unionized	Wage Variable Included
	(1)	(2)	(3)	(4)
Summers & Luce (1985)	Yes	Yes	−.22	Yes
Wasylenko & McGuire (1985)	No	No	?	Yes
Mills (1983)	No	No	−.01 (Mean of city and suburban results)	No
Newman (1983)	Yes	Yes	−5.46 (Assumes mean unionization rate = 20%)	No
Plaut & Pluta (1983)	Yes	?	?	Yes
Kieschnick (1981)	Yes	Yes	?	Yes
Browne, Mieszkowski, & Syron (1980)	Yes	Yes	?	Yes
Dye (1980)	?	?	−.86	No

NOTES: See appendix 2.2 for more details on individual studies. All summaries use authors' preferred specification where this can be determined. Summaries in columns (1) and (2) only reflect results for total business activity or manufacturing business. Column (3) long-run effects are for closest dependent variable in study to total business activity. Heywood and Deich use average percentage change in employment, over four years for each of 12 major states and industries. As the unionization variable does not vary over time, this regression essentially looks at how average 4-year growth is related to unionization. Reported Heywood and Deich numbers in above table are simple average of results for seven industries.

Appendix 3.1
Alternative Hysteresis Theories and Local Labor Markets

The text discusses long-run labor market hysteresis due to human capital effects of demand shocks. Two other theories for explaining labor market hysteresis have been offered: the business capital theory, and the insider-outsider theory. This appendix outlines why neither alternative theory seems a plausible explanation of hysteresis effects in *local* labor markets.

The business capital theory of labor market hysteresis is briefly outlined in Phelps' (1972) book, *Inflation Policy and Unemployment Theory*. Phelps argues that during a boom, businesses adjust their technology and management practices to utilize less-trained workers. Because physical and management capital are quite durable, businesses on average will remain more willing to hire and retain less-skilled workers even after the boom period is over. This long-run change in business capital leads to lower unemployment rates and higher occupational attainment for workers of a given skill level, according to Phelps.

Whatever the merits of this theory at a national level, it cannot explain long-run effects of a local demand shock on local earnings. Suppose there is a once-and-for-all shock to local employment. Local businesses would alter their capital and management practices. Less-skilled workers would have a higher probability of being hired for more demanding positions. If there was no in-migration, this higher probability would lead to a higher utility level for less-skilled workers. Less-skilled workers would be attracted to the better job prospects in this metropolitan area, however, and this in-migration would be expected to depress wages and raise unemployment among less-skilled workers. The wage and unemployment effects would continue until average real earnings of unskilled workers in the metropolitan area are equal to the national average again.

The insider-outsider theory examines how demand shocks affect the outcome of negotiations between firms and worker "insiders"—such as labor unions—who have some power to restrict entry by other workers into jobs. This theory has been most completely developed by Lindbeck and Snower (1988) in their book, *The Insider-Outsider Theory of Employment and Unemployment*. Chapter 10 of their book considers the likely effects of a permanent labor demand shock, which is what state and local economic development policy aims to bring about. A permanent negative demand shock is argued by Lindbeck and Snower to have little effect on wages because the interests of the majority of union members are best served by a policy of stable wages with some layoffs. Hence, if we assume a fixed national labor supply, unemployment will tend to go up and stay up after a permanent negative demand shock. In contrast, a permanent positive demand shock will lead to higher wages, with a relatively modest increase in employment, because such a combination best serves the interest of union insiders. In an economy with a fixed overall labor supply, this implies that unemployment will not be much lowered by permanent positive labor demand shocks.

The Lindbeck and Snower argument does not explain long-run real earnings effects of permanent *local* demand shocks. Suppose that a negative demand shock to a local area leads to lower employment but little change in the real wage. In the short run, this sequence of events will increase local unemployment. But at the local level, labor supply is clearly not fixed in the long run. Out-migration would continue until the local unemployment rate and hence local real earnings are restored to their original level.

Consider a permanent positive demand shock at the local level. Suppose that Lindbeck and Snower are right that union insiders would capture the benefits of this demand shock in higher real wages, and that employment would not expand much. In the short run, local unemployment would be unchanged. But in the long run, in-migration would increase, as individuals in other metropolitan areas are attracted by the prospect of getting higher real wages if a vacancy opens up in an insider job. Local unemployment would actually increase, and continue to increase until expected real earnings in the metropolitan area drop back to their original level. The positive demand shock has no hysteresis effects on equilibrium real earnings. Furthermore, the long-run effects of the positive demand shock on local unemployment are opposite of what we would expect, and what the empirical evidence in chapter 4 suggests to be the case.

It is worthwhile considering why the human capital theory of labor market hysteresis is not also destroyed by migration responses when applied to local labor market demand shocks. A positive demand shock, in the human capital theory, has long-run effects in raising the human capital of the original residents. Individuals with given education, age, and other characteristics now have higher human capital. In-migration does not destroy this human capital advantage because the original residents are now permanently part of a higher-skilled group that is part of a different labor submarket. Hence, lower-skilled in-migrants—even those with similar education and other credentials to the original residents—cannot effectively threaten the higher real wages and lower unemployment that the original residents have achieved. A similar argument can be made for why out-migration cannot alleviate the long-run negative effects of negative local labor demand shocks. In that case, the original residents have lost human capital and hence will have higher long-run equilibrium unemployment rates wherever they live.

The basic difference between the human capital theory and other labor market hysteresis theories is that a demand shock in the human capital theory moves the original residents into a skill group that has a different national equilibrium utility level. In contrast, the other hysteresis theories do not alter the national group into which original residents fit. Inter-area migration does have some long-run tendency to equalize utility levels for individuals of similar characteristics. A local demand shock is not likely to alter any national equilibrium variables. Only demand shocks that alter individual characteristics would appear likely to alter their long-run utility prospects.

Appendix 4.1
Local Labor and Land Market Variables as a Function
of Demand-Induced Shocks to Local Employment

Equations estimated in previous studies and in this study that express changes in local labor and land market variables as a function of local employment growth are puzzling in that they do not clearly correspond to any well-defined behavior or model. These equations do not obviously correspond to any "structural equation" describing the supply or demand of labor or land. They cannot be viewed as "reduced form equations" either, as employment growth is an endogenous variable.

The text discussion states that demand shocks to employment growth will have different effects on labor market variables from those of supply shocks to employment growth. This argument, formalized in this appendix, will show that regressions of changes in labor market variables on demand-induced employment growth can be regarded as "quasi-reduced form" equations. Demand shifters can be treated as exogenous variables. The demand-induced employment growth can be used as an indicator of the size of the demand shock to the local economy.

The argument uses a simple model of a local economy. Comparative static analysis will show that, under certain assumptions, the relationship between demand-induced employment growth and changes in city economic variables will be the same, regardless of the source of the demand shocks. On the other hand, the relationship between supply-induced employment growth and changes in city economic variables will be quite different. Hence, estimation procedures that can identify demand shocks to local employment reveal empirical regularities that can be used to predict the response of the economy to other demand shocks causing similar effects to local employment. In contrast, the effect of employment growth, in general, on economic variables will depend on whether the growth is demand-induced or supply-induced.

My model of a city's economy has two markets, the markets for land and labor. The market for land will be assumed to clear. The market for labor will result in an equilibrium unemployment rate due to efficiency wage considerations (Bulow and Summers 1986; Shapiro and Stiglitz 1984). Demand for a city's labor (L^D) and business demand for city land (H^{DB}) will be assumed to depend upon local real wages (w), land prices (r), the unemployment rate (U), and demand shifters (D) affecting business costs. Other output or input prices are implicitly assumed to either be uniform nationally or to depend indirectly on local real wages and land prices (for example, the price of local services will probably vary in this way). Labor supply to the city (L^S) and worker land demand (H^{De}) depend on real wages, land prices, and the unemployment rate, along with worker supply shifters (S_w) affecting worker utility. The land supply (H^S) is assumed to increase with land prices, as land is bid away from agriculture at the urban fringe, and is also altered by land shifters, such as changes in zoning rules or new road construction (S_z). The real wage is equal to the nominal wage (w_n) divided by a local price index (P) which is some function of local nominal wages and land prices. It is assumed that the real wage function is monotonic in w_n, so it can be inverted to solve for w_n as a function of w and r.

The equilibrium conditions for the land and labor market can be expressed as:

(1) $\quad H^{DB}(w,r,U;D) + H^{De}(w,r,U;S_w) - H^S(r;S_z) = 0.$

(2) $\quad L^D(w,r,U;D) - L^S(w,r,U;S_w)(1-U) = 0.$

Equations (1) and (2) contain three endogenous variables: w, r, and U. (Once w and r are determined, nominal wages and the local price index are also determined.) To allow for a solution, I use the efficiency wage hypothesis. According to efficiency wage theory, a firm may increase profits by increasing real wages if the increase discourages shirking, reduces quits, or raises worker morale and productivity. The firm chooses the wage it pays, so the wage variable above must be reinterpreted as the prevailing wage paid by other firms, which is exogenous to any specific firm. The profit-maximizing real wage paid by any specific firm m (w_m) will probably depend positively on the prevailing city real wage, and negatively on the city unemployment rate, as shirking and quits will tend to increase with improvements in workers' alternatives:

(3) $\quad w_m = f(w,U) \qquad\qquad 0 < f_w < 1, f_U < 0$

where f_w and f_U are partial derivitives of f with respect to w and U. If all firms are identical, in equilibrium $w_m = w$, and equation (3) is solved to yield

(4) $\quad w = g(U) \qquad$ where $g_U < 0$ (as $f_w < 1$).

Equations (4), (1) and (2) comprise the equilibrium system.

A demand shock (a small change in D) will cause changes in w, r, U, w_n, and P. To solve for these comparative static effects, the system of equations ((1), (2), and (4)) can be totally differentiated. The resulting solutions will be of the form:

(5) $\quad \dfrac{dY}{dD} = a_1 L^D_D + a_2 H^{DB}_D$

Y represents any of the endogenous variables (w, r, U, w_n, P). The subscript D indicates a partial derivative (assumed positive) with respect to demand shock D. dY/dD is the total equilibrium derivative representing both direct and indirect effects of D on the equilibrium value of Y. a_1 and a_2 are parameters that reflect the appropriate combinations of partial derivatives from a normal comparative static analysis of equation system (1), (2), and (4).

For purposes of this book, the most important subject for analysis is the conditions under which the equilibrium demand-induced change in labor demand can be validly used as an indicator of the size of demand shocks, as has been implicitly assumed by this and other studies. Labor demand is a valid indicator for a set of demand shocks that proportionately affect labor and land demand, or for which $H_D^{DB} = c_1 L_D^D$, where c_1 is a constant. Alternatively, labor demand will be a valid indicator if $a_2 = 0$, so that business land demand does not affect the equilibrium. In either case, the comparative static effect on any endogenous variable Y will be some multiple of the direct shock to labor demand, or

(6) $\quad \dfrac{dY}{dD} = a_3 L_D^D.$

The equilibrium change in labor demand—that is, employment growth—is also an endogenous variable, and can be written as a function of the direct changes in labor demand or

(7) $\quad \dfrac{dL}{dD} = a_4 L_D^D.$

Solving (7) for L_D^D, and substituting into equation (5), we get

(8) $\quad \dfrac{dY}{dD} = (a_3/a_4)(\dfrac{dL}{dD}) = a_5 \dfrac{dL}{dD}.$

Equation (8) states that the equilibrium change in city economic variables—real wages, unemployment, land prices, and other local prices—due to a demand shock to employment will be some stable function of the employment growth induced by that demand shock. Hence, regressions of changes in city economic variables on demand-induced employment growth should give valid predictions of what the effects would be of other demand-induced shocks to employment growth.

But the model expressed in equations (1), (2), and (4) could also be used to show that employment growth not caused by demand shocks will yield different relationships between equilibrium changes in city economic variables and employment growth. The equation system could also be differentiated with respect to the worker supply shifters S_W or the land supply shifters S_Z. An equation similar to equation (8) could be derived, but there would be no reason to expect the parameter relating the endogenous variables and equilibrium employment growth to be the same as in equation (8). Because employment growth in general is caused by either demand shifters, worker supply shifters, or land supply shifters, the equilibrium relationship between all types of employment growth and city economic variables will differ from the relationship between demand-induced employment growth and city economic variables. Furthermore, the observed relationship for one city or time period between actual employment growth and city economic variables cannot be used for prediction for another city or time period unless the sources of employment growth are expected to be the same in the two cases.

Equation (8) could be viewed as a quasi-reduced form in that it expresses changes in city economic variables as a function of exogenous demand shocks. One might ask why equation (8) should be estimated rather than some reduced form relating changes in city economic variables directly to changes in the demand shifters. The basic argument is that equation (8) is more useful for prediction than estimating the direct relationship between city economic variables and the demand shifters. For example, suppose it is valid to view business taxes as an exogenous demand shifter. Then a regression of changes in city economic variables on changes in local business tax rates can only be used to predict the effects of other changes in local business tax rates. But estimation of equation (8) allows prediction of the economic effects of any demand shock that causes local employment effects of similar size.

It would, of course, be preferable to estimate the entire structural equation system rather than just the quasi-reduced form equation (8), but that would be much more demanding of data and time, and potentially more vulnerable to specification error.

Finally, the validity of equation (8) does depend on some special assumptions, namely, that either land demand shocks are proportional to labor demand shocks, or that business land demand shocks do not greatly affect the equilibrium. The latter assumption may not be far from reality. Business land demand is much less important than residential land demand in the land market. Furthermore, to the extent that these special assumptions do not hold, equation (8) still shows the equilibrium relationship between changes in city economic variables and employment growth that occurs for demand shocks that have "typical" relative effects on business labor and land demand. Estimation of this average relationship may still be of interest, even though there will be some error in using it to predict the effects of demand shocks that cause different relative effects on business labor and land demand.

Appendix 4.2
Specification of Estimating Equations and Econometric Issues

This appendix outlines the rationale for the equation specifications and econometric methods used in this book. The specifications and methods are used in chapters 4, 5, 6, and 7.

The book uses two types of data and two types of models. Some of the empirical analyses examine MSA average economic outcomes. Other analyses use micro data for specific individuals.

The models that attempt to explain the change in average unemployment (chapter 4), prices (chapter 5), or real wages (chapter 6) in each metropolitan area from year t-1 to t are specified in the following form:

$$(9) \quad Y_{mt} - Y_{mt-1} = B_0 + B_t + C(L) \, (E_{mt} - E_{mt-1}) + U_{mt}.$$

Y_{mt} is the value of the unemployment rate, or the natural logarithm of the price index, or the natural logarithm of the real wage, for MSA m at year t. B_t is a set of dummy variables for each time period. E_{mt} is the natural logarithm of the aggregate nonagricultural employment for MSA m at time t. $C(L)$ is shorthand for an unrestricted polynomial in the lag operator. That is, lagged values for metropolitan employment growth are included in the specification, with each lagged value having its own coefficient. The cumulative effect of a shock to growth after s years is the sum of the coefficients up to the sth lag. U_{mt} is the disturbance term.

The form of equation (9) is suggested by equation (8) in appendix 4.1. In both cases, the change in some local economic variable depends on local employment growth. (The distinction between demand-induced growth and other growth is ignored for a moment.) Equation (9) is modified from equation (8) in two important ways. First, lagged values of employment growth are included because a growth shock's effects will change with the passage of time. In terms of equation (8), this implies that we expect the parameter a_5, which reflects some combination of the appropriate derivatives of the equation system (1), (2), and (4), to differ depending on the length of time over which the derivatives of equation (8) are evaluated. This makes sense because the elasticity of local supply and demand with respect to most variables will increase over time.

Second, equation (9) differs from equation (8) in including dummy variables for each time period. Equation (8) shows the effects of local growth shocks holding constant everything else. While empirical research can never perfectly hold "all else" constant, we can control for the national economic environment with time-period dummies.

The micro data used in this book contain information on the earnings, wages, unemployment, and labor force participation of specific individuals in identified MSAs during a particular year. This micro data allows us to control for the demographic composition of the MSA in estimating the effects of growth shocks. In addition, the micro data allows us to see how the effects of an employment shock differ across different types of individuals. But one disadvantage of the micro data is that it is impossible to use the "changes" specification of equation (9), as we only observe an individual during one particular year.

To convert the changes specification of equation (9) to a "levels" specification that only requires information on the dependent variable during one time period, we rewrite equation (9) as

$$(10) \quad (1-L)(Y_{mt}) = B_0 + B_t + (1-L)C(L)(E_{mt}) + U_{mt}.$$

L is again the lag operator. "Dividing" both sides of equation (10) by $1-L$, we get:

$$(11) \quad Y_{mt} = A_0 + A_t + F_m + C(L)E_{mt} + W_{mt}.$$

A_0 and A_t are B_0 and B_t divided by $(1-L)$; this division yields the sum of B_0 or B_t back to the initial time period in which the metropolitan economy was formed. F_m is a fixed effect for the metro area, and must be added because $F_m(1-L) = 0$. W_{mt} is U_{mt} divided by $(1-L)$, which is equal to the sum of U_{mt} back to the first time period.

Equation (11) is still in aggregate form. We convert equation (11) to a form suitable for micro estimation by adding in demographic predictors of individuals' economic behavior (age, race, education, etc.) to get

$$(12) \quad Y_{imt} = A_0 + A_t + F_m + \mathbf{B}'\mathbf{X}_{imt} + C(L)E_{mt} + U_{imt}.$$

$\mathbf{X}_{imt}$ is the vector of individual demographic characteristics for individual i.

The two types of equations used for estimation, equation (12) and equation (9), both control for fixed characteristics of MSAs. For example, many studies have shown that local amenities affect wages and prices (Blomquist, Berger, and Hoehn 1988; Smith 1983; Roback 1982; Gyourko and Tracy 1986). In addition to local amenities, other MSA characteristics affecting local economic variables include: topographic features that limit the land available for development in the MSA; zoning practices and transportation infrastructure that affect developable land; union influence in that metropolitan area; levels of fiscal variables, such as taxes and public services, that may be shifted into local wages and prices; and the MSA industrial structure. Instead of trying to control for every local characteristic that might affect local economic variables, this study simply allows a dummy variable for each MSA to control for any idiosyncratic features of the MSA.

One natural confusion about equation (12) should be clarified. It would appear that equation (12) examines the effect of the MSA's employment level on local economic variables, not the effect of shocks to employment. But the inclusion of an MSA fixed effect alters the interpretation of coefficients on the remaining variables. Inclusion of group dummies in a regression is equivalent to a regression in which the new dependent variable and the new independent variables are the original variables differenced from these group means. Therefore, an equation equivalent to (12) is[1]

(13) Y_{imt} – MSA mean $Y = (B_t$ – MSA mean $B_t) + \mathbf{B}'(\mathbf{X}_{imt}$ – MSA mean $\mathbf{X}) + C(L)(E_{mt}$ – MSA mean $E_{imt}) + (W_{imt}$ – MSA mean W).

Thus, the absolute level of employment in the MSA at time t does not determine the estimated relationship, but rather the employment relative to that MSA's average level. Growth matters, not employment levels.

Equations (9) or (12) can be estimated by ordinary least squares (OLS), and provide estimates of interest. The regressions describe the average relationship between shocks to local employment and changes in local economic variables. As discussed in appendix 4.1, this average relationship depends on the proportion of employment shocks arising from shocks to local demand, labor supply, or land supply.

For more specific predictions of how local economic variables will respond to economic development policies, these ordinary least squares estimates may be subject to bias. Economic development policies that assist business are best viewed as policies that seek to increase local labor demand. To predict the effects of these policies, we want to know the effects of job growth occurring due to demand shocks alone, with supply shifters held constant. As discussed in appendix 4.1, demand-induced local employment growth will have a relationship to local economic variables quite different from supply-induced local employment growth.

To put this argument in econometric terms, we can recognize that labor supply shifters (S_w) and land supply shifters (S_z) are part of the disturbance term in equations (9) and (12). These equations can then be rewritten as:

(9a) $Y_{mt} - Y_{mt-1} = B_0 + B_t + C(L) (E_{mt} - E_{mt-1}) + S_{wmt} + S_{zmt} + U_{mt}.$

(12a) $Y_{imt} = A_0 + A_t + F_m + \mathbf{B}'\mathbf{X}_{imt} + C(L)E_{mt} + S_{wmt} + S_{zmt} + U_{imt}.$

To determine the effects of demand shocks to employment, we want to estimate the effect of shocks to employment, holding supply shifters constant. That is, we want to estimate $E^*(Y_{mt} - Y_{mt-1} \mid B_t, E_{mt} - E_{mt-1}, S_{wmt}, S_{zmt})$ and $E^*(Y_{imt} \mid A_t, F_m, \mathbf{X}_{imt}, E_{mt}, S_{wmt}, S_{zmt})$, where $E^*(Q \mid G)$ is the best linear predictor of Q given G. But as supply shifters are not observed, ordinary least squares regression can only estimate

$$(14) \quad E^*(Y_{mt} - Y_{mt-1} \mid B_t, E_{mt} - E_{mt-1}) = B_0 + B_t + C(L)(E_{mt} - E_{mt-1})$$
$$+ E^*(S_{wmt} \mid B_t, E_{mt} - E_{mt-1}) + E^*(S_{zmt} \mid B_t, E_{mt} - E_{mt-1})$$

$$(15) \quad E^*(Y_{imt} \mid A_t, F_m, \mathbf{X}_{imt}, E_{mt}) = A_0 + A_t + F_m + \mathbf{B'X}_{imt} + C(L)E_{mt}$$
$$+ E^*(S_{wmt} \mid A_t, F_m, \mathbf{X}_{imt}, E_{mt}) + E^*(S_{zmt} \mid A_t, F_m, \mathbf{X}_{imt}, E_{mt}).$$

The last two conditional expectations are hypothetical auxiliary regressions of the supply shifters on the observed independent variables. Because the employment terms are correlated with the supply shifters, these auxiliary regressions will have nonzero coefficients on the employment terms, biasing the coefficient estimates on these variables.

The direction of the bias depends on the particular dependent variable and on which type of supply shifter dominates the data. Labor supply shifters will increase employment, unemployment, and land prices, and reduce real wages. The effect on other local prices is uncertain because of opposite effects on land prices and wages. A demand shock to employment should reduce unemployment, and increase land prices, real wages, and local prices. Thus, OLS estimates should be closer to zero than the true effects of demand shocks on unemployment and real wages. On the other hand, OLS estimates of the effects of employment on land prices should be greater than the true effects of demand shocks. The bias in OLS estimates of growth effects on nonland prices is uncertain.

Land supply shifters should increase employment and reduce land prices; the direct effects on other variables are likely to be small. Hence, due to the presence of land supply shifters, OLS estimates of the effects of employment on land prices and other prices are likely to understate the true effects of demand shocks on these prices.

Considering both labor and land supply shifters, OLS estimates are likely to understate the absolute magnitude of demand shock effects on labor market variables such as unemployment and real wages. The bias in OLS estimates is uncertain for variables that involve the local land market, such as land prices or other local prices.

This bias problem can be solved by instrumental variables. Appropriate instruments are variables that are correlated with the employment variables in equations (9a) and (12a), but uncorrelated with the supply shifters that are part of the disturbance term. Obvious candidates for instruments are variables shifting MSA labor demand.

In this book, only one type of labor demand shifter is used to form instrumental variables:[2] the share effect from a shift-share analysis of each metropolitan area and year-to-year employment change.[3] A shift-share analysis decomposes MSA growth into three components: a national growth component, which calculates what growth would have occurred if all industries in the MSA had grown at the all-industry national average; a share component, which calculates what extra growth would have occurred if each industry in the MSA had grown at that industry's national average; and a shift component, which calculates the extra growth that occurs because industries grow at different rates locally than they do nationally. For the aggregate model (estimating equation (9a)), the sum of the national growth component and the share component for each metro area from year t-1 to t and eight lagged values of that sum are used to form a set of instrumental variables. For the micro model (estimating equation (12a)), a set of national growth components and share components are added to each MSA's 1970 employment to simulate its employment level from 1971 to 1986 if the MSA's industries had grown at the same rate locally as nationally throughout the period. Current and eight-lagged values of those employment level predictions are used as instruments in equation (12a).

Formally, the ''growth predictions'' used to form instruments in this book can be written as

$$(16) \quad G_{mt} = \sum_j R_{jmb} \cdot \frac{(R_{nt} - R_{nt-1})}{R_{nb}} + \sum_j R_{jmb} \cdot \left[\frac{(R_{jnt} - R_{jnt-1})}{R_{jnb}} - \frac{(R_{nt} - R_{nt-1})}{R_{nb}} \right]$$

where R represents the absolute level of employment (not the logarithm of employment), the j subscripts indicate employment in industry j, variables without j subscripts are industry totals, the n subscript indicates employment figures for the nation, and b is some base year. $(R_{nt} - R_{nt-1}/R_{nb})$ is the overall growth in national employment from t-1 to t as a percentage of some base year total. $(R_{jnt} - R_{jnt-1})/R_{jnb}$ is industry j's national growth as a percentage of the base year industry total. R_{jmb} is employment in industry j in metro area m at year b. The first term represents what is usually called the national growth effect, and the second term is usually called the share effect. Equation (16) is converted to logarithmic growth terms to be used as an instrument in estimating equation (9a):

$$(17) \quad IV_{agg} \equiv \ln(R_{mt}^{predicted}) - \ln(R_{mt-1})$$
$$= \ln(R_{mt-1} + G_{mt}) - \ln(R_{mt-1}).$$

Current and eight lagged values of equation (17) are used as instruments in estimating equation (9a) by two-stage least squares. The instruments for equation (12a) can be written as:

$$(18) \quad \ln R_{mt}^{predicted} = \ln(R_{m,1970} + \sum_{k=1971}^{t} G_{mk}).$$

Current and eight lagged values of equation (18) are used as instruments for the employment level variables in equation (12a).

Why would this type of instrument be a good proxy for a demand shock to metro area employment? Because the prediction equations for employment include time-period dummies, we are explaining deviations of MSA growth from the U.S. average using deviations of the "growth prediction" variable from the U.S. average. Deviations of the growth prediction variables in equation (16) from the U.S. average will be due to the share effect, as the national growth effect for a given time period is the same for all MSAs. The share effect can be rewritten as

$$(19) \quad \sum_j R_{jmb} \left[\left(\frac{R_{jnt} - R_{jnt-1}}{R_{jnb}} \right) - \left(\frac{R_{nt} - R_{nt-1}}{R_{nb}} \right) \right]$$

$$= \sum_j \left[R_{jmb} - R_{mb} \left(\frac{R_{jnb}}{R_{nb}} \right) \right] \left[\left(\frac{R_{jnt} - R_{jnt-1}}{R_{jnb}} \right) - \left(\frac{R_{nt} - R_{nt-1}}{R_{nb}} \right) \right]$$

where R_{mb} is total employment in MSA m in the base period, and $R_{mb}(R_{jnb}/R_{nb})$ is the MSA's employment in industry j if it had the same employment share as the national average. That is, the value of the share effect depends only on deviations of MSA employment shares from U.S. averages. For industries serving local markets, MSA employment shares will be close to national averages. Hence, local industries contribute little to equation (19). On the other hand, industries that export their products to national or international markets will often have local employment shares that differ dramatically from the national average. These export industries will be the primary cause of differences across MSAs in the value of equation (19), and hence will be the primary cause of differences across MSAs in the instruments derived from equation (19).

The instrumental variables defined by equations (17) and (18) will differ across MSAs and time due to differences in the national economic performance during the time period of the export industries in which that MSA specializes. The national growth of an industry is a rough proxy for the change in national demand for its products. Thus, these instruments measure changes in national demand for the MSA's export industries. This change in demand would have both direct and multiplier effects (on local supplier and retail industries) on MSA employment. Some of these multiplier effects would take place with a lag.

The actual calculation of these instruments was slightly different for the aggregate data estimation and the micro data estimation, largely because the aggregate data estimation was done some time before the micro data estimation. The instruments used in the aggregate data estimation relied solely on data from the BLS 790 program. This program uses surveys to produce official industry employment figures for each MSA and year, with industry coverage differing greatly across MSAs. For each MSA, I used 1964 as a base year for calculating growth predictions from 1964-65 through 1972-73, 1973 as a base year for calculating growth predictions from 1973-74 through 1978-79, and 1979 as a base year for calculating growth predictions from 1979-80 through 1985-86. For each MSA and base year, I used whatever level of industry detail was reported for that MSA and base year, and put other industries into all other manufacturing and all other nonmanufacturing categories. The choice of only three base years, rather than using year t-1 as the base year for the growth prediction from year t-1 to t, was largely due to the complexity of dealing with very different levels of industry detail across MSAs and over time.

The instruments used in the micro data estimation were based on a combination of data from the ES-202 and BLS 790 program. The ES-202 program provides direct counts from all employers covered by unemployment insurance (virtually all private employment) of annual average employment. The industry detail of the ES-202 data is much greater than for the BLS 790 data. For the micro data estimation, 1979 was used as a base year for all the employment level predictions. ES-202 data on private employment by industry, and BLS 790 data on government employment were added together, and the ES-202 industry employment totals were adjusted proportionately so that the resulting sum added up to total nonagricultural employment as reported by the BLS 790 program. A shift-share analysis was then done for each year from 1970-71 to 1985-86 to calculate growth predictions for each year and MSA. These growth-effect predictions were then used to form employment-level predictions, as outlined in equation (18) above.

Are these share-effect variables good instruments? The quality of an instrument depends on two factors: whether the instrument is a good predictor of the endogenous right-hand side variables; and whether the instrument is uncorrelated with the disturbance term. Information on the predictive ability of the share-effect derived instruments can be obtained from the first-stage regressions used in deriving the 2SLS estimates. Representative regressions are presented in table 4A2.1. They show that the instruments are very good predictors.

The magnitude and pattern of effects of the instruments on MSA employment are also reasonable. The micro data estimates imply that the long-run multiplier of a 1 percent shock to an MSA's export industries is about 1.87.[4] The multiplier at first increases, presumably due to lags in how the export shock affects local retailers and suppliers. The multiplier then declines a bit; this may be due to the negative effects of higher land prices and wages caused by the initial growth shock. The multiplier using the aggregate data instruments is about 4.47, which seems too high. This higher multiplier may be due to the lesser industry detail in the aggregate data instruments. An MSA that specializes in fast-growing industries, using relatively aggregated industrial categories, may also specialize in fast-growing industries within those broad industrial categories.

Because supply shifters are unobserved, it is not possible to tell whether the share-effect derived instruments are correlated with labor or land supply shifters. However, such a correlation is unlikely. The share-effect instruments vary over time for a given MSA due to changes in national demand for that area's export industries. It is hard to see why changes in national demand would have much correlation with exogenous changes in local amenities (which might shift labor supply) or exogenous changes in local transportation systems or zoning rules (which might change land supply).

The empirical specifications for the aggregate data estimation (equation (9a)) and the micro data estimation (equation (12a)) allow for lagged values of employment growth or employment to affect local economic variables. One practical question is how to choose the lag length. After all, if one keeps on adding lags forever, eventually all estimates will be driven to statistical insignificance.

To solve this problem, I used a standard model selection criterion, the Akaike Information Criterion (AIC), for analysis of aggregate time series (Amemiya 1985, chap. 2). The basic idea of this selection criterion is to choose the model that will minimize the out-of-sample prediction error. Models with lower within-sample prediction error and smaller numbers of explanatory variables will tend to have lower out-of-sample prediction errors. Hence, the AIC picks the model that minimizes the following weighted average of the within-sample prediction error and the number of explanatory variables:

(20) $\quad \text{AIC} = \ln(e'e) + 2(K)/N$

where $e'e$ is the within-sample sum of squared residuals, K is the number of explanatory variables in the model, and N is the number of observations. In choosing between two nested models, the AIC is approximately equivalent to using a significance value of 2.00 for a F-test of the validity of the restricted model, as choosing the model with the lowest AIC amounts to choosing the unrestricted model if

(21) $\quad \ln(e_r'e_r) - \ln(e_u'e_u) > 2 \ (K_u - K_r)/N$

where the r subscript on e indicates the error terms from the restricted model, the u subscript on e indicates the error terms from the unrestricted model, K_u is the number of variables in the unrestricted model, and K_r is the number of variables in the restricted model.

Some studies have applied this model selection criterion to time series data (Geweke and Meese 1981). The AIC and other similar model selection criteria have been shown to be asymptotically biased towards choosing too long a lag-length in large samples, although the correct lag-length is most likely to be chosen. A bias toward slightly overfitting the model does not seem undesirable.

For the OLS regressions, the AIC is simply used to choose the optimal lag-length, among all lag-lengths up to eight years. The choice of a lag-length of s years means that the cumulative effect of the growth shock does not change enough from s years to eight years to justify including additional lags. Throughout the book, tables also report the long-run effects of a growth shock in a model with eight lags. These reports always confirm that there are no "significant" differences between cumulative effects after s lags and eight lags. However, sometimes the long-run effect is significant in the s-lag specification but not the eight-lag specification. In these cases, the eight-lag, long-run effect is estimated so imprecisely that neither zero nor the optimal lag-length, long-run effect can be rejected.

In the case of 2SLS estimates, there is no equivalent to the AIC for choosing lag-lengths. However, I adopted a modified AIC criterion that is equivalent to sequentially applying a F-test cutoff of 2.00 to models of longer and longer lag-lengths, in each case testing the new model against the previous best model. This modified AIC is based on the sum of squared residuals calculated using fitted values of the explanatory variable. The sum of squared residuals using actual values of the explanatory variables is in virtually all cases larger than the sum of squared residuals using fitted values. Hence, if a model of lag-length s has a smaller modified AIC than a model of lag-length $s + m$, then a F-test with a cutoff of 2.00 would also choose the model of lag-length s. This follows because

$$(22) \quad \ln(SSR_{fit}^{s}) + \frac{2s}{n} < \ln(SSR_{fit}^{s+m}) + \frac{2(s+m)}{n}$$

implies $\ln(SSR_{fit}^{s}) - \ln(SSR_{fit}^{s+m}) < \frac{2m}{n}$. Thus it is probably true that

$$\frac{(SSR_{fit}^{s} - SSR_{fit}^{s+m}) \, / \, m}{SSR_{fit}^{s+m} \, / \, [n-(s+m)]} < 2, \text{ where } SSR_{fit}^{s} \text{ is the sum of squared residuals}$$

using fitted values for lag-length s. Hence, if $SSR_{fit}^{s+m} < SSR_{act}^{s+m}$, where SSR_{act}^{s+m} is the sum of squared residuals using actual values, then

$$(23) \quad \text{Usual 2SLS } F\text{-test} = \frac{(SSR^s_{fit} - SSR^{s+m}_{fit}) \, / \, m}{SSR^{s+m}_{act} \, / \, (n\text{-}s\text{-}m)} < 2.$$

However, if a model of lag-length $s + m$ has a smaller modified AIC than a model of lag-length s, this model would not necessarily be chosen in a F-test with a cutoff of 2.00, as

$$(24) \quad \frac{(SSR^s_{fit} - SSR^{s+m}_{fit}) \, / \, m}{SSR^{s+m}_{fit} \, / \, (n\text{-}s\text{-}m)} > 2 \text{ does not imply}$$

$$F\text{-test} = \frac{(SSR^s_{fit} - SSR^{s+m}_{fit}) \, / \, m}{SSR^{s+m}_{act} \, / \, (n\text{-}s\text{-}m)} > 2, \text{ as } SSR^{s+m}_{act} \text{ can be considerably greater}$$

than SSR^{s+m}_{fit}.

Hence, the procedure used was as follows: Calculate the modified AIC for all 2SLS lag-lengths from zero to eight. Start out with zero as the best lag-length. Go to longer and longer lag-lengths until one is found that has a smaller AIC. Perform a F-test on the model with that lag-length versus the current best lag-length model. Choose the best model based on a F-test cutoff of 2.00. Continue on to longer lag-lengths, rejecting models with larger AIC values than the current best model, and performing F-tests on models with smaller AIC values than the current best model, choosing a new "best" model based on these F-tests. In most cases, this procedure is identical to choosing the model with the smallest modified AIC value.

Once optimal lag-lengths were chosen for both the OLS and 2SLS specifications, the statistical significance of the difference between OLS and 2SLS specifications was compared, for both the OLS and 2SLS optimal lag-lengths, using the well-known Hausman test (Hausman 1978). If OLS estimates are not significantly different from 2SLS estimates, then we cannot reject the restriction implied by OLS that the disturbance term is uncorrelated with the employment variables in equations (9a) and (12a). Hence, we cannot reject the consistency of OLS estimates, and the OLS-imposed restriction allows use of more information and results in greater precision of the estimates. In this case, OLS estimates are preferred. But if OLS and 2SLS estimates do differ, the implication is that OLS estimates are inconsistent and 2SLS estimates are preferred.

In addition to the Hausman F-test, which looks at the overall differences between the entire group of 2SLS and OLS estimates, I also looked at the statistical significance of differences between OLS and 2SLS estimates of the long-run effect of a shock to growth on the dependent variable. The variance of this difference is calculated, following Hausman, as V(2SLS estimate) – V(OLS estimate).

Another statistical problem examined for the micro data OLS regressions is whether the usual standard errors on the estimated effects of the aggregate employment variables are biased by a group structure to these data. A number of recent papers, in particular several papers by Moulton (1990, 1986), have pointed out that when aggregate variables are combined with micro data, the usual standard errors on the coefficients of the aggregate variables may be much lower than the true standard errors. The basic problem is that the disturbance term for the individual micro data observations may have a group structure that closely follows the group structure of the aggregate variables. OLS computer packages assume that all disturbance terms are independent. The reported standard errors on the aggregate variable coefficients will tend to be too low, because the package overestimates the amount of new information that is added by one more observation on the same group. Moulton has shown that the ratio of the true to usual standard errors will be approximately given by the square root of $[1 + (Var(g_i)/\bar{g} + \bar{g} - 1)P]$, where P is the within-group correlation, $\bar{g}$ is the average group size and $Var(g_i)$ is the variance of the average group size.

In the present case, the aggregate employment terms only vary across MSAs and over time. The regression includes dummy variables for both MSA and time effects. Hence, the relevant groups are MSA/time-period groups. The issue is whether, controlling for MSA and time effects, the disturbance terms for all individuals in a given MSA and year are positively correlated.

The standard test for a group structure to the disturbance term is a one-sided Lagrange Multiplier (LM) test. This test examines whether the estimated within-group correlation is significantly greater than zero. Moulton and Randolph (1989) have recently argued that the one-sided LM-test of group structure in regression disturbances, while asymptotically correct, may be misleading if the number of groups or the number of observations is small. They suggest a F-test to detect a group structure to the disturbance term. This F-test basically examines whether including a full set of group dummies in the regression adds significant explanatory power. Moulton (1988a) has outlined a method for using output from the F-test and other information from the GLM procedure of SAS to obtain unbiased estimates of the within-group correlation.

For each dependent variable examined in the micro data portion of this research, for the OLS optimal AIC lag-length, both LM- and F-tests were performed. These test results are reported in table 4A2.2. The LM-tests never indicated a significantly positive correlation, but F-tests, in some cases, did indicate a group structure to the data. Where the F-test statistic was significant at a 10 percent or lower level, I used Moulton's (1988a) suggested GLM procedure for calculating the within-group correlation, and then calculated the approximate ratio of the true to the usual standard errors.

As shown in the table, the implied percentage bias in the usual OLS standard errors is quite small, never more than 16 percent.[5] As will be discussed in later chapters, making the correlation would never make any difference to inferences drawn from tests of significance for the different models, and makes very little difference to the size of confidence intervals. Hence, the fact that this book primarily reports the usual OLS and 2SLS standard errors does not lead to any misleading conclusions.

This finding of little bias in usual OLS standard errors differs from the findings of other researchers who have included MSA variables in micro data models (Moulton 1990; Freeman 1989). The difference probably occurs because this study, unlike Moulton's and Freeman's, includes controls for MSA fixed effects. MSA effects may cause sizable within-group correlation and bias usual standard error calculations, but once these MSA fixed effects are eliminated, the remaining correlation within MSA/time-period groups is apparently small.

Three final points about estimation procedures should be made. First, for all micro data regressions, some additional specifications were run to test whether the results are sensitive to the length of time the individual has been in the MSA. Ideally, we would like to examine separately the effects of growth on long-term residents. The concern is that estimated long-term effects of a growth shock on average economic outcomes for individuals may reflect changes in the composition of the MSA population due to in-migration that are not controlled for with observed demographic characteristics. Unfortunately, the CPS only reports whether the individual was in that MSA t years ago, where t is 1 year in most cases (i.e., was the individual in the MSA in March of the previous year), but is 5 years ago for the 1985 and 1980 March CPS surveys, which report data on the individual's experiences during 1984 and 1979. All estimates excluded individuals not in the same MSA t years ago; this exclusion was done because if the individual was in a different MSA in March of the previous year, the data on their labor market experiences during the previous year may reflect the economic environment of another MSA.

To test whether results differ for long-term residents or not, for each dependent variable, and for the optimal lag-length chosen for the OLS regressions, I added an interaction term between a dummy variable for a 1984 or 1979 observation and all the employment variables, and estimated this augmented model by OLS. If the changing composition of the local population with in-migration is driving the results, one would expect these dummy variable interaction terms to be highly significant. The estimated effects of an employment shock after three or four years would be much less for the 1984 and 1979 cohorts than for other individuals in the sample. The specific results of this test for different dependent variables are reported in the appendices to various chapters. However, in no case did these interaction terms prove to be statistically significant, and the interaction terms were estimated precisely enough to rule out large differences in the long-run effects of employment shocks on the 1979 and 1984 cohorts versus other cohorts.

Second, most of the results reported in the text and text tables are for cumulative effects of a growth shock. These cumulative effects after s years are the sum of the coefficients on all the employment variables up to the sth lag. The standard errors on these coefficient sums could, of course, be calculated using the estimated variance-covariance matrix of the estimates. But for most of the regression results used in this study, the employment variables are manipulated so that the coefficient sums and their standard errors are directly calculated by the computer package. Specifically, it must be true that

$$(25) \quad \sum_{k=0}^{s} C_k(E_{m,t-k} - E_{m,t-k-1}) = \sum_{k=0}^{s-1} \sum_{f=0}^{k} C_f[(E_{m,t-k} - E_{m,t-k-1}) -$$

$$(E_{m,t-k-1} - E_{m,t-k-2})] + \sum_{f=0}^{s} C_f(E_{m,t-s} - E_{m,t-s-1});$$

$$(26) \quad \sum_{k=0}^{s} C_k E_{m,t-k} = \sum_{k=0}^{s-1} \sum_{f=0}^{k} C_f(E_{m,t-k} - E_{m,t-k-1}) + \sum_{f=0}^{s} C_f(E_{m,t-s})$$

where $E_{m,t}$ is the natural logarithm of MSA m's employment at year t. That is, if all except the last employment variable is expressed as a difference from the previous variable, then the coefficient on each variable will represent an estimated cumulative effect of an employment shock.

Finally, some of the micro dependent variables used in this study are subject to some censoring. That is, the labor force participation rate and the employment rate are basically bounded by zero and one. Ideally, one would want to explicitly deal with this censoring using well-known though complex techniques (Amemiya 1985). This approach was rejected due to constraints of time and money. Given the many other econometric issues addressed in this study (demand shocks versus supply shocks, unobserved MSA effects for up to 89 MSAs, the choice of lag-length, and bias due to unobserved group effects), the large number of regressions run (at least 36 for every dependent variable, given all the lag-lengths investigated), and the tens of thousands of observations in all micro data regressions, it simply was not feasible to address the censoring issue. Even with the censoring, it is still valid to interpret the regressions as estimates of best *linear* predictors of the dependent variable; the censoring means that some nonlinear predictors might do somewhat better. I doubt whether allowing for censoring would much change the estimates of the average effects of growth on different groups.

NOTES

1. In fact, in order to avoid including 89 dummy variables for all the MSAs included in this study, all estimations using micro data are based on equation (13) rather than equation (12), with all variables first differenced from MSA means.

2. This discussion is a bit loose. The full set of two-stage least squares instruments also includes all right-hand side variables in (9a) and (12a) except for the employment terms. The appendix discussion focuses on the instruments excluded from the right-hand side of equations (9a) and (12a), and hence provides the needed extra instruments for the endogenous employment variables.

3. This type of demand shock instrument was previously used in the Bradbury, Downs and Small (1982) book; I discovered their use of this instrument after I had already come up with my approach. Thus, I can only claim the originality of ignorance for my use of this type of instrument.

4. This multiplier is derived by summing all the coefficients on the instruments in table 4A2.1.

5. Note in table 4A2.2 that the ratio of true to usual standard errors is approximately equal to the square root of the F-test statistic. This is not an accident. Moulton's procedure for calculating the within-group correlation relies on analysis of covariance. Assume the micro data regression of interest can be written as $Y_{ij} = \mathbf{B}'\mathbf{X} + e_{ij}$, where Y_{ij} is the value of the dependent variable for individual j in group i, and $\mathbf{X}$ is a vector of explanatory variables. Suppose that the disturbance term for each observation is $e_{ij} = d_i + u_{ij}$, where d_i is independently and identically distributed across groups with mean zero and variance σ_d^2, u_{ij} is independently and identically distributed across groups with mean zero and variance σ^2. The within-group correlation is $\sigma_d^2/(\sigma^2 + \sigma_d^2)$, or, for small σ_d^2, is approximately equal to σ_d^2/σ^2. A regression of the dependent variable on the usual X variables, and a vector of group dummies, yields a mean square error of M_u. The expected value of this mean squared error is σ^2. The partial sum of squares for the group dummies, after taking account of the X variables, has a mean square error of M_d, with an expected mean square of $\sigma^2 + k\sigma_d^2$. This term k will be a complicated trace term, divided by a number which will be approximately equal to the number of groups. The trace term in the numerator of k is the sum, over all groups, of the sum of squared residuals from individual regressions of each group membership dummy on the explanatory variables. With large numbers of group dummies, the explanatory power of such regressions will be nil. The sum of squared residuals in each regression will just equal the sum of the dependent variables squared; summed over all regressions, this will simply be the number of observations. Hence, the term k will approximately equal the average group size.

The usual F-test statistic is given by M_d/M_u. The expected value of this statistic, based on the above discussion, is $(\sigma^2 + k\sigma_d^2)/\sigma^2$, or is approximately equal to $1 + \bar{g}p$, where p is the within-group correlation. If the ratio of the variance in group size to the mean group size is small compared to the mean group size, then this F-test statistic is approximately the square of the ratio of true to usual standard error formula given in the appendix text and in the notes to table 4A2.2.

Table 4A2.1
Effect of Share-Effect Derived Instruments
on MSA Employment and Employment Growth

Representative Micro Data Regression, Partial Results
Dependent Variable: MSA Employment Level
No. of observations: 32,558
R-squared: .6197

Variable	Parameter Estimate	Standard Error
LIV0	1.45	.07
LIV1	1.24	.09
LIV2	.73	.06
LIV3	.48	.09
LIV4	−.88	.07
LIV5	.04	.06
LIV6	.10	.07
LIV7	−.78	.07
LIV8	−.51	.07

Sum of coefficients = 1.87

Representative Aggregate Data Regression, Partial Results
Dependent Variable: MSA Employment Growth
No. of observations: 339
R-squared: .6422

Variable	Parameter Estimate	Standard Error
GIV0	1.72	.26
GIV1	1.02	.27
GIV2	.83	.25
GIV3	.52	.22
GIV4	.31	.23
GIV5	.17	.25
GIV6	−.17	.25
GIV7	.04	.26
GIV8	.03	.25

Sum of coefficients = 4.47

NOTES: LIVt is the ln(predicted employment) for the tth lag, using the share effects from the analysis of ES-202 data to generate the predictions. GIVt is the ln(predicted employment t) - ln(actual employment t-1), using the share effects from the analysis of BLS 790 data to generate the predictions. These are the two types of instruments mentioned in the appendix text. Both of these first-stage regressions reported above also included many other instruments, that is, all the right-hand side variables in equations (9a) and (12a), except for the employment variables, are treated as exogenous. Hence, the micro data regression includes MSA dummies, time dummies, and a full set of individual characteristics. The aggregate data regression includes a full set of time dummies.

Table 4A2.2

Tests of Possible Biases in Calculated Standard Errors Caused by a Variance Components Structure in the Micro Data Used

Dependent Variable	LM-Test Statistic	F-Test Statistic	Unbiased Estimate of Intra-Group Correlation	Approx. Ratio of True OLS Standard Error to Computer Package-Generated Standard Error
Employment probability	-2.31	1.127 (df=323,36519; Pr=.0584)	.00147	1.068
Labor force participation	-3.40	1.034 (df=327,32115; Pr=.3252)	NA	NA
Usual weekly hours	-3.05	1.040 (df=325,28576; Pr=.2995)	NA	NA
Real wages	-.07	1.204 (df=167,13080; Pr=.0381)	.00309	1.098
Occupational rank	-.04	1.209 (df=167,13080; Pr=.0349)	.00316	1.100

Wage differential from occupational mean	$-.20$	1.169 (df = 167,13080; Pr = .0682)	.00256	1.082
Real earnings	.84	1.337 (df = 166,14699; Pr = .00099)	.00452	1.156

NOTES: All calculations are based on the OLS lag-length minimizing the AIC. The LM-test statistic is a one-sided test, where the LM-test statistic is asymptotically standard normal, and positive within group correlation should yield a positive test statistic. The unbiased estimate of the within-group correlation, where the relevant group is each MSA/time period combination, is calculated using the GLM procedure from SAS, based on a procedure outlined by Moulton (1988a). This calculation is expensive, and is only done for cases where the F-test indicates that there may well be significant positive within-group correlation. The ratio of the true OLS standard errors for the aggregate employment coefficients to the computer-generated standard errors is calculated following Moulton (1986) as the square root of $\{1 + [\text{var}(g_j)/\bar{g} + \bar{g} - 1]P\}$, where P is the within-group correlation, $\bar{g}$ is the average group size, and $\text{var}(g_j)$ is the variance across groups of the group size. For the three samples of concern here, average group size and the group-size variance are: employment probability ($\bar{g} = 87.2$, $\text{var}(g_j) = 833.7$); all three real-wage variables ($\bar{g} = 66.5$, $\text{var}(g_j) = 57.5$); real earnings ($\bar{g} = 74.6$, $\text{var}(g_j) = 58.3$). Note that the square root of the F-test statistic is approximately equal to this ratio of true OLS standard errors to computer-generated standard errors.

Appendix 4.3
Background Information on Data

This appendix describes the data used in chapter 4. The same micro data are also used in chapters 6 and 7.

Aggregate unemployment rate data were derived from the Bureau of Labor Statistics publication series, *Geographic Profiles of Employment and Unemployment*. Data were obtained for annual average unemployment rates in various metropolitan areas for each year from 1972 to 1986. These data are calculated by the Bureau of Labor Statistics from the 12 monthly Current Population Surveys.

In addition to restricting the unemployment rate data to cities with CPS-based estimates, only metropolitan areas with official CPI data were included in the aggregate unemployment rate sample. This was to ensure that the aggregate estimation in chapter 4 would use the same set of cities as the aggregate estimation in chapters 5 and 6, which are restricted to MSAs with CPI data. With these restrictions, 25 MSAs ended up being included in the data. These 25 MSAs are identified in table 4A3.1.

The employment growth rates used on the right-hand side of the aggregate unemployment rate equations were defined as the year-to-year change in the natural logarithm of nonagricultural employment. Nonagricultural employment data were obtained from BLS 790 data. One potential problem with the BLS 790 data is that definitions of MSA boundaries change over time. If the boundary changed from year t-1 to year t, I used data based on the old boundaries to measure the logarithmic growth rate from t-1 to t, and data on the new boundaries to measure the logarithmic growth rate from t to $t+1$. In going though various old BLS publications, it was always possible to find some such overlap between employment time series using old and new MSA boundaries.

The micro results from this and other chapters are based on analysis of a pooled data set using information from March editions of the Current Population Survey from March 1980 through March 1987. Each March survey contains extensive information on the labor market activities of individuals in over 60,000 households during the preceding year, and this information was used to derive the dependent variables used in the micro data estimation. Only adult males, ages 25 to 64, are used in the micro data estimation. Furthermore, only males in identified MSAs are included in the analysis. From March 1980 through March 1985, only 44 MSAs are identified in the CPS data. Starting in March 1986, over 200 MSAs are indentified in CPS data. However, many of these MSAs have a relatively small number of observations. Furthermore, each MSA added to the analysis required a new shift-share analysis using the industrial categories reported for that MSA (see appendix 4.2). Hence, only individuals from the top 100 MSAs in population were selected from the March 1986 and March 1987 data tapes, in order to limit the number of shift-share analyses to only MSAs for which there actually was a fair amount of data on individual economic performance. In addition, some of the top MSAs went through such extensive boundary changes that it is difficult to construct a realistic time series of employment growth. MSAs with very extensive boundary changes were therefore excluded from the analysis. The net result was the inclusion of 89 MSAs in the analysis of the micro data. These MSAs are listed in table 4A3.1.

Even after these exclusions, the resulting data set would have had over 100,000 observations. To reduce computing costs, I chose a random subsample of 100 individuals per year from each of the 44 MSAs included in all the eight March CPS tapes. For the 45 MSAs that were only identified on the March 1986 and 1987 tapes, all individuals were included. Including a nearly equal number of observations from different MSAs maximizes the variation in the independent variable of interest, MSA employment, for a fixed sample size. After these further exclusions, the pooled data set had 44,015 observations. Descriptive statistics for the main independent micro variables are reported in table 4A3.2.

The sample size was further reduced in estimating the various micro data models presented in chapters 4, 6, and 7. First, as mentioned in appendix 4.2, only individuals who had been in the MSA for at least t years, where $t=5$ for the March 1985 and March 1980 tapes, but $t=1$ for all the other tapes, were included in the estimation. Second, some of the dependent variables are only defined for individuals of a particular labor force status. For example, the employment rate (= weeks employed during previous year divided by weeks in the labor force) is only defined for individuals with nonzero weeks in the labor force. The usual weekly hours and hourly wage rate variables are only defined for those with nonzero weeks employed during the previous year. Third, real wage rates and real earnings, used in chapters 6 and 7, can only be measured for individuals in the 25 MSAs with local consumer price indices. Fourth, individuals were excluded from the sample if any data were missing on variables in the regression. This problem mainly occurs for the wage rate and earnings variables, as up to 20 percent of the sample refuses to answer these CPS questions. Fifth, to save on computer time and research time, some dependent variables were analyzed together using the same data base, which allowed much quicker estimation using computer packages. But this required the exclusion of any observation missing for any of the dependent variables that were analyzed together. The labor force participation rate (= number of weeks in the labor force during the previous year divided by 52) was analyzed together with the nominal earnings variable (results not reported in this book), which required excluding any observation with missing values on nominal earnings. The usual weekly hours variable was analyzed together with the nominal hourly wage rate variable (= annual earnings divided by the product of annual weeks employed and usual weekly hours; nominal wage rate results are not reported in this book), which required excluding any observation with missing values on earnings. This type of grouping of dependent variables results in some seemingly puzzling differences in sample size. For example, the sample size used in analyzing the employment rate variable (36,962) is greater than the sample size used to analyze the labor force participation rate variable (32,558), because the labor force participation sample only includes observations with nonmissing values for earnings. Table 4A3.2 reports descriptive statistics on the main micro dependent variables used in this study, together with the sample size used in the analysis.

The MSA employment levels used as explanatory variables in the micro data studies are defined as the natural logarithm of the level of nonagricultural employment in the MSA, and are derived from the same BLS 790 data used in the aggregate data studies. In the case of MSA boundary changes from year t-1 to year t, MSA employment growth is calculated using the same method outlined above: using the old boundaries to calculate growth from year t-1 to t, and the new boundaries to calculate growth from year t to year $t+1$. The log MSA employment level for years $t+1$ and following is then calculated by adding in the appropriate amount of logarithmic growth in employment, calculated using the new MSA boundaries, to the log employment level using the old MSA definitions in year t. Because an MSA fixed effect is included in the empirical work, whether employment levels are adjusted to correspond to the old MSA definition, as is done here, or the new MSA definition is irrelevant because what matters is the year-to-year deviations of the MSA employment level from its overall average.

Finally, the detailed empirical results presented in the appendices to chapters 4, 5, 6, and 7 use a great many computer acronyms for the independent variables. Table 4A3.3 presents a guide to these computer acronyms. All demographic variables listed are included as controls in all micro regression results described in this book. All aggregate and micro regressions include a full set of time dummies. As described in appendix 4.2, all micro regressions in this book implicitly include a full set of MSA dummies by differencing all variables (both dependent and independent) from MSA means.

Table 4A3.1
MSAs Included in Research

Akron, OH	Los Angeles, CA *
Albany, NY	Memphis, TN
Albuquerque, NM	Miami, FL *
Allentown, PA	Milwaukee, WI *
Anaheim, CA	Minneapolis-St. Paul, MN *
Atlanta, GA *	Mobile, AL
Austin, TX	Nashville, TN
Bakersfield, CA	Nassau-Suffolk, NY
Baltimore, MD *	New Haven, CT
Baton Rouge, LA	New Orleans, LA
Birmingham, AL	New York, NY *
Boston, MA *	Newark, NJ
Bridgeport, CT	Norfolk, VA
Buffalo, NY *	Oklahoma City, OK
Charleston, SC	Omaha, NE
Charlotte, NC	Orlando, FL
Chicago, IL *	Oxnard-Ventura, CA
Cincinnati, OH *	Philadelphia, PA *
Cleveland, OH *	Phoenix, AZ
Columbia, SC	Pittsburgh, PA *
Columbus, OH	Portland, OR *
Dallas, TX *	Providence, RI
Dayton, OH	Raleigh-Durham, NC
Denver, CO *	Richmond, VA
Detroit, MI *	Riverside, CA
El Paso, TX	Rochester, NY
Flint, MI	Sacramento, CA
Fort Lauderdale, FL	St. Louis, MO *
Fresno, CA	Salt Lake City, UT
Gary, IN	San Antonio, TX
Grand Rapids, MI	San Diego, CA *
Greensboro, NC	San Francisco-Oakland, CA*
Greenville-Spartanburg, SC	San Jose, CA
Harrisburg, PA	Seattle, WA *
Hartford, CT	Springfield, MA
Honolulu, HI	Syracuse, NY
Houston, TX *	Tampa, FL
Indianapolis, IN	Toledo, OH
Jacksonville, FL	Tucson, AZ
Jersey City, NJ	Tulsa, OK
Kansas City, MO *	Washington, DC *
Knoxville, TN	West Palm Beach, FL
Las Vegas, NV	Wilmington, DE
Little Rock, AR	Youngstown, OH
Louisville, KY	

* Included in 25-MSA Sample, used in analyses involving local prices, and aggregate unemployment rate study.

Table 4A3.2
Descriptive Statistics for Main Variables in Micro Data

Variable	Mean	Standard Deviation	Sample Size
Education	13.0	3.2	44,015
Experience	22.3	12.4	44,015
Black	.097	.297	44,015
Spouse Present	.72	.45	44,015
Veteran	.41	.49	44,015
Family Size	3.04	1.56	44,015
No. of Children < 6	.27	.60	44,015
Current Employment Growth	.0228	.0300	44,015
Employment Probability (No. weeks employed ÷ weeks in labor force)	.946	.177	36,962
LFP Probability (No. weeks in labor force ÷ 52)	.875	.309	32,558
Usual Hours (during weeks employed in previous year)	42.67	8.94	29,019
Real Wages (= Real Earnings ÷ product of weeks worked and usual hours)	13.50	8.32	13,299
Real Earnings (during previous year)	24,880	18,334	14,918

Table 4A3.3
Guide to Computer Acronyms Used in Chapter Appendices

Acronym	Descriptive Name	Brief Additional Definition If Needed
Demographic Controls Included in All Micro Equations		
EDUC	Education	No. of years of education completed
EXPER	Experience	$\equiv$ Age - Education - 6
EDUC2	(Education)^2	
EXPER2	(Experience)^2	
EDEX	Education * Experience	
SPOPRE	Spouse Present	= 1 if Spouse is Present, 0 otherwise
FPERS	Family Size	No. of individuals in family
FREC14	No. of children < 6 years old	
VETSTA	Veteran Status	= 1 if veteran, 0 otherwise
BLACK	Black	= 1 if black, 0 otherwise
BEDUC	Black * Education	
BEXPER	Black * Experience	
BEDUC2	Black * (Education)^2	
BEXPER2	Black * (Experience)^2	
BEDEX	Black * Education * Experience	
BSPOPRE	Black * (Spouse Present)	
BFSIZ	Black * (Family Size)	
BCHL6	Black * (No. of children < 6 years old)	
BVETSTA	Black * (Veteran Status)	
Other Variables		
T74 to T86	Dummy Variables for time periods; = 1 if time is 1974, 0 otherwise, etc.	
EM0-EM8	Employment	$EMk = \ln$(MSA employment, year t-k) = kth lag of log employment
GR0-GR8	Employment Growth	$GRk = EM,k - EM,k+1$
ACC0-ACC7	Acceleration of Growth	$ACCk = GR,k - GR,k+1$

NOTES: In micro data portion of study, all variables are first-differenced from MSA means. This gives results equivalent to including a full set of MSA means. All micro equations include a full set of demographic controls and time dummies. All aggregate equations include a full set of time dummies.

Appendix 4.4
Background Information on Empirical Results Used in Chapter 4

Table 4A4.1 presents the least squares estimates from which figures 4.1 through 4.4 in chapter 4 are derived. These estimates are presented to ensure readers know the exact specification of the estimating equations and to inform readers interested in the coefficients on the control variables.

The results reported in figures 4.2 and 4.3 come directly from the employment variable coefficients in the micro employment and labor force participation rate regressions reported in table 4A4.1. The results in figure 4.1 come from summing up the employment variable coefficients in the unemployment rate regression in table 4A4.1 to get cumulative effects. The results in figure 4.4 come from dividing weekly hour coefficients and standard errors in table 4A4.1 by 42.67, the mean value of weekly hours, to get results expressed in percentage terms.

This appendix does not present detailed results for the "growth squared" specifications summarized in table 4.3, or the specifications summarized in table 4.4 that allow growth's effects to vary across different types of individuals. Full sets of these results are available upon request to interested readers. The "growth squared" results add a squared growth term for each growth term included in the regression. The "interaction" results interact the education, experience, and black variables with all employment variables included in the regression.

Using this interaction specification, the results reported in table 4.4 are based on the derivative with respect to a demographic characteristic of the long-run derivative with respect to employment of the dependent variable, and are then multiplied by a "standardized change," as described in the notes to table 4.4. The weekly hours results are adjusted to get the effect of a change in the demographic variable on the *percentage* effect of an employment shock on weekly hours. The expected percentage effect of an employment shock on weekly hours, for individuals with some particular set of demographic characteristics, is the absolute effect (call it A) of the employment shock on weekly hours for that group, which is calculated directly from the regression coefficients, divided by the expected weekly hours (H) for that demographic group, or A/H. The derivative of this percentage effect with respect to demographic characteristic z is given by the following formula:

(27) $\partial\,(A/H)/\partial z = (1/H^2)\,[H(\partial A/\partial z) - A(\partial H/\partial z)]$
$= (\partial A/\partial z)/H - (A/H)\,(\partial H/\partial z) \div H.$

In making this calculation, all derivatives are calculated from the estimated "interaction" specification at the means of all variables, and the mean value of the hours variable is used. The variance of this percentage effect of z is calculated conditional on the sample mean values of all variables and all derivatives, as

$$(1/H^2) \bullet [\text{Variance of } (\partial A/\partial z)].$$

Table 4A4.2 presents the two-stage least squares (2SLS) results for the effects of demand shocks to MSA employment growth on the labor market activity variables of chapter 4, using share-effect derived instrumental variables. All these 2SLS estimates are for the optimal lag-length, as chosen by the modified AIC procedure (see appendix 4.2). These tables also present Hausman tests examining the statistical significance of the overall differences between the 2SLS and OLS specifications, and Hausman tests of the statistical significance of differences in the long-run effects of employment growth between the two specifications. Hausman tests are reported for both the lag-length chosen as optimal in the OLS specification, and the lag-length chosen as optimal in the 2SLS specification. These tests all show that 2SLS estimates are not significantly different from OLS estimates.

Table 4A4.3 summarizes the results of micro data specifications that include interaction terms between the years 1979 and 1984 and the employment variables. Again, coefficient estimates and standard errors are only reported for the employment-related variables. This interaction specification is meant to test whether the effects of a growth shock differ for long-term residents versus more recent residents (see appendix 4.2). The 1979 and 1984 samples only include individuals who have been in the MSA more than five years, while the other years include all individuals who have been in the MSA more than one year. No statistically or substantively significant differences are found between growth effects in 1979 and 1984 and growth effects in other years.

Table 4A4.1

Full Least Squares Estimates Underlying Figures 4.1 through 4.4

Independent Variable	Δ in MSA Average Unemployment Rate, t-1 to t	Dependent Variable		
		Employment Rate, Micro Data	Labor Force Participation Rate, Micro Data	Weekly Hours
INTERCEPT	-0.004 (0.003)			
EDUC		0.0208 (0.0024)	0.0334 (0.0040)	0.25 (0.14)
EXPER		0.00550 (0.00077)	0.0286 (0.0013)	0.461 (0.045)
EDUC2		-0.000269 (0.000072)	-0.00060 (0.00012)	0.0115 (0.0043)
EXPER2		-0.0000359 (0.0000088)	-0.000565 (0.000015)	-0.00726 (0.00051)
EDEX		-.000235 (0.000034)	-0.000626 (0.000057)	-0.0099 (0.0020)
SPOPRE		0.0360 (0.0027)	0.1001 (0.0046)	1.80 (0.16)
FPERS		-0.00226 (0.00078)	-0.0069 (0.0014)	-0.152 (0.046)
FREC14		0.0002 (0.0018)	-0.0015 (0.0031)	0.22 (0.10)
VETSTA		0.0002 (0.0022)	-0.0009 (0.0038)	-0.44 (0.12)
BLACK		-0.375 (0.082)	-0.75 (0.12)	5.0 (5.2)

Variable			
BEDUC	0.0164 (0.0094)	0.086 (0.013)	-1.00 (0.60)
BEXPER	0.0140 (0.0027)	0.0077 (0.0044)	-0.21 (0.17)
BEDUC2	0.00007 (0.00029)	-0.00233 (0.00041)	0.034 (0.018)
BEXPER2	-0.000123 (0.000029)	0.000075 (0.000047)	0.0025 (0.0018)
BEDEX	-0.00050 (0.00013)	-0.00093 (0.00020)	0.0086 (0.0082)
BSPOPRE	0.0644 (0.0078)	0.065 (0.013)	0.13 (0.47)
BFSIZ	-0.0077 (0.0021)	-0.0098 (0.0035)	0.16 (0.13)
BCHL6	-0.0012 (0.0062)	0.029 (0.011)	0.17 (0.36)
BVETSTA	-0.0046 (0.0068)	0.007 (0.012)	1.07 (0.40)
T74	0.007 (0.004)		
T75	0.022 (0.004)		
T76	0.003 (0.004)		
T77	0.003 (0.003)		
T78	0.001 (0.003)		
T79	0.006 (0.004)		

Table 4A4.1 (continued)

Independent Variable	Δ in MSA Average Unemployment Rate, t-1 to t	Dependent Variable		
		Employment Rate, Micro Data	Labor Force Participation Rate, Micro Data	Weekly Hours
T80	0.008	-0.0084	-0.0032	-0.39
	(0.004)	(0.0047)	(0.0074)	(0.26)
T81	0.010	-0.0127	-0.0232	-0.83
	(0.004)	(0.0055)	(0.0074)	(0.30)
T82	0.013	-0.0245	-0.0215	-0.79
	(0.003)	(0.0059)	(0.0074)	(0.32)
T83	0.003	-0.0120	-0.0371	-0.26
	(0.003)	(0.0063)	(0.0074)	(0.36)
T84	-0.007	-0.0146	-0.0444	-0.19
	(0.003)	(0.0068)	(0.0079)	(0.34)
T85	-0.003	-0.0084	-0.0437	-0.67
	(0.003)	(0.0061)	(0.0075)	(0.26)
T86	0.006	-0.0094	-0.0505	-0.40
	(0.004)	(0.0056)	(0.0080)	(0.29)
GR0		0.422		4.1
		(0.066)		(3.8)
GR1		0.254		10.6
		(0.071)		(3.8)
GR2		0.109		
		(0.068)		
GR3		0.269		
		(0.061)		
EM0			0.137	
			(0.042)	

	Col 1	Col 2	Col 3	Col 4
EM2				2.8 (1.5)
EM4		0.066 (0.028)		
GR0	−0.320 (0.033)			
GR1	0.147 (0.043)			
GR2	0.009 (0.044)			
GR3	−0.021 (0.045)			
GR4	0.107 (0.049)			
GR5	−0.058 (0.047)			
GR6	0.078 (0.034)			
R-Squared	0.735	0.0565	0.1820	0.0374
No. of observations	350	36,962	32,558	29,019

NOTES: Standard errors are in parentheses. Blank means that variable was not included in that particular equation. Unemployment rate results were corrected for first-order auto correlation of −.189 (s.e. = .056). Auto correlation correction makes little difference to results. Other three equations were estimated by OLS. All micro variables were differenced from MSA means. This eliminates the intercept term in these equations. The reported standard errors correct for these extra implicit independent variables. However, the reported standard errors do not correct for the "Moulton effect." As discussed in appendix 4.2, this correction would make little difference.

Table 4A4.2

2SLS Estimates of Employment Growth Effects on Labor Market Activity Variables

Variable	Immediate Effect	Cumulative Effect After: 1 year	2 years	3 years	4 years	5 years	6 years	Long-Run Effect	Hausman F-test of Overall Difference: OLS lag-length	2SLS lag-length	Difference in Estimated Long-Run Effect: OLS lag-length	2SLS lag-length
Aggregate Unemployment Rate	-.51 (.11)	-.13 (.11)	-.08 (.10)	-.19 (.10)	-.05 (.12)	-.20 (.10)	-.08 (.06)	-.08 (.06)	1.05 (Prob. = .396)	1.05 (Prob. = .396)	-.02 (.06)	-.02 (.06)
Micro Employment Rate	.17 (.26)	.58 (.26)	.097 (.049)					.097 (.049)	.28 (Prob. = .924)	.61 (Prob. = .608)	.001 (.060)	-.007 (.042)
Labor Force Participation Rate	.232 (.074)							.232 (.074)	2.39 (Prob. = .122)	2.39 (Prob. = .122)	.094 (.061)	.094 (.061)
Weekly Hours	-.01 (2.5)							-.01 (2.5)	.71 (Prob. = .546)	3.35 (Prob. = .067)	-.015 (.024)	-3.771 (2.058)

NOTES: All estimated effects of shocks are for the 2SLS optimal lag-length for each variable, unless otherwise indicated. Standard errors of estimated effects are in parentheses below estimates. The Hausman F-tests show whether the entire set of estimates resulting from 2SLS differs significantly from the entire set of OLS estimates. F-test statistics are calculated both for the OLS optimal lag-length, and 2SLS optimal lag-length, which often differ. The probabilities in parentheses below the F-test show the probability of an F-test statistic of the size reported resulting from chance if the true value of the coefficients in the 2SLS and OLS specifications were actually the same. The last two columns report the difference between the 2SLS and OLS estimated long-run effects of an employment shock (i.e., 2SLS LR effect – OLS LR effect). Standard errors of these differences are in parentheses.

Table 4A4.3

OLS Estimates of Effects of MSA Employment Shocks on Labor Market Activity, with Inclusion of Interaction Term Between Employment Variables and 1979/1984 Dummy

Dependent Variable	Cumulative Effect of Employment Shocks (Except for 1979 and 1984)						Differential Employment Shock Effect for 1979 and 1984						F-Test on Interaction Terms
	Immediate Effect	1 year	2 years	3 years	4 years	Long-Run Effect	Immediate Effect	1 year	2 years	3 years	4 years	Long-Run Effect	
Employment Rate	.445 (.069)	.226 (.082)	.144 (.072)	.278 (.066)	.059 (.028)	.059 (.028)	-.24 (.20)	.27 (.19)	.43 (.24)	.01 (.18)	-.0038 (.0037)	-.0038 (.0037)	2.099 (df=5; 36837; Prob.=.062)
Labor Force Participation Rate	.138 (.042)					.138 (.042)	-.0107 (.0066)					-.0107 (.0066)	2.647 (df=1; 32441; Prob.=.104)
Weekly Hours	4.9 (4.0)	7.4 (4.4)	3.3 (1.5)			3.3 (1.5)	-2.00 (11.00)	12.0 (9.2)	-.09 (.22)			-.09 (.22)	1.14 (df=3; 28898; Prob.=.331)

NOTES: First set of columns shows coefficients on regular MSA employment variables, while second set of columns shows coefficients on interaction terms between MSA employment variables and dummy variable that is one for 1979 and 1984, zero otherwise. Standard errors are in parentheses. Note that F-test statistics never show significance at the conventional 5 percent level of significance. Furthermore, the estimated difference in the long-run effect of growth, between the 1979/1984 cohort and other cohorts, is always substantively small (compared to the estimated average size of the long-run effect) and statistically insignificant at the 5 percent level.

Appendix 5.1
Background Information on Chapter 5 Results

Table 5A1.1 presents the full OLS estimates of the effects of shocks to employment growth on various types of housing prices and overall prices. All results are only for the lag-length chosen as optimal for that particular specification, based on the Akaike Information Criterion (AIC).[1]

These OLS results were summarized in figures 5.1 through 5.4 in the text of chapter 5, along with the results for overall prices. The OLS results reported in this appendix also include information on the estimated time period effect dummies, the number of observations in each regression, and the proportion of variance explained by the regression. The reader will note that the number of observations is different for various dependent variables, because some price indices have been radically changed over time and data on computer tape are only available for more recent years.

Full OLS results are not reported for the nonhousing price regressions, but are available on request.[2] Table 5A1.2 reports 2SLS estimates of the effects of employment growth on different price variables with "share effect" predicted growth terms used as instrumental variables. (Appendices 4.2 and 4.3 have more information on the share effect instrument and its rationale. The share instrument used here is identical to that used in 2SLS estimates of the effects of growth on unemployment.) To save space, the 2SLS table does not report estimated coefficients and standard errors for the time dummies, although they are, of course, part of the estimation.

The 2SLS tables also report Hausman tests that compare the 2SLS estimates to OLS estimates. The F-test examines whether the 2SLS and OLS estimates overall are significantly different. In addition, I report estimates of differences in the estimated long-run effect of growth between the 2SLS and OLS specifications, as well as the standard error of this estimated difference. Much of the discussion of this book has focused on estimating the long-run effects of growth; hence, differences between 2SLS and OLS in the long-run effects of growth are viewed here as of greater importance than differences in estimated short-run effects or estimated time period effects. Hausman test comparisons of 2SLS and OLS estimates are performed both for the lag-length chosen (using the AIC) as optimal for OLS, and the lag-length chosen as optimal for 2SLS.

Of these 13 different inflation indices, Hausman F-tests indicate a difference between 2SLS and OLS, using both possible lag-lengths, for only four of the variables: shelter inflation, homeownership inflation (the old index), transportation inflation, and medical care inflation. In addition, F-test statistics indicate a significant difference between 2SLS and OLS estimates, for the 2SLS

optimal lag-length but not the OLS optimal lag-length, for the new homeownership cost inflation variable and the other goods and services inflation variable.
However, the estimated difference between 2SLS and OLS estimates of the
long-run effect of growth is only statistically significant for the transportation
inflation and new homeownership cost inflation variables. In both cases, 2SLS
estimates indicate somewhat greater long-run effects of a one-time growth shock
on the price level. On the whole, however, the 2SLS estimates do not appear
to require any significant change in the conclusions reached on the basis of
the OLS estimates.

NOTES

1. The chosen lag-length for 2SLS is based on a slight modification to the AIC. See appendix
4.2 for details.
2. The number of observations for the other OLS regressions is as follows: food and beverages,
household furnishings, entertainment, and other goods prices have 247 observations; transportation, apparel, and medical care prices have 343 observations; and household fuel and utility prices
have 339 observations.

Table 5A1.1
Full OLS Estimates of Effects of Employment Growth on Housing Prices and Overall Prices

			Dependent Variable		
Independent Variable	Shelter Prices	Dwelling Rent Price Index	Old Homeownership Price Index	Owners' Equivalent Rental Price Index	Overall CPI
INTERCEP	0.038	0.035	0.030	0.043	0.056
	(0.008)	(0.005)	(0.009)	(0.011)	(0.003)
ACC0	0.054	0.181	-0.095	0.205	0.022
	(0.112)	(0.063)	(0.181)	(0.176)	(0.041)
ACC1	0.361	0.494		0.632	0.118
	(0.116)	(0.066)		(0.159)	(0.042)
ACC2	0.528	0.738		0.684	
	(0.123)	(0.070)		(0.154)	
ACC3	0.554	0.727		0.757	
	(0.119)	(0.068)		(0.156)	
ACC4	0.562	0.577		0.551	
	(0.130)	(0.074)		(0.178)	
ACC5		0.430		0.503	
		(0.075)		(0.209)	
ACC6				0.822	
				(0.227)	
GR1			0.451		
			(0.116)		
GR2					0.200
					(0.031)

	Col 1	Col 2	Col 3	Col 4	Col 5
GR5	0.340 (0.092)				
GR6		0.252 (0.053)			
GR7				0.250 (0.146)	
T74	0.043 (0.011)	-0.003 (0.006)	0.048 (0.014)		0.040 (0.004)
T75	0.046 (0.013)	0.009 (0.008)	0.065 (0.015)		0.026 (0.004)
T76	0.016 (0.012)	0.020 (0.007)	0.037 (0.013)		-0.000 (0.004)
T77	0.033 (0.009)	0.029 (0.006)	0.031 (0.011)		0.008 (0.003)
T78	0.056 (0.011)	0.018 (0.006)	0.065 (0.011)		0.014 (0.003)
T79	0.079 (0.012)	0.014 (0.007)	0.099 (0.012)		0.046 (0.004)
T80	0.106 (0.013)	0.029 (0.007)	0.139 (0.014)		0.065 (0.004)
T81	0.068 (0.012)	0.041 (0.007)	0.084 (0.012)		0.038 (0.004)
T82	0.029 (0.011)	0.055 (0.006)	0.023 (0.014)		0.002 (0.004)
T83	0.022 (0.011)	0.046 (0.006)			-0.016 (0.004)
T84	0.016 (0.010)	0.024 (0.006)			-0.016 (0.003)

Table 5A1.1 (continued)

Independent Variable	Shelter Prices	Dwelling Rent Price Index	Dependent Variable Old Homeownership Price Index	Owners' Equivalent Rental Price Index	Overall CPI
T85	0.003	0.009		0.008	-0.026
	(0.010)	(0.006)		(0.014)	(0.003)
T86	-0.007	-0.010		0.002	-0.046
	(0.012)	(0.007)		(0.016)	(0.004)
No. of observations	339	343	229	74	343
R-Squared	.6521	.5758	.6187	.4062	.8978

NOTES: Standard errors are in parentheses. Blank means variable is not included in that particular regression. As explained in appendix 4.2, coefficients on ACCk variable is cumulative effect after k lags; coefficient on the one included GRt variable is the long-run effect. Reported estimates for each dependent variable are for lag-length that minimized the Akaike Information Criterion (AIC).

Table 5A1.2
2SLS Estimates of Effects of Employment Growth on Various Categories of Prices

Variable	Immediate Effect	Cumulative Effect After: 1 year	2 years	3 years	4 years	5 years	6 years	Long-Run Effect	Hausman F-test of Overall Difference OLS lag-length	2SLS lag-length	Difference in Estimated LR Effect OLS lag-length	2SAS lag-length
Shelter	-0.719 (0.344)	-0.298 (0.343)	0.235 (0.161)					0.235 (0.161)	2.792 (Prob. = .012)	3.359 (Prob. = .010)	-0.242 (0.172)	-0.189 (0.137)
Dwelling Rent	0.237 (0.195)	0.564 (0.092)						0.564 (0.092)	1.477 (Prob. = .175)	1.630 (Prob. = .197)	.125 (.094)	.134 (.077)
Old Homeownership	-1.365 (0.531)	-0.380 (0.529)	0.441 (0.249)					0.441 (0.249)	7.249 (Prob. = .001)	4.649 (Prob. = .004)	-.113 (.196)	-.067 (.216)
Owner's Equivalent Rent	0.700 (0.191)							0.700 (0.191)	.516 (Prob. = .839)	3.981 (Prob. = .050)	.178 (.336)	.268 (.145)
Overall Price Index	-0.111 (0.120)	-0.065 (0.120)	0.150 (0.056)					0.150 (0.056)	1.254 (Prob. = .290)	1.254 (Prob. = .290)	-.050 (.047)	-.050 (.047)
Food and Beverage	0.113 (0.112)	-0.055 (0.107)	0.158 (0.053)					0.158 (0.053)	.564 (Prob. = .639)	.564 (Prob. = .639)	.011 (.042)	.011 (.042)
Transportation	0.249 (0.077)							0.249 (0.077)	7.718 (Prob. = .006)	7.718 (Prob. = .006)	.177 (.066)	.177 (.066)

Table 5A1.2 (continued)

Variable	Immediate Effect	Cumulative Effect After: 1 year	2 years	3 years	4 years	5 years	6 years	Long-Run Effect	Hausman F-test of Overall Difference OLS lag-length	2SLS lag-length	Difference in Estimated LR Effect OLS lag-length	2SLS lag-length
Household Fuel and Utilities	-0.245 (0.188)							-0.245 (0.188)	2.920 (Prob. = .088)	2.920 (Prob. = .088)	-.270 (.160)	-.270 (.160)
Household Furnishings and Operations	0.112 (0.063)							0.112 (0.063)	.380 (Prob. = .538)	.380 (Prob. = .538)	.032 (.052)	.032 (.052)
Apparel	0.173 (0.087)							0.173 (0.087)	.253 (Prob. = .615)	.253 (Prob. = .615)	.037 (.074)	.037 (.074)
Medical Care	0.387 (0.175)	0.100 (0.082)						0.100 (0.082)	3.170 (Prob. = .014)	5.411 (Prob. = .005)	-.015 (.072)	.014 (.073)
Entertainment	0.053 (0.109)							0.053 (0.109)	.263 (Prob. = .953)	.090 (Prob. = .765)	.073 (.069)	.027 (.090)
Other Goods and Services	-0.071 (0.165)	-0.069 (0.158)	-0.132 (0.163)	-0.143 (0.174)	0.268 (0.083)			0.268 (0.083)	1.522 (Prob. = .210)	3.337 (Prob. = .006)	.040 (.055)	.121 (.070)

NOTES: All estimates, unless otherwise indicated, are for 2SLS optimal lag-length. Hausman F-test provides test of overall differences between the OLS and 2SLS sets of estimates, both for the lag-length judged optimal by OLS, and the lag-length judged optimal by 2SLS. The probability below these F-test statistics is the probability of an F-test statistic of this size if there were no significant differences between the true OLS and 2SLS parameters. The last two columns report the difference between the long-run 2SLS effect and the long-run OLS effect (i.e., LR 2SLS − LR OLS). The standard error of these differences are reported in parentheses.

Appendix 6.1
Background Information on Chapter 6 Results

This appendix presents some of the estimates from chapter 6 in more detail.
The full least squares results using Area Wage Survey data on occupational
real wages are presented in table 6A1.1. These are the same aggregate data
results reported in table 6.2 in chapter 6. Table 6A1.1 shows results for the
optimal AIC specification for each variable. The estimated equations are corrected for first-order autocorrelation. The cumulative effect of a growth shock
after three years in the skilled worker real wage specification is the sum of
the coefficients on all the growth variables. The standard errors reported in
the text are calculated based on the variance-covariance matrix of all the
parameters, which is not reproduced here.

Each of the Area Wage Survey wage inflation indices are weighted averages
for specific occupations. Each occupation's wage inflation from t-1 to t is
calculated by a survey of average employers who were located in the MSA
both years.

These aggregate equations were also estimated using share effect instruments
for the lag-length chosen as optimal by OLS. (See chapter 4, appendices 4.2
and 4.3.) A Hausman test was run to compare these estimates using share effect instruments with ordinary least squares estimates. The Hausman test
statistics are reported in table 6A1.2. As can be seen in the table, all of these
test statistics indicate no significant differences between the OLS and share
effect estimates.

I also added employment growth squared terms as explanatory variables in
these equations to see whether a growth shock's effect on real wages varied
with the initial level of growth. The Akaike Information Criterion (AIC) suggested that adding terms in growth squared improved the specification for skilled
real wages and office and clerical worker real wages, but did not improve
the specification for unskilled real wages. More conventional F-tests also showed that the growth squared terms were collectively significant at the 5 percent
level for the skilled real wages equation and the office and clerical real wages
equation, but were not significant in the unskilled real wages equation.

Based on these growth squared regressions, table 6A1.3 shows, for skilled
real wages and office and clerical real wages, how the effects of a 1 percent
shock to growth vary at different initial levels of growth at different times
after the shock. Although the growth squared terms are collectively significant in both these equations, the only individually significant growth squared
effect is for the long-run effect of growth on skilled worker real wages. The
results show that variations in growth have greater effects on skilled real wages
at lower initial levels of growth.

The full basic ordinary least squares results using micro data from the CPS on real wages are presented in table 6A1.4. This table only reports results for the lag-length chosen as optimal for each dependent variable regression by the AIC. The dependent variable in these equations is expressed as real dollars per hour, with the MSA's 1986 price index being assumed to be 1.00 in all cases. All these equations implicitly assume a full set of dummy variables for each MSA; this is done by differencing all variables from their MSA mean before estimation. In addition to controlling for MSA fixed effects, these MSA dummy variables control for any differences across MSAs in the 1986 price level. Also, the inclusion of an MSA fixed effect means that what is important is not the absolute level of employment in the MSA, but its level of employment compared to some typical level for the MSA; that is, what is important is employment growth since some base year.

The percentage effects reported in the chapter 6 text and in table 6.3 are derived by dividing the absolute dollar effects of employment shocks reported in these appendix tables by the sample mean for real wages per hour, which is $13.50. The standard errors of the percentage effects incorporate the stochastic nature of the estimated absolute dollar effects, but condition on the sample mean as a fixed parameter. That is, the percentage effect = absolute dollar effect/sample mean. The calculated standard error to this percentage effect is (standard error to absolute dollar effect)/(sample mean). Thus, these standard errors are best interpreted as the uncertainty in the percentage effect of employment shocks, calculated at this particular fixed value of $13.50; the standard errors do not tell us the uncertainty in our percentage effects if we interpret our calculations as giving consistent estimates of the percentage effects of employment shocks calculated at the population mean.

As was discussed in appendix 4.1, the usual estimates of OLS standard errors of coefficients on aggregate variables in micro data equations may be biased if the disturbance term has a variance components structure. Table 4A2.2 showed the true standard errors on the employment terms should be about 9.8 percent higher than the usual standard errors for the real wage regression, 10.0 percent higher for the occupational rank regression, and 8.2 percent higher for the wage differential regressions. These adjustments were not made in the tables or figures for this chapter, but making this adjustment would have no effect on any inferences.

The OLS real wage estimates were also tested by including an interaction term between the employment variables and a dummy variable for an observation from 1979 or 1984. As discussed in the chapter 4 appendices, the 1979 and 1984 samples only included individuals who had been in the MSA at least five years, while other years' samples included all individuals with at least one year of residence in the MSA. If this study's estimated effects of growth are biased by the special characteristics of in-migrants, then this interaction term should be statistically significant and large. But, as shown in table 6A1.5, the interaction term has only a small and statistically insignificant effect on the real wage.

These micro real wage equations were also estimated using share effects, and all explanatory variables except for the employment terms, as instrumental variables. (See appendices 4.2 and 4.3.) Hausman test statistics were calculated to compare these instrumental variable estimates with ordinary least squares estimates. Comparisons were performed both for the lag-length chosen as optimal by OLS, and the lag-length chosen as optimal by the 2SLS estimates using the share effect instruments. These Hausman test statistics are reported in table 6A1.6. As can be seen in the table, the Hausman test statistics clearly indicate significant differences between the two sets of estimates. As the share effect instrument estimates in theory are always consistent, the instrumental variable estimates become the preferred estimates, given that there are significant differences.

I also compared the 2SLS and OLS estimates of individual coefficients on the employment terms. This comparison is reported in table 6A1.7. As can be seen in the table, the only statistically significant differences in estimates of individual coefficients are that employment shocks have significantly greater short-run effects on the real wage and wage differential variables using the 2SLS estimates, and have significantly greater short-run and long-run effects on the occupational rank variable using the 2SLS estimates. The long-run effects of employment shocks on the real wage or wage differential variables do not differ significantly between the 2SLS and OLS estimates.

I do not report in this appendix the 2SLS estimates that lie behind table 6.4, which show the effects of employment shocks on real wages when interaction terms are included between the employment terms and education, experience (age-education-6) and race. In addition to using share effect projected MSA employment as instruments, these 2SLS regressions used as instruments interaction terms between the share effect instruments and education, experience, and race. A full set of these results are available to interested readers upon request.

To get the change in the percentage effects reported in table 6.4 in the text, I calculated the derivative of the percentage effect with respect to the individual characteristic. The percentage effect is A/W, where A is the absolute dollar effect, and W is the real wage. The derivative of this with respect to individual characteristic X, where X is education, experience, or race, is $d(A/W)/dX = (1/W^2)(W(dA/dX) - A(dW/dX)) = (dA/dX)/W - (A/W)(dW/dX)/W$. This derivative was calculated at the mean values of A, W, and all other individual characteristics, and then multiplied by the standardized change in X to get the figures in table 6.4. This multiplication will only give an approximation to the actual discrete change, but some checks on this calculation indicate that it is a fairly good approximation. The standard errors in table 6.3 were calculated as (standard error of dA/dX) times $(1/W)$ times standardized change. In other words, these standard error calculations take into account the stochastic nature of estimates of dA/dX, but are conditional on the sample mean values of A/W, dW/dX, and W. This simplified approach was adopted because of the complexity of taking into account the true variance and covariance of all these estimates.

Table 6A1.1
Full Least Squares Estimate for Effects of Employment Growth
on Various Real Wage Indices

Variable	Real Wage		
	Skilled Workers	Unskilled Workers	Office & Clerical Workers
INTERCEPT	.001	.008	−.006
	(.005)	(.004)	(.004)
GR0	−.127	−.110	−.029
	(.071)	(.051)	(.045)
GR1	.159		
	(.090)		
GR2	−.200		
	(.091)		
GR3	.153		
	(.074)		
T74	−.019	−.022	−.025
	(.006)	(.005)	(.005)
T75	.014	.006	.006
	(.008)	(.006)	(.005)
T76	.026	.021	.024
	(.007)	(.005)	(.005)
T77	.012	.013	.010
	(.005)	(.005)	(.005)
T78	.012	.004	.005
	(.006)	(.005)	(.005)
T79	−.025	−.027	−.025
	(.006)	(.005)	(.005)
T80	−.028	−.035	−.033
	(.007)	(.005)	(.005)
T81	−.003	−.006	.004
	(.007)	(.005)	(.005)
T82	.006	.007	.026
	(.007)	(.006)	(.005)
T83	.008	.002	.028
	(.007)	(.006)	(.005)
R-Squared	.55	.54	.65
No. of observations	241	234	253

Table 6A1.2
Hausman Test Statistics for Endogeneity
of Employment Growth Variables
in Aggregate Real Wage Equations

Dependent Variable	Value of Hausman Test Statistic	2SLS Estimated Long-Run Effect −GLS Estimated Long-Run Effect
Real wage change, skilled workers	1.46 (df = 4,222) (Prob. = .215)	.12 (.09)
Real wage change, office and clerical workers	.53 (df = 1,241) (Prob. = .467)	.09 (.07)
Real wage change, unskilled workers	.15 (df = 1,221) (Prob. = .699)	−.03 (.07)

NOTES: Hausman F-test statistic examines overall differences between 2SLS and GLS specification. Probabilities stated are probabilities of F-test statistic of this size if there were no true overall differences. Last column reports 2SLS estimated long-run effect of a growth shock minus GLS estimate of long-run effect. Standard error of this difference is in parentheses.

Table 6A1.3

Estimated Elasticity of Aggregate Real Wages with Respect to Employment Growth, Allowing for Differential Effects at Different Initial Levels of Growth

Initial Annual Employment Growth Rate	Real Wages, Skilled Workers	
	Initial Effect	Long-Run Effect = 1 Year
−.01	−.04(.08)	.18(.09)
.025	−.04(.08)	−.02(.06)
.06	−.04(.12)	−.22(.10)
t-Test	.01	2.58

Initial Annual Employment Growth Rate	Real Wages, Office/Clerical Workers	
	Initial Effect	Long-Run Effect = 1 Year
−.01	−.00(.07)	.01(.08)
.025	.09(.07)	−.04(.05)
.06	.18(.11)	−.09(.09)
t-Test	1.47	.74

NOTES: Estimates are based on GLS specifications, allowing for serial correlation, that include squared terms in all employment growth variables. Average annual employment growth rate for this sample of MSAs from 1972 to 1986 is .025; .031 is standard deviate of MSA employment growth rates in this sample, so −.01 and .06 are slightly more than one standard deviation away from the mean. *t*-test row reports *t*-statistic on growth squared term for that particular lagged effect of growth.

Table 6A1.4
Full OLS Estimate of the Effects of Employment Growth
on Various Measures of Real Wages, Using Micro Data

Variable	Real Wage	Occupational Rank	Wage Differential
EDUC	0.264	−0.079	0.343
	(0.175)	(0.062)	(0.170)
EXPER	0.520	0.090	0.430
	(0.057)	(0.020)	(0.056)
EDUC2	0.029	0.027	0.002
	(0.005)	(0.002)	(0.005)
EXPER2	−0.008	−0.00089	−0.007
	(0.001)	(0.00023)	(0.001)
EDEX	−0.001	−0.002	0.001
	(0.002)	(0.001)	(0.002)
SPOPRE	2.457	0.739	1.718
	(0.198)	(0.071)	(0.193)
FPERS	−0.026	−0.042	0.016
	(0.058)	(0.021)	(0.057)
FREC14	−0.111	−0.016	−0.095
	(0.129)	(0.046)	(0.126)
VETSTA	0.189	0.004	0.184
	(0.161)	(0.057)	(0.157)
BLACK	4.518	2.135	2.382
	(6.161)	(2.198)	(6.017)
BEDUC	−0.707	−0.492	−0.215
	(0.712)	(0.254)	(0.695)
BEXPER	−0.093	−0.020	−0.073
	(0.200)	(0.072)	(0.196)
BEDUC2	0.026	0.019	0.007
	(0.022)	(0.008)	(0.022)
BEXPER2	0.002	0.000047	0.002
	(0.002)	(0.00077)	(0.002)
BEDEX	−0.003	0.002	−0.005
	(0.010)	(0.003)	(0.009)
BSPOPRE	−1.070	−0.528	−0.541
	(0.569)	(0.203)	(0.556)
BFSIZ	0.042	0.049	−0.007
	(0.161)	(0.057)	(0.157)

315

Table 6A1.4 (continued)

Variable	Real Wage	Occupational Rank	Wage Differential
BCHL6	−0.030	0.006	−0.036
	(0.465)	(0.166)	(0.454)
BVETSTA	0.082	−0.050	0.133
	(0.487)	(0.173)	(0.476)
T80	−0.767	−0.012	−0.755
	(0.263)	(0.094)	(0.257)
T81	−0.931	−0.167	−0.764
	(0.265)	(0.095)	(0.259)
T82	−1.130	−0.522	−0.608
	(0.264)	(0.094)	(0.258)
T83	−1.041	−0.574	−0.467
	(0.268)	(0.095)	(0.261)
T84	−1.362	−0.567	−0.795
	(0.293)	(0.101)	(0.276)
T85	−1.544	−0.693	−0.852
	(0.285)	(0.101)	(0.279)
T86	−1.257	−0.665	−0.592
	(0.300)	(0.106)	(0.292)
EM0	3.515	1.372	2.143
	(1.575)	(0.562)	(1.538)
R-Squared	0.1699	0.2946	0.0739
No. of observations	13,299	13,299	13,299

NOTES: Standard errors are in parentheses. Full set of MSA dummies is implicitly included by first-differing all variables from MSA means.

Table 6A1.5
Selected Results for Real Wages When Interaction Term is Included
Between Employment Variable and 1979/1984 Dummy

Variable	Parameter Estimate	Standard Error
EM0	3.516	1.572
SEM0	−.169	.279

NOTES: Regression also includes a full set of demographic variables and time dummies. SEM0 is interaction term between EM0 and dummy variable equal to one for 1979 and 1987.

Table 6A1.6
Hausman Test Statistics for Overall Differences
Between Effects of Demand-Induced Growth
and Overall Growth, Micro Real Wage Variables

Variable	Hausman Test Statistic
Real Wages	F-test $(1,13182) = 6.86$; Prob. $= .009$ (OLS optimal lag-length) F-test $(4,13176) = 4.99$; Prob. $= .001$ (2SLS optimal lag-length)
Occupation Rank	F-test $(1,13182) = 5.52$; Prob. $= .019$
Wage Differential from Occupation Mean	F-test $(1,13182) = 3.31$; Prob. $= .069$ (OLS optimal lag-length, F-test $(4,13176) = 3.24$; Prob. $= .011$ (2SLS optimal lag-length)

Table 6A1.7
Comparison of 2SLS and OLS Estimates of Individual Coefficients
on Employment Terms, Micro Real Wage Variables

		Cumulative Effect After:			
		0 years	**1 year**	**2 years**	**3 years**
Real Wages	2SLS	−.2360 (.1676)	.0367 (.2364)	.5963 (.2060)	−.0047 (.0423)
	OLS	.0377 (.0444)	.0481 (.0497)	.0423 (.0427)	.0305 (.0175)
	Difference	−.2737 (.1616)	−.0114 (.2311)	.5540 (.2015)	−.0352 (.0385)

Long-run 2SLS effect is significant up to 2-lag specification; 8-lag specification effect is −.0242 (.0800)

Occupation Rank	2SLS	.0321 (.0096)			
	OLS	.0137 (.0056)			
	Difference	.0184 (.0078)			

Long-run 2SLS effect is significant up to 2-lag specification; 8-lag specification LR effect is .0450 (.0283)

Wage Differential from Occupation	2SLS	−.1651 (.1633)	.0296 (.2302)	.4793 (.2006)	−.0149 (.0412)
	OLS	.0392 (.0433)	.0226 (.0486)	.0324 (.0417)	.0166 (.0171)
	Difference	−.2043 (.1575)	.0070 (.2250)	.4469 (.0384)	−.0017 (.0375)

Long-run 2SLS effect is significant up to 1-lag specification; 8-lag specification LR effect is −.0692 (.0781)

NOTES: OLS and 2SLS dynamics are compared for lag-length chosen by 2SLS estimation technique. Standard errors are in parentheses. Standard error of difference is calculated as V(diff) = V(2SLS) − V(OLS) (Hausman 1978).

318

Appendix 7.1
Detailed Results for Real Earnings Regressions

The data and methodology used are generally similar to those used to estimate the effects of growth on individual labor market activity and real wage variables. The data are pooled CPS data on adult males, ages 25-64, for the years 1979 through 1986. The reader is referred to the appendices to chapter 4 for more details.

As in the real wage regressions for individuals, the sample was restricted to the 25 MSAs for which we have consistent CPI data. As with the real wage regressions, the 1986 price index was arbitrarily set to 1.0 for all MSAs. Any cross-MSA differences in price as of 1986 will be absorbed by the MSA fixed effect included in the regression. (As in previous chapters, the MSA effect is implicitly included by first-differencing all variables from MSA means. This first-differencing also eliminates the intercept.)

The main effects of all growth and demand-induced growth on real earnings have already been presented in figures 7.1 and 7.2. The actual regression includes an extensive list of demographic variables and time dummies. Table 7A1.1 shows the original OLS regression.

The original OLS and 2SLS regressions use the actual value of real earnings as a dependent variable, not the log of real earnings, as real earnings can take on nonpositive values. The percentage effects on real earnings reported in the figures are calculated by dividing the originally estimated dollar effects on real earnings by the mean value of real earnings, $24,880. The standard errors in the figures are also calculated by dividing the originally estimated standard errors by $24,880. This approach yields standard errors in percentage effects at mean real earnings that are conditional on the sample mean value of real earnings. In other words, the sample mean is treated as a datum rather than as a stochastic variable. The *unconditional* standard error in estimates of the percentage effect at the *population* mean would be quite difficult to calculate.

As in previous micro data results, I also re-estimated the OLS regression with a dummy variable for the year 1984 or 1979 interacted with the employment variable. All estimates exclude individuals who were not in the MSA as of "t" years ago. For most of the sample, t is one year, but it is five years ago for 1979 and 1984. Hence, this interaction of the "*8479*" dummy with the employment variables enables us to see whether employment growth has any less—or greater—effect on the real earnings of long-term residents compared to short-term residents. It thus addresses the argument that the growth effects measured here are due to growth attracting new residents with better economic prospects.

Table 7A1.2 shows the relevant results for the equation with these interaction terms. The interaction terms are individually statistically insignificant, and an F-test on their joint significant yields a value of .50 ($df = 2$, 14799; Prob. = .607), which is clearly insignificant. Furthermore, the point estimates clearly show that the long-run effect of an employment shock is very little different for the 1979 and 1984 sample compared to other years. Hence, there is no evidence that growth has different effects on short-term residents compared to long-term residents.

In addition, as discussed in appendix 4.2, I examined whether the usual OLS standard errors or these aggregate employment variables were biased due to a variance components structure of the data. As shown in table 4A2.2, the true OLS standard errors are probably about 15.6 percent higher than the usual OLS standard errors. Making this minor adjustment would have no effect on any inferences made in this chapter.

As was done in previous chapters, the effects of growth were re-estimated with the employment terms treated as endogenous in a 2SLS regression. The instrumental variables used in estimation were all other included variables in the regression, plus the current and eight lagged values of share effect predictions of the logarithm of employment. Appendix 4.1 details how these calculations were done.

Hausman tests were done comparing OLS and 2SLS estimates. Comparisons used both the OLS and 2SLS optimal lag-lengths. The F-test statistic for the OLS optimal lag-length is 5.34 ($df = 2$, 14797; Prob. = .0011). The F-test statistic for the 2SLS optimal lag-length is also 5.34 ($df = 4$, 14795; Prob. = .0003). Both F-test statistics are clearly statistically significant. However, a coefficient by coefficient comparison of the 2SLS and OLS results, for the 2SLS optimal lag-length, shows that the long-term effect of growth is not significantly different. Table 7A1.3 presents this comparison, showing the differences between the two sets of estimates and the standard errors.

Estimates were also done with terms in growth squared added to the employment growth terms. Table 7A1.4 reports the estimated parameters for the employment variables in a growth squared specification with two lags in the employment variable, estimated by 2SLS. This two-lag specification minimized the AIC. To do 2SLS, terms in the square of share effect predicted growth were added as instruments. The F-test statistic for this specification versus the specification without terms in growth squared is .44 ($df = 2$, 14862; Prob. = .644, which is clearly insignificant. Also, the individual coefficients on growth squared are both insignificant and switch signs from the initial effect at zero lags to the effect at one lag. Hence, there is no strong evidence that 1 percent extra growth has different effects at different initial levels of growth.

Finally, estimates were also done allowing interactions between all employment terms and the individual's education, experience (defined as age-education-6 years), and race. Table 7A1.5 shows the 2SLS version of the interaction specification, among all lag-lengths up to eight, that minimizes the AIC. Additional instruments were created by interacting all the original share effect instruments with education, experience, and race. The AIC for this interaction specification (1.2615) is clearly lower than the AIC for the no interaction specification (1.2638), and an F-test rejects the hypothesis that the interaction terms do not matter. (Test statistic is 4.31; $df = 15, 14847$; Prob. $= .8$ times 10^{-7}).

Table 7A1.5 shows how the absolute real *dollar* effect of a growth shock varies with certain individual characteristics. To calculate how variations in these characteristics alter the *percentage* effect of growth on real earnings, we must also calculate how expected real earnings vary with those individual characteristics. As outlined in appendix 6.1, this is done by calculating the derivative of the percentage effect with respect to the individual characteristic at the mean value of all variables. For the present case, the appropriate calculation is

$$\partial P/\partial x = \partial(D/E)/\partial x$$
$$= (1/E^2) [E(\partial D/\partial x) - D(\partial E/\partial x)]$$
$$= (1/E) (\partial D/\partial x) - P(\partial E/\partial x)/E$$

where P is the percentage effect of employment growth on real earnings, D is the dollar effect of employment growth on real earnings, E is expected real earnings for an individual with a particular set of demographic characteristics, and x is one of three demographic characteristics (education, experience, race). E, $\partial D/\partial x$, P, and $\partial E/\partial x$ are all calculated at sample means.

This derivative is then multiplied by the "standardized" change ($= 3.0$ for education, 11.8 for experience, 1.0 for black) to get the percentage changes reported in table 7.4. Because this calculation is a derivative, this is only an approximation to the actual alteration in the percentage effect from a discrete change in an individual characteristic. However, actual calculations show the approximation is quite close in this range. The reported standard error of the percentage effect in table 7.4 is equal to the standard error of ($\partial D/\partial x$) multiplied by the standardized change and divided by mean earnings. In other words, this calculation is conditional on the sample value of mean earnings, the mean effect of growth on earnings, and the mean effect of x on earnings. A standard error calculation that did not condition on these sample values would be extraordinarily complex to calculate.

Table 7A1.1
Basic OLS Results for Real Earnings

Dependent Variable: REARN
Analysis of Variance

Source	DF	Sum of Squares
Model	28	1.38469×10^{12}
Error	14890	3.52766×10^{12}
U Total	14918	4.91236×10^{12}
R-Squared:	0.2819	
Adj. R-Sq.:	0.2805	

Parameter Estimates

Variable	Parameter Estimate	Standard Error
EDUC	1303	324
EXPER	2205	108
EDUC2	77	10
EXPER2	−33	1
EDEX	−37	5
SOPRE	7336	376
FPERS	−13	112
FREC14	−93	257
VETSTA	564	314
BLACK	4616	9,614
BEDUC	−721	1,073
BEXPER	−360	341
BEDUC2	24	33
BEXPER2	9	4
BEDEX	−10	16
BSPOPRE	−2098	1,010
BFSIZ	−423	271
BCHL6	974	874
BVETSTA	738	901
T80	−2591	565
T81	−3675	570
T82	−4091	651
T83	−4549	576
T84	−4479	547
T85	−4171	560
T86	−4229	606
GR0	26802	7,324
EM1	10917	3,065

NOTE: Full set of MSA dummies is implicitly included by first-differencing all variables from MSA means.

Table 7A1.2
Partial Report of Results When Allowing Growth Effects on Real Earnings to be Different for Years in Which Sample Consists Solely of Long-Term Residents

Variable	Parameter Estimate	Standard Error
GR0	27222	7,518
SGR0	−10354	15,314
SEM1	−446	540
EM1	10588	3,114

NOTES: SGR0 and SEM1 are interaction terms between a dummy variable for the 1979 or 1984 year, and the corresponding employment term. Only the employment terms are reported in this table. All the demographic characteristics from the previous table were also included.

Table 7A1.3
Comparison of 2SLS and OLS Estimates of the Effects of Growth

	Cumulative Effect After:			
	0 years	1 year	2 years	3 years
2SLS	−261	635	832	95
	(320)	(429)	(376)	(80)
OLS	241	116	167	95
	(86)	(96)	(82)	(34)
Difference	−502	519	665	0
	(308)	(418)	(367)	(72)

NOTES: All estimated effects show dollar effect of 1 percent growth shock. Standard error of difference is calculated, per Hausman, as square root of the 2SLS variance minus the OLS variance. Standard errors are in parentheses.

Table 7A1.4
Partial Results for 2SLS Estimates that Allow Growth Squared to Affect Real Earnings

Variable	Parameter Estimate	Standard Error
EM2	17245	5,914
GRSQ0	−331999	225,794
GRSQ1	161587	196,939
GR0	−9658	27,178
GR1	99569	26,599

NOTES: Regression also includes full set of demographic characteristics and time dummies. GRSQ0 and GRSQ1 are the squares of the corresponding employment growth variables.

Table 7A1.5
Partial Results for 2SLS Specification that Allows
Demographic Characteristics to Alter Absolute Dollar Effects
of Growth on Real Earnings

Variable	Parameter Estimate	Standard Error
EM4	3437	8,767
EDEM4	404	79
BLEM4	−863	796
EXEM4	60	20
EDGR0	−2563	3,059
EDGR1	2078	2,993
EDGR2	−2494	2,963
EDGR3	−4954	2,557
BLGR0	11320	29,586
BLGR1	−6080	29,914
BLGR2	27150	30,135
BLGR3	−1027	27,761
EXGR0	−1101	720
EXGR1	1283	744
EXGR2	−900	742
EXGR3	1021	630
GR0	16503	5,5965
GR1	16986	62,239
GR2	138482	65,287
GR3	28318	53,907

NOTES: Regression also includes full set of demographic characteristics and time dummies. The variables with an ED, BL, or EX prefix, followed by the acronym for an employment variable, are interaction terms equal to one of three demographic characteristics (EDUC, BLACK, or EXPER) times that employment or growth variables.

Appendix 7.2
Estimates of "Permanent" Real Earnings

The estimates of permanent real earnings used in constructing table 7.5 are based on a somewhat unusual regression analysis. Specifically, real earnings for each individual in the real earnings sample were regressed on the individual's education, experience (again defined as age–education–6), and race. The predicted value of real earnings from this regression was used as an estimate of permanent real earnings. This estimate is somewhat unusual in that earnings equations typically include many determinants in addition to the three that were included in this case.

This inclusion of just three determinants was to make consistent the factors allowed to alter the effects of growth on real earnings and the factors allowed to alter real earnings. Only education, experience, and race were allowed to alter growth's effects on real earnings in the equations described in table 7.4 and in appendix 7.1. These estimating equations describe how the real dollar effects of growth change with these variables, but implicitly do not allow other variables to change the real dollar effects of growth. If other variables, either observed or unobserved, play a role in our estimates of permanent real earnings, there is an inevitable bias toward finding a progressive effect of growth. For those individuals who are predicted by variables other than education, experience, and race to have low permanent earnings, the predicted percentage effect will tend to be high, as these other variables are not allowed to alter the real dollar effects of growth.

Regression estimates of how education, experience, and race affect real earnings are reported in table 7A2.1. The estimates are all highly significant, and have the expected sign and magnitudes.

Table 7A2.1
Regression Analysis of Effects of Education, Experience, and Race on Adult Male Earnings

Dependent Variable: Real Earnings
Mean of Dependent Variable: 24,880

Model SSR: 4.092 times 10^{12}
R-Squared: .1838

Variable	Parameter Estimate	Standard Error
Intercept	−9293	785
Education	2440	47
Experience	148	12
Black	−7178	441

NOTES: Education and experience are measured in years. Experience = Age–education–6. Black = 1 if racial status = black, = 0 otherwise.

Appendix 8.1
Illustrative Arguments
for Why State and Local Economic Development Policies
May Provide National Employment Benefits

This appendix presents two diagrams that strengthen two arguments made in chapter 8: the benefits of an extra job are higher in high-unemployment areas than in low-unemployment areas; and nationwide wage subsidies can increase national employment in labor markets suffering from involuntary unemployment.

Figure 8A1.1 compares the benefits of a job in high-unemployment and low-unemployment local labor markets. I assume the areas have identical labor supply curves. Each point on the labor supply curve represents the reservation wage to some individual of supplying an additional unit of labor. Both the areas have identical efficiency wages of w_e. I assume this efficiency wage does not vary with labor demand conditions in the local labor market; the implications of relaxing this assumption are discussed below.

Area 1 differs from Area 2 in having lower labor demand. As a result, the equilibrium employment in Area 1 is N_1, and in Area 2 is N_2. Involuntary unemployment in Area 1 is equal to line segment fb ($= L_S^* - N_1$), and is higher than involuntary unemployment in Area 2, which is given by line segment fe ($= L_S^* - N_2$).

Another assumption is that scarce jobs are rationed among individuals according to their reservation wages. Individuals with lower reservation wages are assumed to out-compete individuals with higher reservation wages for the scarce jobs, because their job search intensity is higher, and their quit rate lower. In Area 1, the available jobs go to individuals with reservation wages less than w_r^1. In Area 2, the available jobs go to individuals with reservation wages less than w_r^2.

One more job in a local labor market has benefits to the individual obtaining the job equal to the wage paid minus that individual's reservation wage. In Area 1, this benefit is equal to line segment ba, or $w_e - w_r^1$. In Area 2, this benefit is equal to line segment ec, or $w_e - w_r^2$.

A symmetric argument can be made for the cost of losing a job from a local labor market. The cost is equal to the wages lost minus the individual's reservation wage. In Area 1, the cost of losing one job is line segment ba, while in Area 2 the cost of losing one job is line segment ec.

Hence, transferring a job from Area 2 to Area 1 could have net efficiency benefits. The marginal individual who gains a job in Area 1 enjoys benefits of ba, while the marginal individual losing a job in Area 2 suffers a loss equal

326

Figure 8A1.1
Variations in the Value of a Job in High vs. Low Unemployment Areas

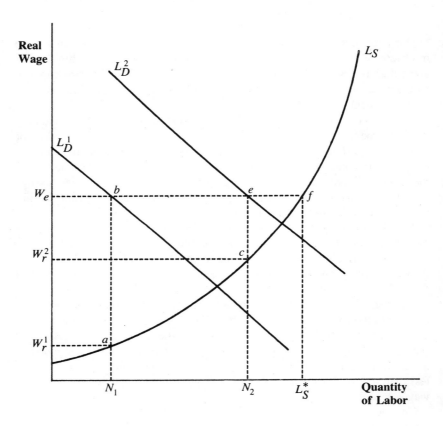

NOTES: L_D^1 and L_D^2 represent high and low unemployment markets.

to *ec*. The net national benefits of the transfer for workers are *ba – ec*. Transferring a job from Area 2 to Area 1 also distorts business location decisions, and the efficiency costs of this distortion should be weighed against the benefits for workers. Presumably, gross profits (without economic development subsidies) of having this job in Area 1 are less than the gross profits associated with having the job in Area 2. But as long as the reduction in gross profits is less than the net worker gain of *ba – ec*, national economic efficiency will be enhanced by this geographic reallocation of jobs.

The assumption that efficiency wages in a local labor market do not change with labor market conditions could be relaxed. It would be reasonable to assume that there is some tendency for the equilibrium efficiency wage to increase as unemployment is reduced. This would be true, for example, in models in which above-market efficiency wages are in part designed to give workers an incentive to work hard to avoid being fired. As unemployment is reduced, higher wages would be required to give the proper incentive to workers. In the diagram, this efficiency wage variation with unemployment could be depicted by drawing the efficiency wage locus as an upward sloping curve, rather than the horizontal line that figure 8A1.1 actually shows.

Even with this relaxation of assumptions, the conclusion that extra jobs benefit higher unemployment areas the most would not change as long as the efficiency wage locus is flatter than the reservation wage/labor supply curve. If the efficiency wage locus is flatter than the reservation wage curve, then the difference between efficiency wages and reservation wages will increase for local unemployment increases caused by reduced labor demand. A relatively flat efficiency wage locus seems reasonable for local labor markets, as workers will make comparisons with other local labor markets to determine whether the wages they receive are fair. The empirical evidence (Dickens and Katz 1987) suggests that fairness considerations are probably more important in setting efficiency wages than the need to avoid employee monitoring costs by giving workers an incentive to avoid being fired; for example, industry profits seem a more important determinant of industry wage differentials than differences across industries in the difficulty of monitoring worker productivity.[1]

Figure 8A1.1 assumes that differences in local unemployment are largely due to differences in local labor demand conditions. However, the argument that an extra job has greater benefits in high-unemployment local labor markets will still probably be valid if labor supply shifts cause differences in local unemployment rates. For example, the benefits of an extra job in Area 1 or Area 2 would tend to be higher after a parallel rightward shift in the labor supply curve, which would cause both greater unemployment and lower reservation wages for the marginal individual who gains that extra job.

Figure 8A1.2 considers the employment and efficiency effects of worker-financed subsidies for business labor demand. I consider first the case of involuntary unemployment in a national labor market. The efficiency wage is fixed at w_e, with employment of N, and unemployment equal to line segment ak.

Consider a national wage subsidy of sn paid to businesses and financed by workers. This will cause an upwards shift in the labor demand curve of $sn = bm$, and an upward shift in the labor supply curve of $ec = sn$. Employment will increase from N to N'. The reduction in labor supply has no effect on equilibrium employment, as at the new equilibrium point (point m in the diagram), labor supply still exceeds labor demand, resulting in involuntary unemployment. Labor demand is still the key constraint that determines employment.

Will there be enough increased product demand to purchase the increased output produced by these additional workers? As shown below the diagram, when one considers the increase in business profits, the increase in workers' gross incomes (before paying increased taxes to finance the wage subsidy), as well as the decrease in worker income caused by the increased taxes on workers, the net increase in income exactly equals the value of the increased production resulting from the extra employment. In a model such as this, where there is only one good, all of this income will be spent on the one good.

The increased employment is associated with efficiency benefits for the national economy. Businesses gain profits and the additional employed workers gain, ignoring taxes, a surplus equal to the gross wages they receive minus their reservation wages. Counterbalancing these benefits is the tax cost to workers of financing the subsidy. The net effect, shown below the figure, is equal to area $amfg$, that is, the area bounded by points $a,m,f,$ and g. The area can also be seen as the net difference between the value of what additional workers produce ($amxz$), minus the opportunity cost of their time, equal to their reservation wages ($fxzg$).

This analysis of wage subsidy effects implicitly assumes that unemployment is of the variety that economists label "classical unemployment": unemployment due to wages being above-market-clearing levels. If product markets are also in disequilibrium, with prices such that product supply exceeds product demand, then wage subsidies may not increase employment. Any individual firm will not find it in its interest to increase employment, even with a wage subsidy, as there will not be product demand for the firm's increased output. This is the case of what economists label "Keynesian unemployment." Because economic development policies are aimed at increasing long-run employment levels, it seems more appropriate to consider the case of classical unemploy-

Figure 8A1.2
Effects of Wage Subsidies
in Labor Markets with Involuntary Unemployment

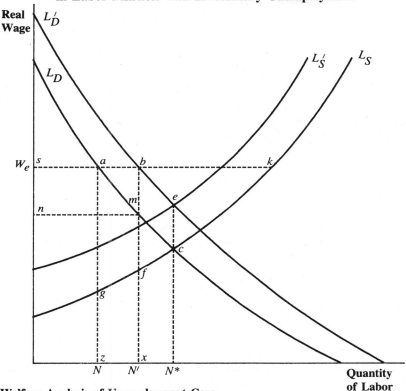

Welfare Analysis of Unemployment Case

Cost of subsidy $= (-sbmn)$
Δ in profits $= +samn$
Gross Δ in workers' surplus $= +abfg$
$$\overline{\text{Net} = +amfg}$$

Demand/Supply Analysis of Unemployment Case

Δ in value of production $= +amxz$
Δ in income available for demand $= \Delta$ profits $+ \Delta$ gross workers' incomes $-$ subsidy costs
$\qquad\qquad\qquad\qquad\qquad\qquad = samn + abxz - sbmn$
$\qquad\qquad\qquad\qquad\qquad\qquad = amxz$
Hence $\Delta S = \Delta D$

NOTES: Subsidy to labor demand shifts L_D to $L'_D D$, L_S to L'_S.

ment rather than the case of Keynesian unemployment. While insufficient product demand may be the main constraint to employment expansion during a recessionary period, long-run chronic unemployment seems more likely to be due to above-market-clearing wages rather than above-market-clearing product prices.[2]

In the case of full employment, worker-financed wage subsidies are unlikely to lead to much employment expansion. The initial full employment equilibrium will be at a point such as point c. Worker-financed wage subsidies will shift both labor demand and labor supply curves up. The most straightforward assumption is that each firm receives a flat dollar wage subsidy, and each worker pays a flat dollar tax to finance that subsidy. Under that assumption, both labor demand and labor supply curves shift up by the same amount. The equilibrium shifts from point c to point e. Employment is unchanged.[3]

NOTES

1. The efficiency wage locus will not be flatter than the reservation wage locus if efficiency wages' only purpose is to give workers a greater incentive to avoid unemployment. For example, in the model of Bulow and Summers (1986), the reservation wage of workers is flat up to the fixed available labor supply, while efficiency wages increase as employment goes up and unemployment goes down. Hence, in their model, low-unemployment labor markets gain more from an extra job than high-unemployment labor markets, because wage rates are higher in low-unemployment labor markets, but reservation wages of the marginal individual are no different in the two labor markets.

If this model were true, there would be efficiency benefits from transferring jobs from high-unemployment areas to low-unemployment areas. Furthermore, we would expect low-unemployment areas to more vigorously pursue economic development policies than high-unemployment areas. Economic development competition would reallocate jobs to low-unemployment areas, but this reallocation would be economically efficient. Hence, even under a Bulow/Summers model, there would still be national benefits from state and local competition for jobs.

However, as outlined in the appendix text, the evidence suggests that fairness is a more important determinant of efficiency wages than the need to provide incentives for workers to want to avoid being fired. Hence, it seems unlikely that the Bulow/Summers model is a good guide to how the benefits of an extra job vary in different local labor markets.

2. For an excellent recent discussion of different theories of unemployment, see Davidson (1990).

3. One could make different assumptions about the form of the subsidies and taxes that might lead to some effects of this wage subsidy policy on employment, either positive or negative. However, any such distortion of employment from the full employment equilibrium level could be shown to be inefficient.

REFERENCES

Advisory Commission on Intergovernmental Relations. 1981. "Regional Growth: Interstate Tax Competition." Advisory Commission on Intergovernmental Relations Report A-76, March 1981.

Ambrosius, Margery Marzahn. 1989. "The Effectiveness of State Economic Development Policies: A Time-Series Analysis." *Western Political Quarterly* 42 (3): 283-300.

Amemiya, Takeshi. 1985. *Advanced Econometrics*. Cambridge, MA: Harvard University Press.

Apgar, William C., Jr. 1987. "Recent Trends in Real Rents." Joint Center for Housing Studies Working Paper W87-5. Massachusetts Institute of Technology and Harvard University.

Armington, Catherine, Candee Harris, and Marjorie Odle. 1984. "Formation and Growth in High Technology Firms: A Regional Assessment." In *Technology, Innovation and Regional Economic Development*. Washington, DC: Office of Technology Assessment.

Baily, Martin N., and James Tobin. 1978. "Inflation-Unemployment Consequences of Job Creation Policies." In *Creating Jobs: Public Employment Programs and Wage Subsidies*, ed. John L. Palmer. Washington, DC: The Brookings Institution.

_____. 1977. "Macroeconomic Effects of Selective Public Employment and Wage Subsidies." *Brookings Papers on Economic Activity*, Washington, DC: The Brookings Institution.

Bania, Neil and Linsay Noble Calkins. "Trends in State and Local Taxation of Business." 1988. Working Paper. Center for Regional Economic Issues, Case Western Reserve University.

Bartik, Timothy J. 1991. "The Effects of Property Taxes and Other Local Public Policies on the Intrametropolitan Pattern of Business Location." Forthcoming in *Industry Location and Public Policy*, ed. Henry Herzog and Alan Schlottmann. Knoxville, TN: University of Tennessee Press.

_____. 1990. "The Market Failure Approach to Regional Economic Development Policy." *Economic Development Quarterly* 4, 4 (November): 361-370.

_____. 1989a. "Small Business Start-Ups in the United States: Estimates of the Effects of Characteristics of States." *Southern Economic Journal* 55, 4 (April): 1004-1018.

_____. 1989b. "The Effects of Demand Shocks on Local Labor Markets." W.E. Upjohn Institute for Employment Research, Kalamazoo, MI, September.

_____. 1988a. "Who Benefits from Local Economic Development Policies?" Paper presented at the annual meetings of the Association for Public Policy Analysis and Management, Seattle, WA, October 28.

_____. 1988b. "The Effects of Environmental Regulation on Business Location in the United States." *Growth and Change* 19, 3 (Summer): 22-44.

_____. 1986. "Neighborhood Revitalization's Effects on Tenants and the Benefit-Cost Analysis of Government Neighborhood Programs." *Journal of Urban Economics* 19 (1986): 234-248.

332

_____. 1985. "Business Location Decisions in the United States: Estimates of the Effects of Unionization, Taxes, and Other Characteristics of States." *Journal of Business and Economic Statistics* 3, 1 (January): 14-22.

Bartik, Timothy J. and V. Kerry Smith. 1987. "Urban Amenities and Public Policy." In *Handbook of Regional and Urban Economics,* ed. E.S. Mills. New York: Elsevier Science Publishers.

Bartik, Timothy J., Charles Becker, Steve Lake, and John Bush. 1987. "Saturn and State Economic Development." *Forum for Applied Research and Public Policy* (Spring): 29-41.

Bartik, Timothy J., J.S. Butler, and Jin-Tan Liu. Forthcoming. "Maximum Score Estimates of the Determinants of Residential Mobility: Implications for the Value of Residential Attachment and Neighborhood Amenities," *Journal of Urban Economics.*

Bauer, Paul W. and Brian A. Cromwell. 1989. "The Effect of Bank Structure and Profitability on Firm Openings." *Economic Review* 25, 4: 29-39.

Beeson, Patricia and Edward Montgomery. 1990. "The Effects of Colleges and Universities on Local Labor Markets." NBER Working Paper No. 3280 (March).

Benson, Bruce L. and Ronald N. Johnson. 1986. "The Lagged Impact of State and Local Taxes on Economic Activity and Political Behavior." *Economic Inquiry* 24 (July): 389-401.

Bernstein, Jeffrey I. and M. Ishaq Nadiri. 1988. "Interindustry R&D Spillovers, Rates of Return, and Production in High-Tech Industries." *The American Economic Review* 78, 2 (May): 429-434.

Blair, John P. and Robert Premus. 1987."Major Features in Industrial Location: A Review." *Economic Development Quarterly* 1, 1 (February): 72-85.

Blair, John P., Rudy H. Fichtenbaum, and James A. Swaney. 1984. "The Market for Jobs: Locational Decisions and the Competition for Economic Development." *Urban Affairs Quarterly* 20, 1 (September): 64-77.

Blomquist, Glenn, Mark Berger, and John Hoehn. 1988. "New Estimates of Quality of Life in Urban Areas." *American Economic Review* 78, 1 (March): 89-107.

Bolton, Roger. 1989a. " 'Place Prosperity vs. People Prosperity' Revisited." Working paper presented at the Regional Science Association meetings in Santa Barbara, CA, November.

_____. 1989b. "An Economic Interpretation of A 'Sense of Place'." Research Paper No. 130, Department of Economics, Williams College, Williamstown, MA, January.

Bowman, Ann O'M. 1987a. "The Visible Hand: Major Issues in City Economic Policy." Research Report of the National League of Cities, Washington, DC, November.

_____. 1987b. "Tools and Targets; The Mechanics of City Economic Development." Research Report of the National League of Cities, Washington, DC, October.

Bradbury, Katherine, Anthony Downs, and Kenneth Small. 1982. *Urban Decline and the Future of American Cities.* Washington, DC: The Brookings Institution.

Browne, Lynn E. 1990. "Why Do New Englanders Work So Much?" *New England Economic Review* (March/April): 33-46.

_____. 1987. "Too Much of A Good Thing? Higher Wages in New England." *New England Economic Review* (Jan/Feb): 39-53.

Browne, Lynn E., Peter Mieszkowski, and Richard F. Syron. 1980. "Regional Investment Patterns." *New England Economic Review* (July/August): 5-23.

Brueckner, Jan K. 1987. "The Structure of Urban Equilibria: A Unified Treatment of the Muth-Mills Model." In *Handbook of Regional and Urban Economics*, ed. E.S. Mills. New York: Elsevier Science Publishers.

Bulow, Jeremy and Lawrence Summers. 1986. "A Theory of Dual Labor Markets with Application to Industrial Policy, Discrimination, and Keynesian Unemployment." *Journal of Labor Economics* 4, 3: 376-414.

Burdett, Kenneth and Tara Vishwanath. 1988. "Declining Reservation Wages and Learning." *Review of Economic Studies* 55: 655-666.

Canto, Victor A. and Robert I. Webb. 1987. "The Effect of State Fiscal Policy on State Relative Economic Performance." *Southern Economic Journal* 54, 1 (July): 186-202.

Carlino, Gerald. 1979. "Increasing Returns to Scale in Metropolitan Manufacturing." *Journal of Regional Science* 19, 3: 363-373.

Carlton, Dennis W. 1983. "The Location and Employment Choices of New Firms: An Econometric Model with Discrete and Continuous Endogenous Variables." *The Review of Economics and Statistics* 65 (August): 440-449.

Carlton, Dennis W. 1979. "Why Do New Firms Locate Where They Do: An Econometric Model." In *Interregional Movements and Regional Growth*, ed. William C. Wheaton. Washington, DC: The Urban Institute.

Carroll, Robert and Michael Wasylenko. 1989. "The Shifting Fate of Fiscal Variables and Their Effect on Economic Development." In *Proceedings of the Eighty-Second Annual Conference on Taxation*, Atlanta, GA, October 8-11, 1989: 283-290.

Case, Karl E. 1986. "The Market for Single-Family Homes in the Boston Area." *New England Economic Review* (May/June): 38-48.

Charney, Alberta H. 1983. "Intraurban Manufacturing Location Decisions and Local Tax Differentials." *Journal of Urban Economics* 14: 184-205.

Church, Albert M. 1981. "The Effects of Local Government Expenditure and Property Taxes on Investment." *Journal of the American Real Estate and Urban Economics Association* 9 (Summer): 165-180.

Citizens Research Council of Michigan. 1986. "Municipal Government Economic Development Incentive Programs in Michigan." Citizens Research Council of Michigan Report No. 280, February.

Clark, David, James Kahn, and Haim Ofek. 1988. "City Size, Quality of Life, and the Urbanization Deflator of the GNP: 1910-1984." *Southern Economic Journal* 54 (January): 701-714.

Clarke, Marianne K. 1986. *Revitalizing State Economies.* Washington, DC: National Governors Association.

334

Committee for Economic Development. 1986. *Leadership for Dynamic State Economies.* New York, NY.

Coughlin, Cletus C., Joseph V. Terza, and Vachira Arromdee. Forthcoming. "State Characteristics and the Location of Foreign Direct Investment within the United States." *Review of Economics and Statistics.*

_____. 1989. "State Characteristics and the Location of Foreign Direct Investment within the United States: Minimum Chi-Square Conditional Logit Estimation." Working Paper. Federal Reserve Bank of St. Louis, July.

Coughlin, Cletus C. and Phillip A. Cartwright. 1987. "An Examination of State Foreign Export Promotion and Manufacturing Exports." *Journal of Regional Science* 27, 3: 439-449.

Crihfield, John B. 1990. "Manufacturing Supply." *Regional Science and Urban Economics* 20: 327-349.

_____. 1989. "A Structural Empirical Analysis of Metropolitan Labor Demand." *Journal of Regional Science* 29, 3 (August): 347-371.

Cross, Rod (ed.). 1988. *Unemployment, Hysteresis, and the Natural Rate Hypothesis.* New York: Basil Blackwell.

Cross, Rod and Andrew Allan. 1989. "On the History of Hysteresis." In *Unemployment, Hysteresis, and the Natural Rate Hypothesis.* New York: Basil Blackwell.

Davidson, Carl. 1990. *Recent Developments in the Theory of Involuntary Unemployment.* Kalamazoo, MI: W.E. Upjohn Institute for Employment Research.

Deich, Michael. 1990. "An Empirical Analysis of State Taxation and Manufacturing Plant Location." Ph.D. dissertation, The University of Michigan.

_____. 1989. "State Taxes and Manufacturing Plant Location." In *Proceedings of the Eighty-Second Annual Conference on Taxation,* Atlanta, GA, October 8-11, 1989.

Dickens, William T. and Lawrence F. Katz. 1987. "Inter-Industry Wage Differences and Industry Characteristics." In *Unemployment and the Structure of Labor Markets,* eds. Kevin Lang and Jonathan S. Leonard. New York: Basil Blackwell.

Doeringer, Peter B., David G. Terkla, and Gregory C. Topakian. 1987. *Invisible Factors in Local Economic Development.* New York: Oxford University Press.

Due, John F. 1961. "Studies of State-Local Tax Influence on Location of Industry." *National Tax Journal* (June):163-173.

Duffy-Deno, Kevin T. and Randall W. Eberts. 1989. "Public Infrastructure and Regional Economic Development: A Simultaneous Equations Approach." Federal Reserve Bank of Cleveland Working Paper 8909, August.

Dunn, L. F. 1979. "Measuring the Value of Community." *Journal of Urban Economics* 6: 371-382.

Dye, Thomas R. 1980. "Taxing, Spending, and Economic Growth in American States." *The Journal of Politics* 42: 1085-1107.

Eberts, Randall W. 1991. "Some Empirical Evidence on the Linkage between Public Infrastructure and Local Economic Development." In *Industry Location and Public Policy* eds. Henry Herzog and Alan Schlottmann. Knoxville, TN: University of Tennessee Press.

Eberts, Randall W. and Joe A. Stone. 1988. "Wage and Employment Determination in Local Labor Markets." W.E. Upjohn Institute for Employment Research Report, September.

Economic Report of the President: 1990. Washington, DC: U.S. Government Printing Office.

Eisinger, Peter. 1988. *The Rise of the Entrepreneurial State.* Madison: University of Wisconsin Press.

Erickson, Rodney A. and Susan W. Friedman (with Richard E. McCluskey). 1989. "Enterprise Zones: An Evaluation of State Government Policies." Final report prepared for the U.S. Department of Commerce, Economic Development Administration, Technical Assistance and Research Division, April.

Erickson, Rodney A. and Paul M. Syms. 1986. "The Effects of Enterprise Zones on Local Property Markets." *Regional Studies* 20 1: 1-14.

Erickson, Rodney A. and Michael Wasylenko. 1980. "Firm Relocation and Site Selection in Suburban Municipalities." *Journal of Urban Economics* 8: 69-85.

Fallows, James. 1989. *More Like Us.* Boston: Houghton Mifflin.

Feiock, Richard. 1989. "The Adoption of Economic Development Policies by State and Local Governments: A Review." *Economic Development Quarterly* 3, 3 (August): 266-270.

_____. 1987. "Urban Economic Development: Local Government Strategies and Their Effects." In *Research in Public Policy Analysis and Management,* ed. Stuart S. Nagel. London: JAI Press, Ltd.

Fishe, Raymond P.H. 1982. "Unemployment Insurance and the Reservation Wage of the Unemployed." *The Review of Economics and Statistics* 64 (February): 12-17.

Fleisher, B. and G. Rhodes. 1976. "Unemployment and the Labor Force Participation of Married Men and Women: A Simultaneous Model." *Review of Economics and Statistics* 58, 4 (November): 398-406.

Fosler, R. Scott. n.d. "Does Economic Theory Capture the Effects of New and Traditional State Policies on Economic Development?" Working Paper. Committee for Economic Development.

Fox, William F. 1981. "Fiscal Differentials and Industrial Location: Some Empirical Evidence." *Urban Studies* 18: 105-111.

Fox, William F. and Matthew N. Murray. 1990. "Local Public Policies and Interregional Business Development." *Southern Economic Journal* 57, 2 (October): 413-427.

Freeman, Richard. 1989. "Labor Market Tightness and the Declining Economic Position of Young Less Educated Male Workers in the United States." Working Paper. Harvard University, December.

_____. 1981. "Economic Determinants of Geographic and Individual Variation in the Labor Market Position of Young Persons." In *The Youth Labor Market Problem: Its Nature, Causes and Consequences,* ed. R. Freeman and D. Wise. Chicago: University of Chicago Press.

Friedman, Joseph, Daniel A. Gerlowski, and Jonathan Silberman. 1989. "Foreign Direct Investment: The Factors Affecting the Location of Foreign Branch Plants in the United States." Working Paper. University of Baltimore, September.

Garber, Carter and Verna Fausey. 1986. "Today's Jobs at Yesterday's Wages." *Southern Changes* 8, 4/5 (October/November): 16-24.

Gardner, Mona J., Han Bin Kang, and Dixie L. Mills. 1987. "Japan, U.S.A.: The Impact of the Diamond Star Plant on the Bloomington-Normal Economy and Housing Market." Office of Real Estate Research Paper No. 54, University of Illinois at Urbana-Champaign, October.

Garofalo, Gasper A. and Devinder M. Malhotra. 1983. "Regional Capital Formation in U.S. Manufacturing During the 1970s." *Journal of Regional Science* 27, 3 (August): 391-401.

Geweke, John and Richard Meese. 1981. "Estimating Regression Models of Finite But Unknown Order." *International Economic Review* 22, 1 (February): 55-70.

Gillingham, Robert. 1980. "Estimating the User Cost of Owner-Occupied Housing." *Monthly Labor Review* 103, 2 (February): 31-35.

Gillingham, Robert and Walter Lane. 1982. "Changing the Treatment of Homeowner-ship in the CPI." *Monthly Labor Review* 105, 6 (June): 9-14.

Glickman, Norman and Douglas Woodward. 1989. *The New Competitors.* New York: Basic Books.

————. 1987. "Regional Patterns of Manufacturing Foreign Direct Investment in the United States." A special project report prepared for the U.S. Department of Commerce, Economic Development Administration, Research and Evaluation Division.

Gold, Steven D. 1988. "A Review of Recent State Tax Reform Activity." In *The Unfinished Agenda for State Tax Reform,* ed. S. Gold. Denver, CO: National Conference of State Legislatures.

Goldstein, Harvey A. and Michael I. Luger. 1988. "Science/Research Parks as Instruments of Technology-Based Regional Policy: An Assessment." Presented at the Association for Public Policy Analysis and Management, 10th Annual Research Conference in Seattle, WA, October 27-29.

Gordon, Robert J. 1973. "The Welfare Cost of Higher Unemployment." *Brookings Papers on Economic Activity.* Washington, DC: The Brookings Institution.

Grady, Dennis O. 1987. "State Economic Development Incentives: Why Do States Compete?" *State and Local Government Review* (Fall): 86-94.

Graham, Stephen G. 1982. "The Determinants of the Geographical Distribution of the Formation of New and Small Technology-Based Firms." Ph.D. dissertation, Michigan State University.

Gramlich, Edward M. 1987. "Subnational Fiscal Policy." *Perspectives on Local Public Finance and Public Policy.* Greenwich, CT: JAI Press.

————. 1981. *Benefit-Cost Analysis of Government Programs.* Englewood Cliffs, NJ: Prentice Hall.

Graves, Philip E. 1980. "Migration and Climate." *Journal of Regional Science* 20, 2: 227-237.

Greenwood, Michael J. and Gary L. Hunt. 1989. "Jobs versus Amenities in the Analysis of Metropolitan Migration." *Journal of Urban Economics* 25: 1-16.

_____. 1984. "Migration and Interregional Employment Redistribution in the United States." *American Economic Review* 74, 5 (December): 957-969.

Greenwood, Michael J., Gary L. Hunt, and John M. McDowell. 1986. "Migration and Employment Change: Empirical Evidence on the Spatial and Temporal Dimensions of the Linkage." *Journal of Regional Science* 26, 2 (May): 223-234.

Grieson, Ronald E. 1980. "Theoretical Analysis and Empirical Measurements of the Effects of the Philadelphia Income Tax." *Journal of Urban Economics* 8: 123-137.

Grubb, W. Norton. 1982. "The Flight to the Suburbs of Population and Employment, 1960-1970." *Journal of Urban Economics* 11, 3 (May): 348-367.

Gyourko, Joseph. 1987a. "Effects of Local Tax Structures on the Factor Intensity Composition of Manufacturing Activities Across Cities." *Journal of Urban Economics* 22: 151-164.

_____. 1987b. "New Firm Activity and Employment Changes Among the Localities in the Philadelphia Area, 1980-1983." In *Economic Development Within the Philadelphia Metropolitan Area,* eds. Anita Summers and Thomas Luce. Philadelphia: University of Pennsylvania Press.

_____. 1984. "Effects of Differences in Local Economic Conditions on the Scale and Composition of Manufacturing Activity." Ph.D. dissertation, University of Chicago.

Gyourko, Joseph and Joseph Tracy. 1986. "The Importance of Local Fiscal Conditions in Analyzing Local Labor Markets." NBER Working Paper No. 2040.

Hamilton, Bruce and Robert Schwab. 1985. "Expected Appreciation in Urban Housing Markets." *Journal of Urban Economics* 18: 103-118.

Harris, Candee S. 1986. "Establishing High-Technology Enterprises in Metropolitan Areas." In *Local Economies in Transition,* ed. Edward M. Bergman. Durham, NC: Duke University Press.

Hatry, Harry P., Mark Fall, Thomas O. Singer, and E. Blaine Liner. 1990. *Monitoring the Outcomes of Economic Development Programs.* Washington, DC: Urban Institute Press.

Hausman, Jerry A. 1981. "Labor Supply." In *How Taxes Affect Economic Behavior,* eds. Henry J. Aaron and Joseph A. Pechman. Washington, DC: The Brookings Institution.

_____. 1978. "Specification Tests in Econometrics." *Econometrica* 46: 1251-71.

Helms, L. Jay. 1985. "The Effect of State and Local Taxes on Economic Growth: A Time Series Cross Section Approach." *The Review of Economics and Statistics* 67 (February): 574-582.

Henderson, J. Vernon. 1988. *Urban Development.* New York: Oxford University Press.

Heywood, John S. and Michael D. Deich. 1987. "Do Unions Discourage Economic Activity?" *Economic Letters* 25: 373-377.

Hodge, James. H. 1981. "A Study of Regional Investment Decisions." In *Research in Urban Economics,* Vol. 1, ed. J. Vernon Henderson. Greenwich, CT: JAI Press.

338

Hoehn, John P., Mark C. Berger, and Glenn C. Blomquist. 1987. "A Hedonic Model of Interregional Wages, Rents, and Amenity Values." *Journal of Regional Science* 27 (4): 605-620.

Holzer, Harry J. 1991. "Employment, Unemployment and Demand Shifts in Local Labor Markets." *Review of Economics and Statistics* 73, 1 (February).

Holzer, Harry J. and Edward B. Montgomery. 1989. "Asymmetries and Rigidities in Wage Adjustments By Firms." Working Paper. Michigan State University.

Houseman, Susan N. and Katharine G. Abraham. 1990. "Regional Labor Market Responses to Demand Shocks: A Comparison of the United States and West Germany." Paper presented at the Association for Public Policy Analysis and Management meetings in San Francisco, October 18-20.

Howland, Marie. 1988. *Plant Closings and Worker Displacement: The Regional Issues.* Kalamazoo, MI: W.E. Upjohn Institute for Employment Research.

_____. 1985. "Property Taxes and the Birth and Intraregional Location of New Firms." *Journal of Planning, Education and Research* 4 (April): 148-156.

Howland, Marie and George Peterson. 1988. "The Response of City Economies to National Business Cycles." *Journal of Urban Economics* 23: 71-85.

Hovey, Harold A. 1986. "Interstate Tax Competition and Economic Development." In *Reforming State Tax Systems,* ed. S. Gold. Denver, CO: National Conference of State Legislatures.

Inman, Robert P. with Sally Hines, Jeffrey Preston, and Richard Weiss. 1987. "Philadelphia's Fiscal Management of Economic Transition." In *Local Fiscal Issues in the Philadelphia Metropolitan Area,* eds. Thomas F. Luce and Anita A. Summers. Philadelphia: University of Pennsylvania Press.

Isserman, Andrew M. and Paul M. Beaumont. 1989. "New Directions in Quasi-Experimental Control Group Methods for Project Evaluation." *Socio-Economic Planning Science* 23, 1/2: 39-53.

Isserman, Andrew, Carol Taylor, Shelby Gerking, and Uwe Schubert. 1986. "Regional Labor Market Analysis." In *Handbook of Regional and Urban Economics,* ed. P. Nijkamp. New York: Elsevier Science Publishers.

James, Franklin J. 1991. "The Evaluation of Enterprise Zone Programs." In *Enterprise Zones,* ed. Roy E. Green. Newbury Park, CA: Sage Publications.

_____. 1988. "Federal Economic Development Programs and National Urban Policy." *Economic Development Quarterly* 2, 2 (May): 68-181.

_____. 1984. "Urban Economic Development: A Zero-Sum Game?" In *Urban Economic Development,* eds. Richard D. Bingham and John Blair. Beverly Hills, CA: Sage Publications.

Jones, Bryan D. 1990. "Public Policies and Economic Growth in the American States." *Journal of Politics* 52, 1 (February): 219-233.

Jones, Stephen R.G. 1989. "Reservation Wages and the Cost of Unemployment." *Econometrica* 56 (May): 225-246.

Jones, Susan A., Allen R. Marshall, and Glen E. Weisbrod. 1985. "Business Impacts of State Enterprise Zones." Paper presented to the U.S. Small Business Administration, September.

Kasper, Hirschel. 1969. "The Asking Price of Labor and the Duration of Unemployment." *The Review of Economics and Statistics* 49 (May): 165-172.

Kenyon, Daphne A. 1988. "Interjurisdictional Tax and Policy Competition: Good or Bad for the Federal System?" Report submitted to the U.S. Advisory Commission on Intergovernmental Relations, February 29.

Kiefer, Nicholas M. and George R. Neumann. 1979. "An Empirical Job-Search Model, with a Test of the Constant Reservation-Wage Hypothesis." *Journal of Political Economy* 87, 11: 89-107.

Kieschnick, Michael. 1983. "Taxes and Growth: Business Incentives and Economic Development." In *State Taxation Policy,* ed. Michael Barker. Durham, NC: Duke University Press.

_____. 1981. *State Taxation Policy.* Durham, NC: Council of State Planning Agencies, Duke University Press.

Lau, L. 1978. "Applications of Profit Functions." In *Production Economics: A Dual Approach to Theory and Applications,* Vol. 1. Amsterdam: North-Holland.

Levy, Frank. 1982. "Migration's Impact on the Economic Situation of Minorities and the Disadvantaged." Urban Institute Report under contract HC-6065 to HUD. Washington, DC: The Urban Institute.

Levy, John M. 1990. "What Local Economic Developers Actually Do: Location Quotients versus Press Releases." *Journal of the American Planning Association* 56, 2 (Spring): 153-160.

_____. 1981. *Economic Development Programs for Cities, Counties, and Towns.* New York: Praeger.

Lichtenberg, Frank R. 1990. "Aggregation of Variables in Least-Squares Regressions." *The American Statistician* 44, 2 (May): 169-171.

Lindbeck, Assar and Dennis J. Snower. 1988. *The Insider-Outsider Theory of Employment and Unemployment.* Cambridge, MA: MIT Press.

Lindsay, Franklin A. 1986. *Leadership for Dynamic State Economies.* Washington, DC: Committee for Economic Development.

Logan, John and Harvey Molotch. 1987. *Urban Fortunes: The Political Economy of Place.* Berkeley, CA: University of California Press.

Luce, Thomas F., Jr. 1990a. "The Determinants of Metropolitan Area Growth Disparities in High-Technology and Low-Technology Industries." Working Paper. Department of Public Administration, Pennsylvania State University.

_____. 1990b. "Local Taxes, Public Services, and the Intrametropolitan Location of Firms and Households." Working Paper. Department of Public Administration, Pennsylvania State University.

_____. 1987. "High Technology in the Region." In *Local Fiscal Issues in the Philadelphia Metropolitan Area,* eds. Thomas F. Luce and Anita A. Summers. Philadelphia: University of Pennsylvania Press.

Luger, Michael I. 1987. "The States and Industrial Development: Program Mix and Policy Effectiveness." In *Perspectives on Local Public Finance and Public Policy,* Vol. 3, ed. John M. Quigley. Greenwich, CT: JAI Press.

Luger, Michael I. and Harvey A. Goldstein. 1990. "Technology in the Garden: Research Parks and Regional Economic Development." Final report to The Ford Foundation Program in Human Governance and Public Policy, January.

Luger, Michael I. and Sudhir Shetty. 1985. "Determinants of Foreign Plant Start-ups in the United States: Lessons for Policymakers in the Southeast." *Vanderbilt Journal of Transnational Law* 18, 2 (Spring).

Manning, Christopher A. 1988. "The Determinants of Intercity Home Building Site Price Differences." *Land Economics* 64, 1 (February): 1-14.

Marston, Stephen T. 1985. "Two Views of the Geographic Distribution of Unemployment." *Quarterly Journal of Economics* (February): 57-79.

McConnell, Virginia D. and Robert M. Schwab. 1990. "The Impact of Environmental Regulation on Industry Location Decisions: The Motor Vehicle Industry." *Land Economics* 66, 1 (February): 67-81.

McGuire, Therese J. 1985. "Are Local Property Taxes Important in the Intrametropolitan Location Decisions of Firms? An Empirical Analysis of the Minneapolis-St. Paul Metropolitan Area." *Journal of Urban Economics* 18: 226-234.

McGuire, Therese J. and Michael Wasylenko. 1987. "Employment Growth and State Government Fiscal Behavior: A Report on Economic Development for States From 1974 to 1984." Report prepared for The New Jersey State and Local Expenditure and Revenue Policy Commission, July 2.

McHone, W. Warren. 1986. "Supply-Side Considerations in the Location of Industry in Suburban Communities: Empirical Evidence from the Philadelphia SMSA." *Land Economics* 62, 1 (February): 64-73.

_____. 1984. "State Industrial Development Incentives and Employment Growth in Multistate SMSAs." *Growth and Change* 15, 4 (October): 8-15.

McLure, Charles E. 1986. "Tax Competition: Is What's Good for the Private Goose Also Good for the Public Gander?" *National Tax Journal* 39, 3 (September): 341-348.

Mehay, Stephen L. and Loren M. Solnick. 1990. "Defense Spending and State Economic Growth." *Journal of Regional Science* 30, 4 (November): 477-488.

Mills, Edwin S. 1983. "Metropolitan Central City Population and Employment Growth During the 1970's." Working Paper No. 83-7, Federal Reserve Bank of Philadelphia, September.

Mills, Edwin S. and Bruce W. Hamilton. 1984. *Urban Economics,* 3rd edition. Glenview, IL: Scott, Foresman.

Mills, Edwin S. and Richard Price. 1984. "Metropolitan Suburbanization and Central City Problems." *Journal of Urban Economics* 15: 1-17.

Milward, H. Brinton and Heidi Hosbach Newman. 1989. "State Incentive Packages and the Industrial Location Decision." *Economic Development Quarterly* 3, 3 (August): 203-222.

Minnesota Department of Trade and Economic Development. 1988. "State Technology Programs in the United States, 1988." Office of Science and Technology, July.

Mofidi, Alaeddin and Joe A. Stone. 1990. "Do State and Local Taxes Affect Economic Growth?" *The Review of Economics and Statistics* 72, 4 (November): 686-691.

Moomaw, Ronald L. 1988. "Agglomeration Economies: Localization or Urbanization?" *Urban Studies* 25, 2: 150-161.

Moore, Thomas S. and Aaron Laramore. 1990. "Industrial Change and Urban Joblessness: An Assessment of the Mismatch Hypothesis." *Urban Affairs Quarterly* 25, 4 (June): 640-658.

Moulton, Brent R. 1990. "An Illustration of a Pitfall in Estimating the Effects of Aggregate Variables on Micro Units." *The Review of Economics and Statistics* 72, 2 (May): 334-338.

————. 1988a. "Using SAS to Estimate a Regression with Two Variance Components." Working Paper. Division of Price and Index Number Research, U.S. Bureau of Labor Statistics, April.

————. 1988b. "An Illustration of A Pitfall in Estimating the Effects of Aggregate Variables on Micro Units." Bureau of Labor Statistics Working Paper 181, April.

————. 1986. "Random Group Effects and the Precision of Regression Estimates." *Journal of Econometrics* 32: 385-397.

Moulton, Brent R. and William C. Randolph. 1989. "Alternative Tests of the Error Components Model." *Econometrica* 57, 3 (May): 685-693.

Mullen, John K. and Martin Williams. 1991. "Supply-Side Effects and State Economic Growth." Revised version of paper presented at the 37th North American Meetings of the Regional Science Association International, Boston, November 1990.

Munnell, Alicia H. 1990. "How Does Public Infrastructure Affect Regional Economic Performance?" *New England Economic Review* (September/October) 11-33.

Muth, Richard F. 1971. "Migration: Chicken or Egg?" *Southern Economic Journal* 37: 295-306.

Nakosteen, Robert A. and Michael A. Zimmer. 1987. "Determinants of Regional Migration by Manufacturing Firms." *Economic Inquiry* 25, 2 (April): 351-362.

National Association of State Development Agencies. 1990. "1990 State Economic Development Expenditure Survey." Washington, DC.

Netzer, Dick. 1990. "An Evaluation of Interjurisdictional Competition Through Economic Development Incentives." Working Paper. New York University.

Newman, Robert J. 1983. "Industry Migration and Growth in the South." *Review of Economics and Statistics* 65: 76-86.

Nichols, Donald A. 1987. "Effects on the Noninflationary Unemployment Rate." In *Jobs for Disadvantaged Workers: The Economics of Employment Subsidies,* eds. Robert H. Havemen and John L. Palmer. Washington, DC: The Brookings Institution.

O'hUallacháin, Breandán and Mark A. Satterthwaite. 1990. "Sectoral Growth Patterns at the Metropolitan Level: An Evaluation of Economic Development Incentives." Discussion Paper No. 29, J. L. Kellogg Graduate School of Management, April.

Oates, Wallace E. and Robert M. Schwab. 1988a. "Economic Competition Among Jurisdictions: Efficiency Enhancing or Distortion Inducing?" *Journal of Public Economics* 35: 333-354.

————. 1988b. "The Allocative and Distributive Implications of Local Fiscal Competition." Working Paper No. 88-38, Economics Department, University of Maryland, June.

Osborne, David. 1988. *Laboratories of Democracy*. Boston: Harvard Business School Press.

Palumbo, George, Seymour Sacks, and Michael Wasylenko. 1990. "Population Decentralization within Metropolitan Areas: 1970-1980." *Journal of Urban Economics* 27, 2 (March): 151-167.

Papke, James A. 1990. "The Role of Market Based Public Policy in Economic Development and Urban Revitalization: A Retrospective Analysis and Appraisal of the Indiana Enterprise Zone Program." Year Three Report prepared for The Enterprise Zone Board, Indiana Department of Commerce, August 31.

Papke, James A. and Leslie E. Papke. 1986. "Measuring Differential Tax Liabilities and Their Implications for Business Investment Location." *National Tax Journal* (September): 357-366.

Papke, Leslie E. 1991. "Tax Policy and Urban Development: Evidence from an Enterprise Zone Program." Working Paper, Boston University.

_____. 1989a. "Taxes and Other Determinants of Gross State Product in Manufacturing: A First Look." In *Proceedings of the Eighty-Second Annual Conference on Taxation,* Atlanta, GA, October 8-11.

_____. 1989b. "Interstate Business Tax Differentials and New Firm Location: Evidence From Panel Data." NBER Working Paper No. 3184, November.

_____. 1987. "Subnational Taxation and Capital Mobility: Estimates of Tax-Price Elasticities." *National Tax Journal* 40, 2 (June): 191-204.

_____. 1986. "The Location of New Manufacturing Plants and State Business Taxes: Evidence From Panel Data." In *Proceedings of the Seventy-Ninth Annual Conference on Taxation* held under the auspices of the National Tax Association - Tax Institute of America, Hartford, CT, November 9-12.

Peirce, Neal, Jerry Hagstrom, and Carol Steinbach. 1979. *Economic Development: The Challenge of the 1980s.* Washington, DC: Council of State Planning Agencies.

Phelps, Edmund. 1972. *Inflation Policy and Unemployment Theory.* New York: Norton.

Place, Frank. 1986. "The Relationship of State and Local Government Spending and Taxing to Economic Performance: An Econometric Analysis of the States from 1972 to 1984." Wisconsin Department of Development, Division of Policy Development, Bureau of Research Report No. RP-86-7, September.

Plaut, Thomas R. and Joseph E. Pluta. 1983. "Business Climate, Taxes and Expenditures, and State Industrial Growth in the United States." *Southern Economic Journal* 50: 99-119.

Pollakowski, Henry O. 1988. "Owner-Occupied Housing Price Change in the U.S., 1974-1983: A Disaggregated Approach." Joint Center for Housing Studies of the Massachusetts Institute of Technology and Harvard University Report No. R87-1.

Pomp, Richard. 1985. "Modernization and Simplification of Tax Administration and the Tax Law." *Tax Notes* (November 4).

Power, Thomas Michael. 1989. "Broader Vision, Narrower Focus in Local Economic Development." *Forum for Applied Research and Public Policy* 4 (Fall).

Premus, Robert. 1982. "Location of High Technology Firms and Regional Economic Development." A staff study prepared for use by the Subcommittee on Monetary and Fiscal Policy of the Joint Economic Committee, Congress of the United States, June 1.

President's Commission for a National Agenda for the Eighties. 1980. *Urban America in the Eighties.* Report of the Panel on Policies and Prospects for Metropolitan and Nonmetropolitan America. Washington, DC: U.S. Government Printing Office.

Quan, Nguyen T. and John H. Beck. 1987. "Public Education Expenditures and State Economic Growth: Northeast and Sunbelt Regions." *Southern Economic Journal* 54, 2 (October): 361-376.

Rasmussen, David, Marc Bendick, and Larry Ledebur. "A Methodology for Selecting Economic Development Incentives." *Growth and Change* 15, 2 (January 1984): 18-25.

Reese, Laura A. 1991. "Municipal Fiscal Health and Tax Abatement Policy." *Economic Development Quarterly* 5, 1 (February): 23-32.

Reynolds, Paul D. 1990. "Predicting New Firm Births: Interactions of Organizational and Human Populations." Working paper presented at State of the Art in Entrepreneurship Research Conference, Frank Hawkins Kenan Institute of Private Enterprise, University of North Carolina, October 5-6.

Reynolds, Paul D. and Steve Freeman. 1987. "1986 Pennsylvania New Firm Survey," Prepared under contract for the Appalachian Regional Commission, Washington, DC (January).

Reynolds, Paul D. and Wilbur Maki. 1990. "U.S. Regional Characteristics, New Firms, and Economic Growth." Working paper presented to the Cross-National Workshop on the Role of Small, Medium Enterprises in Regional Economic Growth at the University of Warwick, Coventry, United Kingdom, March 28.

Rinehart, James R. and William E. Laird. 1972. "Community Inducements to Industry and the Zero-Sum Game." *Scottish Journal of Political Economy* (February): 73-90.

Riordan, William. 1963. *Plunkitt of Tammany Hall.* New York: Dutton.

Roback, Jennifer. 1982. "Wages Rents and the Quality of Life." *Journal of Political Economy* 90: 1257-1278.

Romans, Thomas and Ganti Subrahmanyam. 1979. "State and Local Taxes, Transfers and Regional Economic Growth." *Southern Economic Journal* 46, 2 (October): 435-444.

Rosen, Harvey S. 1988. *Public Finance,* second ed. Homewood, IL: Irwin.

Rosen, Sherwin. 1979. "Wage-Based Indexes of Urban Quality of Life." In *Current Issues in Urban Economics,* eds. P. Mieszkowski and M. Straszheim. Baltimore: Johns Hopkins University Press.

_____. 1974. "Hedonic Prices and Implicit Markets: Product Differentiation in Pure Competition." *Journal of Political Economy* 82: 34-55.

Rubin, Barry M. and Margaret G. Wilder. 1989. "Urban Enterprise Zones: Employment Impacts and Fiscal Incentives." *APA Journal* (Autumn): 418-431.

344

Rubin, Barry M. and C. Kurt Zorn. 1985. "Sensible State and Local Economic Development." *Public Administration Review* (March/April): 333-339.

Rubin, Irene S. and Herbert J. Rubin. 1987. "Economic Development Incentives: the Poor (Cities) Pay More." *Urban Affairs Quarterly* 23, 1 (September): 37-62.

Rubin, Marilyn Marks. 1991. "Urban Enterprise Zones in New Jersey: Have They Made A Difference?" In *Enterprise Zones,* ed. Roy E. Green. Newbury Park, CA: Sage Publications, 105-121.

Salinas, Patricia Wilson. 1986. "Urban Growth, Subemployment, and Mobility." In *Local Economies in Transition,* ed. E. Bergman. Durham, NC: Duke University Press.

Sander, William. 1989. "Local Taxes, Schooling, and Jobs in Illinois." Office of Real Estate Research Paper No. 75, College of Commerce and Business Administration, University of Illinois at Urbana-Champaign, December.

Schmenner, Roger W. 1982. *Making Business Location Decisions.* Englewood Cliffs, NJ: Prentice Hall.

Schmenner, Roger W., Joel C. Huber, and Randall L. Cook. 1987. "Geographic Differences and the Location of New Manufacturing Facilities." *Journal of Urban Economics* 21: 83-104.

Schneider, Mark. 1984. "Suburban Fiscal Disparities and the Location Decisions of Firms." *American Journal of Political Science* 29 3 (August): 587-695.

Shapiro, Carl and Joseph Stiglitz. 1984. "Equilibrium Unemployment as a Worker Discipline Device." *American Economic Review,* 74: 433-444.

Smith, V.K. 1983. "The Role of Site and Job Characteristics in Hedonic Wage Models." *Journal of Urban Economics* 11: 296-321.

Steinnes, Donald N. 1984. "Business Climate, Tax Incentives, and Regional Economic Development." *Growth and Change* 15, 2 (April): 38-47.

Stephenson, Stanley P., Jr. 1976. "The Economics of Youth Job Search Behavior." *Review of Economics and Statistics* 58 (February): 104-111.

Stiglitz, Joseph E. 1988. *Economics of the Public Sector,* second ed. New York: Norton.

Summers, Anita and Thomas F. Luce. 1987. *Economic Development Within the Philadelphia Metropolitan Area.* Philadelphia: University of Pennsylvania Press.

_____. 1985. *Economic Report on the Philadelphia Metropolitan Area 1985.* Philadelphia: University of Pennsylvania Press.

Summers, Gene, et al. 1976. *Industrial Invasion of Nonmetropolitan America.* New York: Praeger.

Summers, Lawrence H. 1986. "Why Is the Unemployment Rate So Very High Near Full Employment." *Brookings Papers on Economic Activity.* Washington, DC: The Brookings Institution.

Testa, William A. 1989. "Metro Area Growth from 1976 to 1985: Theory and Evidence." Working Paper. Federal Reserve Bank of Chicago, January.

Testa, William A. and Natalie A. Davila. 1989. "Unemployment Insurance: A State Economic Development Perspective." Working Paper. Federal Reserve Bank of Chicago, January.

Thibodeau, Thomas G. 1988. "Explaining Inter-Metropolitan Variation in Real Housing Price Fluctuations." Center for Research in Real Estate and Land Use Economics Working Paper No. 88-3, Southern Methodist University, March.

Tiebout, Charles. 1956. "A Pure Theory of Local Expenditures." *Journal of Political Economy* 64: 416-24.

Topel, Robert. 1986. "Local Labor Markets." *Journal of Political Economy* 94: S111-S143.

Treyz, George I., Dan S. Rickman, and Gang Shao. 1990. "The REMI Economic-Demographic Forecasting and Simulation Model." Working Paper, Regional Economic Models, Inc.

Treyz, George and Benjamin Stevens. 1985. "The TFS Regional Modelling Methodology." *Regional Studies* 19, 6: 547-562.

U.S. Advisory Commission on Intergovernmental Relations. 1981. *Regional Growth: Interstate Tax Competition.* Washington, DC: U.S. Government Printing Office, March.

U.S. Bureau of the Census. 1986. *Statistical Abstract of the United States: 1987,* 107th edition. Washington, DC.

U. S. General Accounting Office. 1988. "Enterprise Zones, Lessons From the Maryland Experience." Report to Congressional Requesters, December.

Vaughan, Roger J., Robert Pollard and Barbara Dyer. 1985. *The Wealth of States: Policies for a Dynamic Economy.* Washington, DC.

Vedder, Richard K. 1981. "State and Local Economic Development Strategy: A 'Supply-Side' Perspective." A staff study prepared for the use of the Subcommittee on Monetary and Fiscal Policy of the Joint Economic Committee, Congress of the United States, October 26.

Venti, Steven F. and David A. Wise. 1984. "Moving and Housing Expenditure: Transaction Costs and Disequilibrium." *Journal of Public Economics* 23: 207-243.

Walker, Robert and David Greenstreet. 1989. "Public Policy and Job Growth in Manufacturing: An Analysis of Incentive and Assistance Programs." Paper presented at the 36th North American meetings of the Regional Science Association, Santa Barbara, CA, November 10-12.

Wasylenko, Michael J. 1991. "Empirical Evidence on Interregional Business Location Decisions and the Role of Fiscal Incentives in Economic Development." In *Industry Location and Public Policy,* eds. Harry Herzog and Alan Schlottmann, Knoxville, TN: University of Tennessee Press.

_____. 1988. "Economic Development in Nebraska." Nebraska Comprehensive Tax Study Staff Paper No. 1, Metropolitan Studies Program, The Maxwell School, Syracuse University, revised.

_____. 1980. "Evidence of Fiscal Differentials and Intrametropolitan Firm Relocation." *Land Economics* 56, 3 (August): 339-349.

Wasylenko, Michael J. and R. Carroll. 1989. "Employment Growth and State Government Fiscal Behavior: A Report on Economic Development for States From 1973 to 1987." Preliminary report prepared for The Arizona Joint Select Committee on State Revenues and Expenditures, February.

346

Wasylenko, Michael and Therese McGuire. 1985. "Jobs and Taxes: The Effect of Business Climate on States' Employment Growth Rates." *National Tax Journal* 38, 4 (December): 497-512.

Weinstein, Bernard and Harold Gross. 1988. "The Rise and Fall of Sun, Rust, and Frost Belts." *Economic Development Quarterly* 2, 1 (February): 9-18.

Wheat, Leonard F. 1986. "The Determinants of 1963-77 Regional Manufacturing Growth: Why the South and West Grow." *Journal of Regional Science* 26, 4: 635-659.

Wheaton, William C. 1983. "Interstate Differences in the Level of Business Taxation." *National Tax Journal* 36, 1 (March): 83-94.

White, Michelle J. 1986. "Property Taxes and Firm Location: Evidence from Proposition 13." In *Studies in State and Local Public Finance,* ed. Harvey S. Rosen. Chicago: National Bureau of Economic Research Project Report Series. University of Chicago Press.

Wildasin, David E. 1989. "Interjurisdictional Capital Mobility: Fiscal Externality and a Corrective Subsidy." *Journal of Urban Economics* 25, 2 (March): 193-212.

_____. 1986. *Urban Public Finance.* New York: Harwood.

Wilson, John D. 1986. "A Theory of Interregional Tax Competition." *Journal of Urban Economics* 19: 296-315.

_____. 1985. "Optimal Property Taxation in the Presence of Inter-Regional Capital Mobility." *Journal of Urban Economics* 18: 73-89.

Winnick, Louis. 1966. "Place Prosperity vs. People Prosperity: Welfare Considerations in the Geographic Redistribution of Economic Activity." In *Essays in Urban Land Economics in Honor of the Sixty-Fifth Birthday of Leo Grebler.* Los Angeles: Real Estate Research Program, University of California at Los Angeles.

Witte, Ann Dryden. 1975. "The Determination of Interurban Residential Site Price Differences: A Derived Demand Model With Empirical Testing." *Journal of Regional Science* 15, 3: 351-364.

Woodward, Douglas P. 1990. "Locational Determinants of Japanese Manufacturing Start-Ups in the United States." Working Paper. University of South Carolina.

Yandle, Bruce. 1984. "Environmental Control and Regional Growth." *Growth and Change* 15, 3 (July): 39-42.

INDEX

Abraham, Katherine, 86-87 (Table 4.1), 88, 110nn7, 9, 111n14
Advisory Commission on Intergovernmental Relations (ACIR), 61n28
Age demographic group
effects of local growth on, 206
long-run growth effects on wages by, 153-55
Akaike Information Criterion (AIC), 89, 121, 143, 161, 276-78, 300, 307
Allan, Andrew, 16n8
Ambrosius, Marjorie M., 18, 21 (Table 2.1)
Amemiya, Takeshi, 89, 276, 281
Apgar, William C., Jr., 134n8
Area Wage Survey (AWS), 142-44
Armington, Catherine, 225, 236 (App. 2.2), 257 (App. 2.4)
Arromdee, Vachira, 21 (Table 2.1), 216, 238 (App. 2.2), 248 (App. 2.3), 254 (App. 2.4), 259 (App. 2.5)

Bailey, Ralph E., 12
Baily, Martin, 203n10
Bartik, Timothy J., 15n6, 28, 48, 54, 56, 57, 62n32, 65, 80n6, 133n4, 201n1, 203n9, 214, 219, 224, 237 (App. 2.2), 250, 252 (App. 2.3), 255, 256 (App. 2.4), 259, 260 (App. 2.5)
Bauer, Paul W., 57, 219, 237 (App.2.2), 255 (App. 2.4)
Bean, Ed, 75
Beaumont, Paul M., 58n5
Beck, John H., 223, 245 (App. 2.2), 251 (App. 2.3)
Becker, Charles, 15n6, 28, 133n4
Beeson, Patricia, 216, 237 (App. 2.2)
Bendick, Marc, 59n10
Benson, Bruce L., 223, 237(App. 2.2), 251 (App. 2.3), 256 (App. 2.4)
Berger, Mark, 155n1, 270
Blair, John P., 44, 188
Blomquist, Glenn, 155n1, 270
Bloomington, Illinois, 115
BLS. *See* Bureau of Labor Statistics (BLS)
Bolton, Roger, 66, 211n1
Bowman, Ann O'M., 195

Bradbury, Katherine, 87 (Table 4.1), 110n7, 158, 159 (Table 7.1), 160, 227, 231, 237 (App. 2.2), 282n3
Browne, Lynn E., 108n4, 140, 141 (Table 6.1), 228, 237 (App. 2.2), 257 (App. 2.4), 261 (App. 2.5)
Bulow, Jeremy, 265, 328n1
Bush, John, 15n6, 28, 133n4
Business location decision
effect of taxation on, 36-44
empirical analyses of, 38-39, 216-47
environmental regulations as factor in, 54, 56-57
local unionization as factor in, 52-54
measurement in, 31-33
patterns related to tax effects of, 39-44
problems of modeling, 30-36
public services as variable for, 44-48, 248-53
survey evidence on, 26-27
wages as variable for, 49-52, 254-58
See also Chrysler/Mitsubishi auto plant location; General Motors Saturn plant
Butler, J. S., 65

Canto, Victor A., 221, 237 (App. 2.2)
Carlton, Dennis W., 226, 229, 238 (App. 2.2), 257, 258 (App. 2.4)
Carroll, Robert, 219, 246 (App. 2.2), 250 (App. 2.3)
Cartwright, Phillip A., 18, 22 (Table 2.1)
Case, Karl E., 116 (Table 5.1)
Charney, Alberta H., 231, 238 (App. 2.2)
Chrysler/Mitsubishi auto plant location, 115
Church, Albert M., 231, 233, 238 (App. 2.2)
Citizens Research Council of Michigan, 15n5
Clark, David, 155n1
Clarke, Marianne, 194-95
Committee for Economic Development, 7, 12
Competition for jobs
effect of, 190
higher subsidies to national business from, 197
national effects of subsidies generated by, 197-99

347